Transnationalism And Civic Engagement: Diasporic Formation And Mobilization In Denmark And The UAE

Abdulkadir Osman Farah

Adonis & Abbey
Publishers Ltd

Published by

Adonis & Abbey Publishers Ltd
P.O. Box 43418
London
SE11 4XZ
Tel: + 44 845 388 7248
Website: http://www.adonis-abbey.com
Email: editor@adonis-abbey.com

Nigeria
Adonis & Abbey Publishing Company
P.O. Box 10546 Abuja,
Nigeria
Tel: +234 816 5970458

First Edition, June 2012

British Library Cataloguing-in-Publication Data
A catalogue record for this book is available from the British Library

ISBN: 978-1- 909112-00-1

TABLE OF CONTENTS

iv

ACKNOWLEDGEMENTS

This book resulted from three years of meticulous research efforts in three different continents, Africa, Asia and Europe. The working process has been both intensely challenging and significantly exhilarating. The research also reflects intellectual accumulation with inputs and sources stretching over decades. In this regard I am greatly in debt to my parents who sacrificed a lot and raised me to balance passion with critical sense and to contribute to the world positively. I am equally and deeply grateful to the rest of my family, my wife, my children and my brothers and sisters, many of them unfortunately due to the grave circumstances in my homeland, find themselves scattered around the world. In addition, I thank my pre-school teacher at Mogadishu who introduced me to the written word, particularly the sacred word *Iqra* (read) that have since shaped and continue to influence my life.

Without the support from Professors Mammo Muchie and Johannes D. Schmidt this work would not have reached its intended goals. Mammo responded quickly and rigorously in commenting my constant inquiries and suggesting valuable alteration and insights. I admire Mammo's sincerity, openness and perpetual search for social justice. Similarly, Johannes has demonstrated, with regard to Somali studies, his global commitment by raising funds and network support for a successful global and Diaspora conference in Denmark bringing together about 300 scholars that has led to the publication of well received book in 2007.

Special thanks to Professor Abdi M. Kusow of Iowa State University who, in our long weekend telephone and skpye exchanges, contributed to this project significantly. I am grateful to Martin Jørgensen for his unreserved guidance and support in relation to numerous research issues. Thanks also to Senior DIIS researcher Bjørn Møller who commented this work and suggested valuable inputs.

Finally I express my gratitude to researchers Mohammed Said Gees, Boobe Yusuf Duale and Mohammed Hassan Ibrahim from the Academy for Peace and Development in Somaliland for facilitating my field work in Somalia and Somaliland. I also thank the employees of the Muntada library in Sharjah UAE, and all the organizations and personalities assisting the field work in the UAE.

Abdulkadir Osman Farah,
Aarhus-Denmark, March 2012

CHAPTER 1

INTRODUCTION

Migration is an integrated part of human life. We migrate to survive and maintain a dignified life. Migrants flee from *fitnah* (widespread intolerance and violence), poverty, exclusion and injustice. Major historic transformations such as the transatlantic slavery, colonization, dictatorship, globalization and procuring civil wars expanded and complicated human migration and mobility (Papastergiadis, 2000: 25-26). In pursuing particularistic gains, dominant social groups and countries displaced less privileged groups from their countries of origin. In certain periods, this was done with the justification of civilizing primitive peoples for modernization and geopolitical resource accumulation (Mazrui, 1993: 23). Migrants often seek economic and social security in environments providing better opportunities than those available in their home environments. Consequently, migrant numbers increase and the migration character changes (Castells, 2001: 118).

Scholars with diverse perspectives tried to explain the Diaspora phenomenon (*cf.* Chapter 2). So far no consensus exists on the link between migration and Diaspora[1]. There is, however, the distinction of essentialist and non-essentialist Diaspora conceptualizations. First are essentialists who see Diaspora as intriguingly homeland oriented and refer to Diaspora's socio-cultural background and biological relations with the homeland. Essentialists perspectives assume that people always rely and refer to basic kin relationships. Thus analysis on Diaspora communities should address the origins of social relationships and ties. The homeland-oriented approaches tend to focus on long distance nationalism, highlighting the ethnic significance of Diaspora attachment (*cf.* Sheffer, 1986: 27). Second are

---

[1] Robin Cohen discusses the possibility of people becoming Diaspora without migration. Such groups could include people who become Diaspora without migrating from their homeland due to colonial and imperial demarcation of national borders, and these also include people with certain ideological commonalities for instance anti-capitalist movements and possibly terror networks (Robin, 2008: p.9).

1

non-essentialist paradigms that consider Diaspora community as more host country oriented than homeland oriented. This approach recognizes the Diaspora's ability to adjust to the host country by eventually abandoning homeland traditions and relations (Bauböck and Faist, 2010: 150).

In addition, recently the so-called trans-nationalist perspectives, portraying Diaspora as dynamic communities linking both to homeland and to host country environments, gained momentum. The approach assumes Diaspora's flexibility to obtain double consciousness. Trans-nationalism and globalization provide opportunities for expanded communication and transportation. Consequently Diaspora pursues multiple, hyphenated identities with simultaneous belonging to homeland and host country contexts (*cf.* Vertovec, 2009: 6-7).

Somalis as immigrants and refugees, originating from a volatile Arab-Afro region, contributed to the global migration development that increasingly influenced in both domestic and international relations. The specificity with the Somali case is that despite their relative homogeneity in terms of common ethnicity, language, culture and religion, Somalis remain one of the most internally divisive societies in the world.

Somalis conducted migration within and beyond the immediate Horn of Africa region for centuries. But on a large scale, trans-national Somali exodus is a recent development, arguably a post cold war phenomenon. The same applies to Somali Diaspora formations in Scandinavia, the rest of Western Europe and North America. The migration intensity coupled with post cold world trans-national opportunities for earlier *"passive"* diasporas generated an increased interest for research on migration and Diaspora studies, including the Somali Diaspora.

This research argues that the English written scholarship on Somali Diaspora, discussed in detail in chapter 3, reflects global, geopolitical developments and the policies of the host countries to cope with and better understand migrants, refugees and Diaspora from developing countries. This explains why the Somali Diaspora studies reflect an essentialist host country-centred perspective. The current western scholarship on Somalia and the Somalis mainly rely on historical, mostly colonial, conceptualization and interpretation that often considered Somalis as subjects, purely antagonistic and *qabiil* (clan) oriented. Such approaches fail to report Somalia as an emigration and Diaspora country for diverse nations from different countries for centuries. In addition, the English written scholarship insists that the majority of the Somali people belong to a nomadic tradition. The fact is that Somalis mainly consist of agro-pastoral people who for centuries inhabited within and the environs of ancient urban city states that traded with ancient civilizations for hundreds of years (Singh, 2002: 51).

Danish research on Somali Diaspora is limited and emphasizes the Somali community's marginal role in the Danish society. Though researchers try to access social realities among the Somalis, they confronted accessibility, networking, observation and interpretation challenges. This study tried to overcome such obstacles by focusing on Somali perspectives and experiences through lengthy observations on Diaspora spaces combined with active participation in community mobilizations.

The preferred methodology (presented in chapter 4) includes a qualitative inductive approach through empirical interviews and observations. The selection of the case approach helps us to better understand the complexities of the Diaspora phenomenon. This study particularly tried to answer three main questions:

- What characterizes Somali migration patterns to DK and UAE?
- How Somali Diaspora describe processes in the two host countries? And where the Somali Diaspora is located in the two countries?
- How do respondents explain Somali Diaspora space formation, organization and mobilization?

Furthermore the fieldwork among the Somali Diaspora represents the core of this study. Thus, data comes from interviews conducted in two stages first from August 2008 to August 2009 in Denmark and the UAE a second field work in the two countries (From January- February 2010). The study also applied indigenous methodologies of information seeking i.e. (*xog warran*) and conversing (*iswareysi*).

The design of this study is comparative as it compares/contrasts Somali Diaspora communities in Denmark and the UAE. Denmark is an advanced, democratic, stable welfare state. The UAE is a traditional, conservative, undemocratic, rentier oil state. The two cases also differ on the historical processes of exit and reception with regard to the Somalis and other immigrants. It was comparatively recent, around two decades ago, when Denmark received a large number of Somalis, while the link between the Somalis and the UAE goes back centuries. So it is not an exaggeration to claim that the UAE hosts old Somali Diaspora while Denmark accommodates an emerging Somali Diaspora, still in its formative stages. Selecting and comparing the two cases is therefore in accordance with the case study method; a research strategy that analyzes a single or two cases (Stake, 1995). The decision to include or exclude cases are based on the criteria of critical and better understanding of the situation and the consideration of which cases provide better insights with regard to the research topic (Stake, 2000: 446). The comparative design entails studying two presumably contrasting cases with the application of similar methods. The reasoning of such comparative approach is that we can understand, in this case the Somali Diaspora better, in comparing two dissimilar cases, the Danish and the UAE contexts.

Preliminary analysis of the data started while conducting and transcribing interviews. The combination provided an opportunity to structure basic ideas and models. The process involves systematic gleaning of themes or basic concepts from transcribed interviews and the observation notes. This early stage of language comparison and assessment represents the early stages of inductive conceptualization (Strauss and Corbin 1998: 101). The study applied particular transcription techniques inspired by (Kvale, 1997) and the data was transferred to a software data management program QSR Nvivo.

Furthermore, the research sought to combine fieldwork and theory with the aim of systematically understanding and interpreting social processes (Snow, Morrill, & Anderson, 2003). Chapter 5 introduces and compare theoretical perspectives. In the study, theory plays an inductive role where the presented theoretical insights inform the interpretation. In the process, the research tries to integrate empirical findings with competing theoretical perspectives. The aim is to better understand and make sense of the collected data. The study considers the theories as containing different, complementing, perspectives and frameworks not necessarily representing universal conceptualization of social reality.

The study linked the empirical data with conceptual perspectives proposed by prominent social scientists such as Durkheim and Ibn-Khaldun. The two scholars propose a modern-centric development model, advocating for a society based not on *"mechanical solidarity"* (badawa) but on *"organic solidarity"* (hadara) with sophisticated division of labour under the protection of hegemonic state, with emphasis on *moral regulation*. The modernization paradigm assumes a natural human primitiveness and underdevelopment that will require social and institutional-oriented dimensions to move to advanced complex stages of social, economic and political structures. Apart from their conceptual similarity, the two thinkers agree on the significance of religion in society. Durkheim argued for the secularization of religion, while Ibn-Khaldun proposed religious superiority.

4

Discussing these classical scholars is important because their conceptual ideas and perspectives continue to influence contemporary researchers on migration and Diaspora. For instance in studying Diaspora's political engagement and homeland relations, a prominent migration and Diaspora scholar, Sheffer (2003) introduced a model comparable to Durkheim's and Ibn-Khaldun's developmental approach. Sheffer divides diasporas into hierarchical, developmental categories depending on how modern, established and state centric the Diaspora community appears.

In modifying the classical evolutionary research, Bourdieu proposes a number of conceptual frames to improve the state macro-centric developmental approach. With the introduction of concepts such as *"habitus"*, "social field", *"symbolic capital"* and *"social capital"*, Bourdieu focuses on the reflexivity and the duality of agency-structure relations (*cf.* Bourdieu,1991: 49). It is no longer just the dominant structure that we all need to adjust. Bourdieu shifts focus from the exclusive macro position to a meso and micro position of social relations. Yet, he partially remains structural oriented as the ultimate aim of social improvement rests on collective society and state formulation.

With the application of the ideas developed by another social thinker Foucault, we are able to challenge the emphasis on objectivity and structural inclusion and assimilation (*cf.* Foucault,1985: 10-11). Foucault proposes we should rather pay more attention to discourses and daily practices. Particularly we need to observe, interpret and analyze how societies and states exclude through persistence discourse and hegemony, and how marginalized constituents mobilize and resist such macro-imposed structures.

Although the world has increasingly become global and people are increasingly mobile, states and their regulations persist. It is thus difficult for Diaspora and other migrants to maintain a proper life without citizenship rights. In this regard, the Somali Diaspora in Denmark have the privilege of accessing formal and expanded citizenship providing them with an opportunity to be mobile and thereby achieve improved social quality compared to pre-migration times. The Somali Diaspora utilizes this citizenship through the participation of social and political mobilizations as well as electoral processes. Apart from accessing welfare benefits, the Diaspora receives state subsidiary for community organization and mobilization efforts. On the negative side, most Somali Diaspora members do not enjoy substantial, informal citizenship in the form of having social contacts with native citizens and their networks. Somalis in Denmark relate almost exclusively to formal institutions and associations. In contrast, most members of the Somali Diaspora in the UAE do not access formal citizenship, as the UAE restricts citizenship privileges to the country's minority population. The lack of formal citizenship makes the Somalis engage more informally with individuals, networks and institutions in the UAE. In the process, they create informal, social relations helping them to access social, financial and political privileges. Denmark and the UAE also differ with regard to their respective attitude towards immigrants. In Denmark, the political rhetoric is negative towards immigrants. Both politicians and the media, particularly those from the right wing constituents, profile immigrants as representing primitive cultures posing a threat to the Danish culture, society and the political system in the long term. The media and politicians in the UAE do not consider immigrants as a threat. The Somali Diaspora in the UAE has the advantage of residing in an Islam Arab country geographically and culturally close to Somalia and with a long historical relationship. Business opportunity structures provide higher levels of competitiveness, which in turn provides access and resources for a homeland-linked trade. The main challenge confronting the Diaspora in the UAE is the lack of citizenship rights. Because of this structural restriction, Somalis choose to operate informally in host country-related mobilization activities, whereas they formally organize in their interaction with the homeland.

Chapter 6 discusses the citizenship concept and the developments and differences on citizenship structures and opportunities in Europe, Africa, Denmark, the UAE and Somalia. In addition the chapter examines the link between citizenship and Diaspora. One of the consequences of Diaspora in a new society is to question the conventional conceptualization of Diaspora. An important point is how the media shapes public opinion in relation to migrants and Diaspora. Considering this reality the chapter analysed the Danish and UAE media reporting and the way they particularly discuss on Somali Diaspora and Somali related issues. The chapter further contrasts the similarities and the differences the media representation entails.

In chapters 7, 8 and 9, the research presents the empirical data, analysis and findings in relation to Somali Diaspora in the two cases. Denmark is a western, secular, democratic welfare state, while the UAE is a traditional, non-democratic, rentier oil state. Despite this difference, in certain aspects the Somali Diaspora in the two cases confronts comparable challenges such as gender and intergenerational dispute more or less directly linked to the state and society in the two host countries. The economically friendly, but

6

legally restrictive, institutional and structural environment in the UAE produces a Somali Diaspora that concentrates on socio-economic entrepreneurship activities influencing Diaspora spaces, internal community dynamics and homeland relations. Consequently, the Diaspora in the UAE continuously reinvents itself, always adjusting to the prevailing circumstances. Currently, this Diaspora succeeded to establish a global contact zone for economic entrepreneurship together with a vibrant Diaspora homeland contact and exchange. The welfare system in Denmark, with expanded citizenship rights but with more restriction on economic entrepreneurship, leads to a Somali Diaspora focusing on cultural and religious aspects together with homeland, ideological development and social remittance.

The Somali Diaspora in Denmark and the UAE also organize and mobilize. Since the September 2001 attacks in the US, similar to other Muslim Diasporas, Somalis have struggled to overcome suspicion and recurring accusations of extremism. In the UAE, the community mobilized and responded to the accusations of financially sponsoring radicalization, warlordism and piracy in the homeland. In Denmark, the community mobilized to counter media and political campaigns accusing the Diaspora for radicalization. In addition, the two Diaspora, though in different ways, utilize cultural mobilizing structures such as traditional leaders and ethnic associations in order to negotiate and promote community interests. Both Diasporas operate at trans-national level by interacting and linking to the homeland, host country and beyond.

In the UAE, *qabiilah* relations, although modified, still prevail. Apart from the mediation of conflicts among the Somalis, the *qabiilah* network provides welfare, particularly for individuals confronting challenges in the host country. Despite the absence of a welfare state that provides social services, Somalis in the UAE exhibit self-confidence in managing their livelihoods and at the same time contributing to the development of the host country and the homeland (Wharfage, 2009).

In contrast, the Somali Diaspora in Denmark organizes and mobilizes formally in relation to host country institutions while pursuing informal activities in relation to the homeland. This is mainly to do with the existence of citizenship opportunities. Most Somalis in Denmark are either citizens or hold a permanent resident status with expanded social and political rights. Although they are often subjected to political rhetoric and exclusion, they have formal rights to organize and pursue civil liberties. Though authorities recently introduced anti-immigrant restrictive legislations, the inclusion of the Somalis into the Danish welfare system affects the community positively. Most obvious is the fact that the state-sponsored social and institutional protection reduces dependency on the Somali *qabiilah* relation and thereby *qabiilah*-ism. *Qabiilah* relations might exist theoretically but in the Danish context, it loses its basic functions, except for limited informal applications for homeland politics among elder, usually unemployed, Somali men engaged in heated *"fadhi kudirir"* sessions. As an institution, qabiilah relation among the Somalis in Scandinavia is, at least officially, replaced by a Pan-Somali framing and sometimes also by multi-ethnic Islamic framing.

Finally the two cases differ on the framing opportunities. Somalis in Denmark frame ideas and values that promote Somali and Islamic identities occasionally combined with the adapted Danish identity. The basic ideas that bring the community together are the state of being Somali and being Muslims while remaining legally part of the Danish society. The Somali Diaspora in the UAE does not formally frame socio-religious and cultural issues, as there are no significant religious and cultural differences between the homeland and the host country. They rather prefer to organize cultural and national festivities linking to the homeland. The Somali Diaspora in the UAE has strategically decided and qualifies as a trade Diaspora[2].

The mobilization of Diaspora depends on the political opportunities (the institutional and legal conditions), the mobilizing opportunities (the associational, organizational and networking possibilities) and the framing opportunities (the opportunity to express ideas and values to mobilize) both in relation to the host environment and to the homeland. The Somali Diaspora cases in Denmark and the UAE illustrate how differences in opportunity structures influence Diaspora mobilization. For instance, the Diaspora in Denmark pursues formal mobilization in relation to the host country. The conduct is in accordance with the associational tradition in Scandinavia, where citizens establish civil society groups to mobilize and participate in the society through specific networking and group formation activities.

In contrast, the Diaspora in the UAE refrains from organizing formally, at least officially, in relation to the authorities in the UAE. Their formal public organization and mobilization targets the homeland. If Somalis in the

---

[2] Cohen 2008 p.83 in his archetypal classification of Diasporas described The Chinese and the Lebanese as trade Diasporas, whereas, he argued, the Jewish, the Palestinians, the Armenians and probably the Africans are victim diasporas.

UAE need to mobilize officially, they will have to do it within business framing pursuit. Such trade-oriented structural priority brings the business elite at the top of the community structure.

In an increasingly complex world, it is difficult to maintain the idea of an agent-structure relationship. We can no longer discuss, as modern social scientists did, a dominant structure that actors have to adjust. It is possible to refer to multiple strategies and structures, *i.e.* more or less objective and subjective structures. A structural-oriented approach can explain some dimensions of the rationality of social change but we obviously need to supplement with an actor-oriented analysis.

There is a need to envision an intermediate position to understand both the structure and actor perspectives. This will require from us to shift to the middle and not to take for granted any grand narratives. Focus will then rest on the actual social construction of social reality. Diaspora processes in the Denmark and the UAE confirm that social constructivism so far provides the most suitable epistemological and ontological frames to study Diaspora communities. In addition, by bringing the perspectives of another Diaspora, namely that of the Somalis in the UAE, the study nuances the discourse in Denmark that some migrants and refugee Diaspora naturally link and depend on state welfare. The study documented that Diaspora can be independent from the state welfare support and instead and in contrast show its contribution to host country and homeland developments. Finally, the presented Somali Diaspora cases illustrate the need to pay more attention to the spiritual human needs and capability to simultaneously adjust and resist.

CHAPTER 2

SOMALI MIGRATION AND DIASPORA FORMATION

Definition of Diaspora

So far no academic consensus exists on the definition of Diaspora. Scholars disagree on the classification and the qualification criteria for Diaspora inclusion. For instance Safran (1991), Cohen (1996 & 2008) and Sheffer (2003) argue for the hierarchization of Diaspora communities, *i.e.* a process of structuring Diaspora into *"original"* real Diaspora and *"less original"* unreal Diaspora. Whereas Diaspora scholars such as Appadurai (1990), Anthias (1998) and Sökefeld (2006) prefer Diaspora horizontalization with lesser Diaspora generalizing definition recognizing the diversity and the ability of each Diaspora to pursue the life world with strategies they find necessary.

It is, however, possible to differentiate two different definitional categories of Diaspora; the essentialist and the non-essentialist approaches. The first approaches are evolutionary oriented and ethno-centric in *e.g.* focusing on ethnic and national identity affiliations. Such definitions link Diaspora to kinship and homeland roots and assume more structured and organized modern Diaspora in contrast to less modern and dynamic Diaspora. The second approaches characterizes and evaluates Diaspora on the actual behaviour and priorities they choose to value more than the cultural background and biological ethnicity they hail from. The latter approach links the Diaspora not directly but indirectly to the kinship and homeland roots. They do it as a consequence of Diaspora relationship that emerges from actual social constructions and modifications. Thus, the distinction has less to do with their *"roots"* and more with experience through their travel *"routes"* (Gilroy, 1993).

The following table 2.1 shows selected propositions in the two approaches. The essentialists argue that Diaspora relate to singular homes, spaces and mobilizations whereas non-essentialists emphasise the dynamics of Diaspora constructing plural homes, space and mobilization activities. The cultural and national relations are significant for essentialists while non-essentialists prefer social processes and interactions. Diaspora spaces and mobilizations are not segregated from the surrounding local, national, international environments. Diaspora ethno-spaces engage and respond to global social, political and economic dynamics with continuing transnational and trans-state interactions and exchanges. Under such circumstances it is difficult to define Diaspora as belonging to singular structural category.

Table 2.1 Diaspora perspectives

Essentialist approaches	Non-essentialist approaches
• Diaspora experience *"departure from a place of origin and limited or lack of acceptance in their places of settlement"* (Cohen, 2006: 4).	• Diaspora is a process of "settling down and putting roots elsewhere". Diaspora might therefore pursue *"homing desire"* from that of *"homeland desire"* (Brah, 1996: 192). • Diaspora construct 'Diaspora space', where people experiment subjective social attitudes and practice (ibid. 208). • Diaspora adapt "Trans-cultural identities' (ibid. 208).
• Diaspora engage in *"long distance nationalism"* (Anderson, 1983)	• Diaspora reflect not *"originality"* and *"true belonging"* (Anthias, 1998).
• Diaspora represent a *"trans-border citizenry"* (Glick Schiller 2005: 164).	• Diaspora is a movement that *"seek opportunities, mobilize communities and frame ideas"* (Sokefeld, 2006)
• Diaspora promote *"Implicit insistence on conformity and homogeneity"* (Ang, 2001) • Diaspora represent *"ethnic fundamentalism"* (Assad 1993, Chhachhi 1991)	• *"Diaspora represent a "resistance both to originality and belonging. It represents a resistance against dominance and exclusion"* (Chariandy, 2006) • Diaspora represent a *"decolonization, emancipatory social movement"* (Papastergiadis, 1998: 121).
• Diaspora represent " Cultural, political and economic exchange trans-state exchange with the homeland" (Hall, 1991).	• Diaspora represent *'ethnoscapes, technoscapes, finanscapes, medias-capes and ideoscapes'* (Appandurai 1990: 296)
	• Diaspora emerge from *"critical dialogism and not from exclusive national identity"* (Mercer, 2003).
	• Diaspora reflect *"Transnational activities through communication, politics, social and economy"* (Portes, 1997: 18)

Scholars on both approaches recognize the significance of migration and mobility for Diaspora. Generally Diaspora involves a movement and settlement process across multiple physical, virtual and spiritual spaces. They also agree on the essence of Diaspora organization and mobilization as well as the significance for citizenship and institutional mechanism for Diaspora community development. Obviously their diverse disciplinary epistemological and ontological lenses influences on whether to highlight essentialist or non-essentialist dimensions of Diaspora experience.

This study takes a critical approach to the essentialist and non-essentialist ways of looking Diaspora. Diaspora reflects a multifaceted community social process that becomes more complex through transnational contacts and exchanges which will make it irreducible to the dichotomy of the essentialist and non-essentialist narratives.

Migration and Diaspora formation

The history of the Somali migration attests that Somalis fled from persecution, *fitnah* (widespread intolerance and violence) and *qabiilah* (*qabiilism*). The Somali Diaspora largely consists of migrants expelled from their country of origin due to dictatorship and warlordism. Somalia in the 1990s became home for notorious warlords (Charlton and May, 1989).

The conventional wisdom considers Somali migration as recent and refugee oriented. This is not the case for Alpers (1986) who researched African migration and Diaspora formations including Somalis in the regions around the Indian Ocean and the Red Sea. Alpers's basic argument is that Africans migrated to Arabia, to Indonesia and to India for trade and colonial related activities. These Africans eventually mixed with the locals but remained attached to their homeland through customs, language, culture and rituals. Despite their long presence, these Diasporas created distinct Diaspora with cultural practices and interaction with other communities in host societies (ibid.). Alpers propose the need to challenge the state and economic centric conventional paradigms of migration and Diaspora analysis (ibid.). With regard to the Somalis Alpers's research is important as he examined the Somali Diaspora in Yemen, Aden and non-Somali Diaspora formations in Mogadishu, among others the Hadramis (immigrants from Yemen) and Persians (Iranians)[3].

---

[3] The name Mogadishu means " The seat of the Shah" indicating its Persian origin. Persian Muslims migrated from Shiraz, Persia to Mogadishu where some of them built one of the oldest and known mosques in the city Arba'a Rukun in the 11th century (Mukhtar in eds. Ahmed, 1995: 5).

In modern times, migration from Somalia was colonial-driven, later post-colonial authorities, civilian and military regimes intensified the process. The post- dictatorship and the subsequent collapse of the state led to mass historic exodus. The different stages produced different migration types. As indicated in figure 2.1, the first was strategic and it took Somalis to Africa, Arabian Peninsula and Asia to sustain colonialism in these regions. The second was partially economic and opposition-driven and resulted in the migration of bureaucrats, army officers and students. The third was global on a much larger scale and included traumatized groups including children and women.

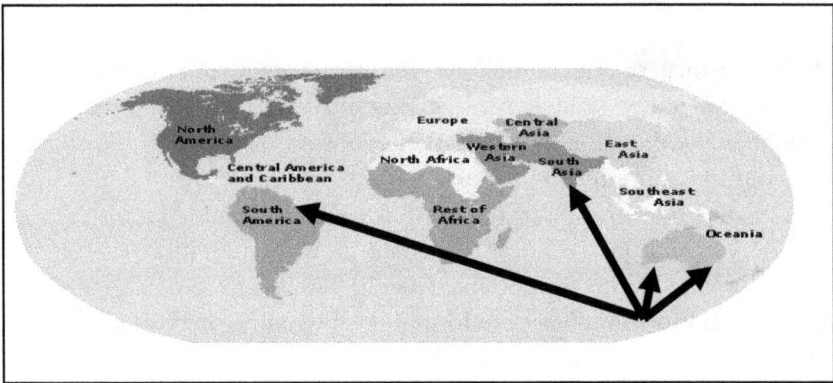

Figure 2.1   Migration pattern

Somali Diaspora

As discussed earlier there is no academic consensus on the definition of Diaspora. The general understanding is that Diaspora should fulfil the conditions of *"dispersion, dealing with reluctant hosts, contest and maintenance of an active relationship with the homeland"* (Cohen, 1996). According to this description Somalis qualify as Diaspora. For centuries, the Somalis travelled and settled in other countries. Some of the earliest destinations were the Arabian Peninsula and East Africa. The devastating traumatic civil war generated the latest phase of the migration. About two million Somalis fled abroad as dictatorship and warlordism shattered their lives. Many of them belong to the most capable in social, political and economic terms. The collapse of the Somali state in 1991 brought havoc and scattered millions to destitute refugee life in many countries. Though arriving in different periods and circumstances, the estimated 1½ million Somalis in Diaspora (table 2.2) consider themselves related and connected to each other. The intensified global telecommunication and internet have since helped create a better organized dispersed community (Issa-Salwe, 2009).

Host country	Estimated number of Somalis
USA	200.000
UK	200.000
Norway	40.000
Sweden	40.000
DK	18.000
UAE	100.000
Saudi Arabia	200.000
Kenya	400.000[4]
Yemen	300.000
Total	1.498.000

Table 2.2   Somali Diaspora

Somalia gained independence in 1960 and the two colonially divided parts (Somaliland and Southern Somalia), unified under a Western-styled parliamentary system, forming the Somali republic (Contini, 1969: 14). Later, General Siyad Barre seized power in 1969, expounding *"scientific socialism"* (Markakis in eds. Markakis and Waller, 1986: 23). Receiving military and development aid from the Soviet Union (1969–77) and the United States (1978–89), the regime funded the war with Ethiopia over the Ogaden region. Internally, while the regime formally banned manifestations of *qabiil* organization, Siyad Barre, in fact used state finances to manipulate different interest groups by entrenching his power and rely on his immediate relatives.

In 1988, insurrection by the Somali National Movement in Northern Somalia met with severe government reprisals. The central region also

---

[4] This is the new Somali Diaspora and refugees, the number of Somali Kenyans are more than 2 million.

suffered. Persecution of dissenting groups and political movements became common throughout the country. Eventually, the United Somali Congress and the Somali Patriotic Movement overthrew Siyad Barre in 1991 (Gundel, 2003). The state collapsed. In 1991–1992, 240,000 to 280,000 people died from starvation or disease in Southern and Central Somalia alone. At least 40,000 people were killed in fighting as the region entered a long period of inter-qabiil warfare, banditry and famine (UNDP, 2001). International efforts to broker a resolution to the political crisis failed miserably. Today, in some areas, localized politics, based on traditional qabiil-based, municipal, Islamic and local business influences, ensure a degree of stability. In January 2009, Sheikh Sharif Sheikh Ahmed became the head of the Transitional Federal Parliament (TFP), but to date, the Transitional Federal Government (TFG) still exerts no clear territorial control in Somalia. In the North, the self-declared Republic of Somaliland (since 1991) and the self-administered Puntland State of Somalia (since 1998) have maintained relatively stable administrations, although internationally unrecognised. Somaliland recently held successful democratic elections with the peaceful transformation of power from one president to another.

Nomadic Migration

Pastoral mobility across Somalia's borders with neighbouring countries to graze livestock, trade or work have been a common feature for centuries. Colonization divided greater Somalia into five regions: British, Italian, and French Somaliland respectively, as well as the Northern Frontier District of the British Kenyan Colony and the Ogaden region of Ethiopia. In 1960, the independent Somali Republic was formed as British and Italian Somaliland merged. The Northern Frontier District, however, remained in independent Kenya and the Ogaden region remained part of Ethiopia. French Somaliland eventually gained independence in 1977 as the Republic of Djibouti. Hence, ethnic Somalis have traditionally inhabited an area that stretches beyond Somalia's 1960–1991 borders, living also in Djibouti, northern Kenya and the Ogaden region of present-day Ethiopia. During the colonial period, men from British Somaliland, many former nomadic pastoralists, worked as employees of the UK's Merchant Navy, some returning after sojourns in the UK, others stayed in respective host countries (Kahin, 1997: 31).

Figure 2.2   Colonial driven migration

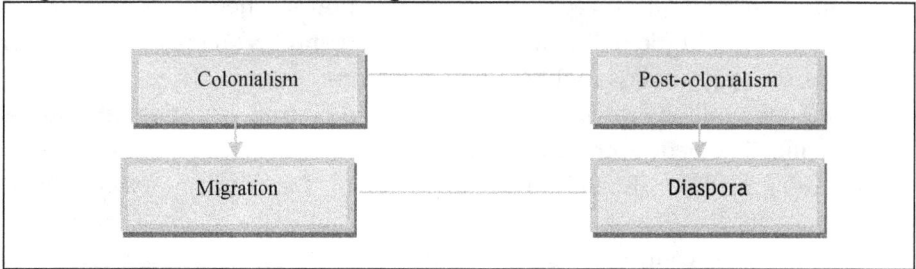

Colonial and Oil Migration

Since the 1960s, significant numbers of Somalis migrated to work in the oil-rich Gulf. By 1987, the number was estimated to 375,000 (Ahmed, 2000). These migrants were often relatively well-educated people looking for better employment than could be found in Somalia (Marchal, 1996). Today, the many Somalis who remained in the Arabian Gulf Arab countries confront certain challenges. Employment opportunities have declined and most migrants including the Somalis suffer from lack of proper legal status.

War Triggered Migration

The next major migration was related to the war over the Ethiopian Ogaden Region between Ethiopia and Somalia. This war provoked a humanitarian crisis, which brought about the first massive refugee movement, sending thousands of ethnic Somalis into Somalia (Waldron and Hasci, 1995). By 1981, these refugees constituted about 20-40 per cent of the population of Somalia (Simons, 1995). From 1984 to 1991, this group of refugees was accompanied by more Ogaden refugees as well as fleeing Ethiopian Oromos (Waldron and Hasci, 1995). Thus, already before the civil war, Somalia hosted one of the largest refugee populations in Africa.

Mass Exodus

The eruption of the civil war in 1988 reversed this situation and generated the third major movement – this time from Somalia into the Ethiopian Ogaden Region. This flow was first caused by the conflict between

SNM (Somali National Movement) rebels and the Siyad Barre regime, and was prompted by the bombing of Hargeysa in 1988. The escalation of the conflict in 1991 produced further refugee flows, when the USC, with the support of SPM (Somali Patriotic Movement) and SNM, ousted Siyad Barre. Thus, the largest mass flight of Somalis occurred from early 1991 when more than one million are estimated to have fled from fighting in southern Somalia. The better-off refugees went abroad to Western countries such as Canada, the US, UK, Italy, Holland, Sweden, Denmark, Norway, Finland, and Australia. Though, most, and significantly the poorest, fled to the neighbouring countries, such as Kenya and Ethiopia, or elsewhere within Somalia illegally and hence elude documentation. According to UNHCR, the number of registered displaced Somalis in Somalia and worldwide is around 2.249,454 (UNHCR, 2010).

Table 2.3   Somali migration and reasons

Period	Reason for Migration	Implications
Colonial times (from 1900-	Work with colonial powers (the army and the economic sea fare sector)	Joining the second world war, wars in Burma and Korea
1960s-early 1970s	Economic migration to Gulf countries	Brain drain
1980s-	Political opposition to the military regime	Opposition centres in Ethiopia, Yemen, Libya and Eastern European countries (mostly students and qualified politicians and military

		officers)
1988-	Civil war victims	Mass refugees (including vulnerable groups such as women and children)

The following sections present a general overview of Somali Diaspora communities in East Africa (Kenya), Middle East (Yemen & UAE), North America (USA & Canada) and the rest of Europe (UK and Italy).

Somali Diaspora in the Middle East

Somalis migrated to the Middle East for hundreds of years. Most of the Somalis who went to work in the Gulf oilfields were young men. Some women were employed as domestic workers or nurses. Almost all were segregated from the local population. Middle East countries do not normally provide citizenships and employee rights to foreigners. Migrants must leave when employment contracts expire. Somalis were often subjected to violations of their basic rights by contractors who rejected to pay their fees or provide them with holiday compensations.

Hence, Somalis in the Middle East remain vulnerable and not properly integrated into the political system. There are, however, few exceptional cases as the UAE, Qatar and Oman provide Citizenship for some Somalis. In Dubai and UAE, Somalis built centres for business engagement that involve global marketing and exchange. Somalis from all over the world generally use Dubai as their financial and trade centre for their businesses with Somalia itself. However, here too, Somalis do not enjoy full rights and there are many uncertainties about their legal residence status. Through their remittances and trade with Somalia, they are considered major players in the reconstruction of Somalia. Hence, a considerable part of the financing as well as educational system in particular Mogadishu are channelled by Somali business people who maintain the Mogadishu – Dubai and Gulf of Arabia linkage.

Somali Diaspora in the United Kingdom, United States and Canada

Somalis in the United Kingdom include British citizens and Somalis with resident permits. Britain has the largest Somali community in Europe. Estimates suggest that up to 200,000 or more Somalis live in the UK. The first Somali immigrants in the UK included seamen and merchants who arrived in the 19th century. During the Second World War, Somalis working for the British Royal Navy settled in the UK. During the 1980s and 1990s, the civil war in Somalia brought large number of Somali immigrants and refugees to the UK. The Somali community represents one of the largest Muslim groups in Britain (Quraishi, 2005: 20).

Table 2.4   British citizenship for Somalis

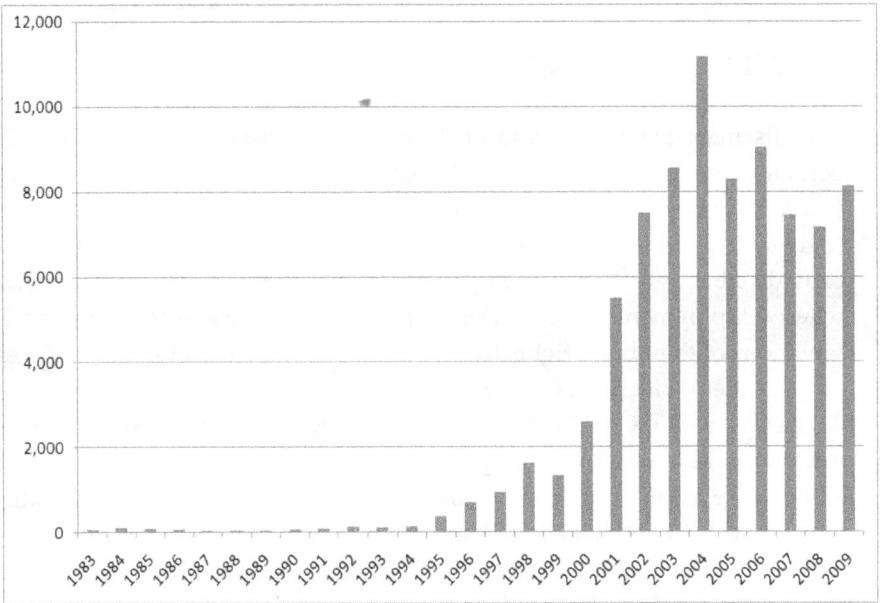

From the late 1990s, the UK attracted secondary migration of Somalis from the Netherlands, Sweden and Denmark. The reason for the secondary migration included declining employment opportunities in other European countries and the possibility to join the more established Somali Diaspora in the UK (Kleist, 2008).

The Somalis in North America are said to be the most resourceful among Somali Diaspora. The reason could be that the USA initially attracted students and well educated groups (Roble and Rudledge, 2008: 10). Later the ruling elite and former government officials chose to migrate to either Canada or the USA. More importantly, Somalis consider North America to provide possible and successful integration opportunities. Somalis in the UK and North America are the most active in the development of Somalia politically, socially and economically.

Remittances are the prime contribution to Somalia from the Northern American and UK Diaspora (World Bank, 2007: 152). However, the UK and North American Diaspora are leading in the recent emerging construction and small enterprises in Somalia itself, as well as in the telecommunications sector. Somalis in the UK, USA and Canada are organised in community associations, which mostly mobilize Somalis to bring assistance to Somalia in periods of emergency such as droughts and floods.

Information technology is increasingly being used to increase the links between Diaspora and the homeland. An interesting case is the new satellite TV station, Universal TV (www.tvuniversal.net). The case of this station shows a typical global Somali business venture as the station is owned by a businessman, based in the UK and Dubai, running businesses in telecommunication and satellite instruments. In an interview with the television, the owners explained that they established the TV station to contribute to the development and reconstruction of Somalia, by helping Somalis abroad and Somalis at home to connect. Recently, the station has taken a significant role in mobilizing Somali Diaspora to support projects in Somalia. During homeland emergencies, the TV airs fundraising humanitarian programs. Time will tell, but it seems that stations such as the Universal TV and the Internet will have impact on the way in which the Somali Diaspora engages with regard to the development in their country.

Somali Diaspora in Italy

Somalia has an historical relationship with Italy. Italy colonized the southern and most productive part of the country. During the Second World War, South Somalia briefly came under British rule. When the war ended, the UN designated Italy to administer under UN mandate to prepare Somalia for independence. Many Somalis, therefore, received their education from Italy. Naturally, many of these Somalis established relationships with Italy. Some even decided to stay in Italy to pursue further careers and education. After independence, Italy and the Soviet Union became the main contributors to the education and development sectors of Somalia (Hamphrey, 2007: 63). Many Somalis in Italy belong to the best educated among the Somalis. When the civil war broke out, Italian expatriates in Somalia assisted the resettlement of their Somali employees in Mogadishu. Thousands of Somalis live in Italy and many have gained Italian citizenship. Younger generations consider Italy as a transit destination on their route to Scandinavia, the UK and North America.

With regard to the development and relationship with the host nation and their country of origin, Somalis joined efforts and established organisations to help themselves and the people back home. One such organization is called Italo-Somalo[5] and is based in Rome. This organization is created by people with a mixture of Italian and Somali backgrounds and by educated Somalis. They organize activities for integration and development to help Somalis in Italy and in Somalia. In addition, there are a number of women organizations involved in helping Somali women in Italy and women and children in Somalia. Unlike Scandinavia and some other western countries, Italy does not have an inclusive welfare system. Thus immigrants and refugees receive a minimum of support (Schierup et al., 2006: 168). This pressures Somalis to look for jobs to survive. The lack of proper welfare also influences the Diaspora organizations that spend more energy and resources on helping people to get jobs rather than building up institutions and supporting their country of origin. On the other hand, Italy is the only country in Western Europe that still provides special favour and treatment for the Somali immigrants[6]. For instance Somali immigrants are entitled to get a one-year residence permit if they are approved to be a proper refugee. This annual residence permit is renewed every year until the individual acquires permanent status and later citizenship.

Somali Diaspora in Kenya

Eastleigh is located in the eastern part of Nairobi, Kenya. There has been a large Somali presence for a very long time, but since the 1990s, Eastleigh

---

[5] http://www.italosomali.org/

[6] Somali refugees in Italy use to get permanent residence. There is also a large network of Italian expatriates who use to work in Somalia. In addition Italy recognizes immigrants from e.g. Somalia and Eritrea as immigrants from former Italian colonies with closer understanding and relationship.

has become the home for thousands of Somalis, mostly refugees from the civil war. Initially, the Somali refugees settled in makeshift refugee camps in the Northern districts bordering Somalia. Subsequently, they resettled in Eastleigh to pursue better opportunities. Though confronting numerous social and political challenges, the new Somali arrivals succeeded to transform this neighbourhood to a large commercial neighbourhood trading a number of goods. There are 2.4 million Somalis in Kenya (Kenya census, 2009).

Eastleigh is probably the second most important Somali Diaspora business centre in the World after Dubai. Among the residents in Eastleigh you find the most prominent business people from Somalia. Some of them own hotels and large properties while conducting huge business international enterprises. The fact is that most Somalis come to Eastleigh as refugees with none or few belongings. Over time, they remarkably succeed in settling and making a living for themselves while providing assistance for relatives back home. Many Somalis in Eastleigh are engaged in small business enterprises. There are also various humanitarian and educational activities taking place in Eastleigh. The neighbourhood also houses numerous private schools that teach children from basic Quran teachings to advanced schooling. As refugees in Kenya, Somalis do not get formal jobs, so most support themselves through informal job undertakings.

Through complex networks of friends and relatives, the business communities in Eastleigh, Dubai and Bakaara market in Mogadishu engage in activities that are not only providing profits for the business community but also for the wider ordinary Somalis. Regardless of where Somalis live, they share their orientation towards the homeland, particularly in their contribution to homeland development through *hawaala* (remittance).

The *qabiilah* research dominated much of Somali scholarship in the past five decades. The research might provide partial explanation of core social structures among the nomads in Northern Somalia. Nonetheless, the explicit essentialist argument, that kinship constitutes the essence of Somali social and organizational behaviour, represents a major epistemological weakness. The fact is that more or less structured socialization efforts from early childhood throughout adulthood make people interact and join diverse social formations locally, nationally and transnationally. With the emergence of other networking forms reflecting ordinary people's aspirations and behaviour, traditional *qabiilah* relations lose their main significance. This does not mean Somalis will abandon *qabiilah* in its entirety. As Muslims, they still have the option to refer to their *qabiilah* relations for verifying their lineage and historical background.

The appropriate application of the Islamic form of *qabiilah* makes way to Diaspora associations that in return have the potential eventually to replace the old nomadic, national and territorial based *qabiilah*. This is because Diaspora *qabiilah* rests not on blood ties but on ties of neighbourhood and friendship, commonality on adapting common host language, acquiring host citizenship in engaging a variety of professional and less professional associations and contributing to homeland development. Among the Somali Diaspora it is already the norm in addressing and recognising each other as *"reer[7] Norway"*, *"reer UK"*, *"reer Denmark"* and *"reer Canada"* rather than *"reer* qansax and *reer* qurac" the real *qabiilah* references.

Furthermore the Diaspora associations operate within triadic relationship of networks in the host country, homeland and trans-Diaspora contacts and exchanges. Thus a successful transformation depends on diasporic strategies of integration, assimilation and segregation in respective diasporic locations and the activities of the Somalis that might engage in *qurbah badinah* "bad Diaspora" (Mishra, 2006: 121). Similarly, the prevailing inequality in the global, political and economic systems determines the level of success and coherence among the global Somali Diaspora. Those in the core might favour moderation instead of traditionalism. In contrast, those in the semi-periphery or periphery might confront a mixture of institutional, traditional and economic challenges.

Due to the protracted civil war, the Somali Diaspora acquires more responsibility and obligations making them most capable Somalis so far in terms of social, economic and professional resources. That places Somali Diaspora in a crucial position by not only overcoming destructive traditional *qabiilism* but also contributing to the long anticipated development and reintegration of Somalia into the world community.

---

[7] *"Reer"* can roughly be translated as constituent- a form of network that resembles *qabiilah*. Linking the *"reer"* concept to host countries is interesting as Diaspora members began to identify themselves not on link *qabiilah* relations in the homeland but host countries people reside.

CHAPTER 3

SOMALI DIASPORA STUDIES

Introduction

Scholars disagree on whether migration leads to significant social transformations affecting not just individuals and less privileged components but also broader social, economic and institutional structures. Some suggest that migration generates significant global economic, political and social changes (Castells, 2010). Others argue that migration is an important part of world development but that the process brings limited social transformation, as people's basic social and cultural values remain unchanged. Instead the changes affect more on marginal communities, who often disperse and transnationalize (Portes, 2010)

Modern Somali migration resulted from Colonialism. European powers such as Britain, France and Italy invaded and divided the country into so-called British, French and Italian Somalilands. The immediate partition led to Somalis in Eastern Ethiopia and Northern Eastern Kenya becoming Diaspora without migrating from their homes[8]. The deal was sealed at the Berlin conference held in 1884 on the scramble for Africa. Equally significant, colonialism introduced capitalist relations production and circulations to the Somalis. Before colonialism Somalis exchanged food, livestock and locally-produced goods with imports from India and Asia (Najjar, 1973: 117). Qabiil relationship were always significant for the Somali nomads, but in its politicised and divisive version came along with colonial powers, mainly employing the techniques to divide and rule (Samatar, 1992).

When Ibnu-batatu, the Arab historian, visited Mogadishu, he described Somalis as peaceful people with administrative skills and command for multiple languages (Mohammed, 1978). He never mentioned *qabiilism* among the Somalis. The first scholar to conceptualize genealogically Somali

---

[8] Robin Cohen discusses the possibility of people becoming Diaspora without migration. Such groups could include people with certain ideological commonalities for instance anti-capitalist movements and possibly terror networks (Robin, 2008: p.9).

qabiilism was A. M. Lewis, a British anthropologist embedded with the imperial army of British Somaliland (Lewis, 1962).

Somalis become transnational in connection with the colonial expansion in the sense of not just occupying Somalia, but also exploiting the Somali labour to contribute to British colonial endeavours in many parts of the world including Europe (Boahen; 1990: 256). Some have even contributed to the liberation of Europe in joining both World Wars (Fremeau; 2006: 174)[9]. Post independent corrupt civilian regimes accelerated the migration of mainly young Somalis to the Arabian Gulf. Later, the military regime forced the migration of opposition groups, mainly professionals, students and the business elite dissatisfied with the military rule.

Literature on Somali migration, particularly the English written scholarship, focuses on Somali Diaspora in the west. Contemporary studies concentrate on the post- Somali state collapse period where mass Somali migration occurred following the collapse of the state and subsequent anarchy, in a situation where Somalia attracted huge global media attention due to the US involvement and recent increase of radicalization in Somalia. The fact is, nonetheless, Somalis migrated for centuries through the land and sea. Some of the earliest Somali Diaspora was formed in Asia and Africa. Later Somali Diaspora settled in Europe and North America.

Turton (1974), reports that David Stanley made a transit via Aden-Yemen, at the time when it was functioning as a major British imperial port. It is been reported he hired Northern Somalis for his mission to Congo. The opening of Suez Canal made the Aden port important making Somalis taking positions in Aden. Consequently at the end of 19th century, ports in Perth and New York had growing Somali Diaspora communities. For instance the Welsh coast of Britain had the largest concentration of Somalis outside Africa and Arabia. The opening of Suez (1869) Canal encouraged Somali migration and the Sayid Mohamed Abdulla Hassan jihad (1899-1921) contributed to the division of the Somalis and further migration (Al-Safi, 1998). Poverty and drought also made Somalis to migrate. Somali transnationalism is therefore not a recent development. The process goes back to colonial times where Somalis in Kenya mobilized Somalis in Somalia, east Africa and Britain to campaign for increased tax and they wanted the British to identify them as Somalis – not as Africans or natives (Chau, 2010). Somalis were for instance recruited for a variety of services

---

[9] There is monument in Marseille, France commemorating the Somali battalion who died for the liberation of France and Europe.

with the British Empire encompassing Africa, Asia, Europe and even America. There are also Kenyan Somalis who became Diaspora without moving, these are the NFD Somalis. Earlier Kenyan Somalis wanted to unite with Somalia. But in recent years, their situation is much more institutionalized in Kenya, following the collapse of the State. This tells us that Somali migration is older contrary to the claim that migration started 1991. The debates on Diaspora often favour institutions and structures rather than Diaspora agency (Hopkins, 2010). There is a need to conceptualize Diaspora as an intermediate social group between two cultures, identities and homelands.

Diaspora Identity

The English-written studies on Somali Diaspora could be roughly divided into two main components. The first include perspectives that emphasise homeland-oriented essentialist Somali identity formation. The assumption is that Somalis continue to behave as inhabitants in their original homeland. Their social organization, space formation and mobilization correspond to homeland priorities and practices. This approach stresses the significance of originality and belonging based on territorial roots. Ontologically essentialist perspectives assume that Somali social organization, economic and political mobilization and space formations mainly reflect homeland relations. Focus rests on history, originality and traditional institutions.

The second perspectives include studies that emphasize the non-essentialist transnational character of Somali Diaspora. Here Somalis emerge as agents trying to navigate or negotiate between host country and homeland opportunities without necessarily fully belonging to both. This places the Somali Diaspora at the core of the analysis where Somalis themselves find suitable place to link and pursue a better life. Such approaches recognize the complexity of Somali socio-economic relationship and organization reflecting combined opportunities and interaction between homeland-host country spaces, mobilization factors, conditions and constraints. Focus, here, rests on the individual agency in pursuing freedom and better social conditions.

Essentialist Diaspora Formation

In recent times, Somalia has seen the expansion of economic activities, especially in telecommunication companies. Though such developments are linked to financial transactions of Diaspora remittance, these are also related to the existence of ethno-cultural traditional solidarity and trust among the Somalis. Kinship relations, and informal networking and trust help Somalis enforce contracts and deal with the harsh conditions of statelessness (Collins , 2009).

Studying Somalis in Denmark, Kleist (2008) finds that Somalis form Diaspora consciousness that rest on homeland identities. Somalis are divided through *qabiil* and regional affiliations. Their engagement towards homeland and host country reflects their frustration of unsuccessful integration and gender transformation within the traditional Somali family. The transnational engagement is male-dominated due to their pursue of status and self reliance (ibid). The study by Nauja and Hansen (2007) conceptualize the Somali Diaspora from essentialist traditional perspective. For instance they consider Somali Diaspora in Denmark homeland-oriented and a male dominated community group divided into competing *qabiil* constituents. This is argued to have resulted from the lack of Somali men maintaining their previous status as undisputed family breadwinners (ibid.). The assumption is that the Somali man confronts difficulties in adjusting into a Danish society that is modern and insists on gender equality. Confused Somali men then congregate in exclusive Somali associations to express masculine attitudes and in this way obtain social status. In addition, Somali men engage in transnational humanitarian and developmental projects to reclaim lost masculinity (Hansen, 2008).

According to Nauja and Hansen, the spaces that Somalis create in Denmark reflect homeland traditions. For instance the Somali associations in Denmark are male- dominated. The activities that take place there say more about male chauvinism and female oppression than integration into the host country (Nauja, 2008; Hansen, 2008). For them, when Somalis remit, they do so to sustain traditional *qabiil* relationship. It is the same with regard to mobilization. Somalis engage in transnational politics through their *qabiil*, sub-*qabiil* and regional affiliations, all leading to more belonging to traditional homeland identity rather than to Danish reality. Absent from their analysis is the Somalis' link to the host opportunities and constraints that often condition their behaviour not just in the host society but beyond.

The description of the Somali Diaspora as traditional-oriented ignores the urban—rural and class distinctions within the Somali Diaspora. In addition, both Nauja and Hansen underestimate the dynamics of the opportunity structures in which Somalis find themselves. For instance, there is no mention of the social exclusion and the challenges Somalis confront in a country that in recent years had a conservative government insisting upon the differences between the Danish society and the immigrants from developing countries and Islamic countries (Olwig and Paerregaard, 2007: 52).

Horst (2008) questions the analytical limitation with macro *qabiil* research focusing mostly on state and society boundaries. Instead she proposes an emphasis on the individual groups and their transnational interactions at sub-community and regional level rather at state level (ibid). Economic transactions, homeland conflicts and peace-making take place not in relation to presumed macro levels but within sub-*qabiil* level (ibid.). Such activities become more intensified with the help of web media, where most are *qabiil* homepages but there are also some serious ones (Salwe &Olden, 2008)

Non-essentialist Diaspora Formation

The proper characteristics of the Somali Diaspora are far from the static social relations and interactions postulated by scholars on the essentialist identity formation perspective. Somali Diaspora forms a politicized Diaspora similar to other Diasporas that e.g. create non-national Muslim Diaspora (Werbner, 2000) and there are diverse Diasporas creating a black Diaspora (Gilroy, 1993). The individual agency of Diaspora is influenced directly and indirectly by local and distant social dynamics introducing a hybrid belonging.

A comparative analysis of Somali women in Toronto and London shows that Somali women form transnational Diaspora practices directly and indirectly linked to by host country constraints and challenges together with homeland traditions (Hobkins, 2010). This is demonstrated through modifications in dress, religious and linguistic practices in the host country (ibid.). Consequently Somali Diaspora identity formation is not just linked and determined by certain originality and geographical location.

The core of transnationalism is its emphasis on social, cultural and political fields that cross geographical boundaries (Basch et al., 1994: 7). It is mainly economic centric and assumes the movement of people in voluntary basis. But scholars find that refugee transnationalism (Sherrell and Hyndman 2006) refers to distinct expressions of such social fields across international borders among refugees who did not choose the conditions of their departure. Compared to voluntary migrants, refugees have distinct relationship with their homeland and also their host countries (Al-Ali, Black, and Koser, 2001). Thus the refugee transnationalism involves ruptures rather than connections, as the conventional transnationalism presumes (Hyndman, 2010).

We need to examine the internal dynamics of migration and Diaspora formation. Traditionally migration studies focus on pre-migration, departure and relationship with the homeland and post-migration context, the conditions under which migrants prevail during their adjustment in the homeland. Likewise, conventional studies ignore the transition period in which many immigrants and refugees find themselves in almost any situation between departure and settlement and between homeland and potential host country. Under such circumstances instead of geographies and institutions, it is rather the psychological dimensions and interactions among peer groups and networking that are the core for social interaction (Rousseau *et al.*, 1998).

Moreover, Griffiths (1997) refers to the difference of adaptation between ordinary migrants and refugees. The initial trauma of departure continues to influence the way of life left behind, to subsequent stages of *"transculturation in which exiles psychologically open their suitcases and try to forge individual projects"* (Joly and Cohen, 1989: 127). Griffiths argues that in tower Hamlets *qabiil* relationship exists but is under transformation due to intergenerational and gender challenges. Somali Diaspora tries to adapt new forms of relationship. The question is which relationships prevail or whether they co-exist.

Adjusting into their host society and joining already existing social opportunities and constraints Diaspora Somalis develop strong religious identity both in London and Canada (McGown, 1999: 228). This is not the revitalization of traditional Islam in Somalia - it is more conservative (ibid.: 229). It is conditioned by the social context and spaces provided by host countries and how the Somali Diaspora react to it (ibid.: 166).

As Muslims, Somalis confront challenges such as secularism in particularly western host countries. In Canada, a country with a multi-cultural tradition, Somalis face challenges with regard to the integration in the country (Collet, 2007). Here, the religious transformation that Somalis undergo is more important than the *qabiil* dimension.

With regard to Diaspora's economic exchanges with the homeland the argument that economic transactions to Somalia follow traditional homeland identities is similarly questionable. Lindley (2009) contends that Somali remittance is complex and depends on a number of factors. The Diaspora perspective can help us better understand remittance not just as a process of money transactions, but also as a social process linked to status formation (ibid.).

There are examples where Somalis are integrated and managed to overcome traditional barriers with the Help of Tabligi movement and the Indian Muslim community in South Africa (Sadouni, 2009). Somalis in South Africa (in the cities Mayfair and Fordsburg) categorize themselves as Muslims by organizing their own mosques and associations, as they gratually develop their own Somali-Muslim identity (ibid.).

Somalis create and mobilize religious institutions such as mosques and schools for teaching their children. In economic terms, they pursue entrepreneurship and economic investment based on traditional ethno-religious solidarity linked to the formal economy of the host country. On certain occasions such as the experiences in Kenya, South Africa and the UAE, Somali Diaspora represents a significant economic factor. Somali Diaspora economy is for instance a significant portion of the formal Kenyan economy (Campbell, 2006).

The level of cultural transformation among the Somalis and the adaptation of the country's culture depend on various factors. Younger Somalis who either arrived at a young age or were born in the UK oppose to FGM. Male and less integrated individuals might approve of FGM (Morison *et* al., 2004). The assumption is that the more people integrate and assimilate the more they abandon homeland traditions. Here one forgets that FGM is also controversial in Somalia. There are urban, rural and class differences. In addition, the practice is non-Islamic.

Non-Western Literature on Somali Diaspora

The Arab Islamic literature on Somali migration and Diaspora is comparatively older than the literature on Somali Diaspora produced in the West in recent years. Similarly the contents and the themes investigated by Arab and Islamic scholars are also different. The Western literature talks about Somali migration for economic reasons while the oriental literature, discusses Somali migration following colonial partition and domination of

31

Somalia. Eastern scholars also focus on the contribution made by those colonized to the colonial economic exploitation and development as well as, on behalf of colonial powers, fighting for imperial wars. In addition, they consider the Somali migration as a serious deficit for the country as the Somalis who migrated were mainly those with educational capabilities, leading to brain drain[10].

The *qabiil* as central organization factor is a research topic that dominates the western, mainly English-written, literature on Somalia and Somalis. It is possible to offer several explanations for the *qabiil* overemphasis. The first is that I. M. Lewis, the grand old man in Somali western scholarship laid the foundation for successive Western Somali *"Knowledge of archeology"* and *"orientalism"*. He has, in other words, succeeded in framing the conceptualiz ation of Somali society through *qabiil* lenses. The second is the modern state societies in the West including researchers who sometimes preoccupied with the dichotomy of modern and less modern, civilized and non-civilized. The Somali project as a *qabiil* research considered the Somali society as antithesis to the progressive bureaucratic societies. Research projects would then investigate how *qabiilistic* and traditional Somalis were. In this regard, the *qabiil* research serves as project for social cohesion and confirmation not for the Somalis but for the involved groups and institutions. For instance, the major *qabiil* analysis project conducted by Lewis among the nomads in Somaliland in 1950s was funded by the British Defence Ministry, which was at the time called the war ministry (Besteman, 1996). Direct colonialism might have ended but post-colonial hegemony prevails.

This research also refers and analyses Somali Diaspora's application of *qabiil*. But unlike the essentialist oriented research focus, the study describes and analyses how Somalis utilize the traditional relationship for strategic rather than for genealogical motives. As indicated in the empirical part of this study, *qabiil* relationships are dynamic and the application by Diaspora depends on prevailing circumstances in the host country, homeland developments, global networks and the overall socio-economic and political conditions in which the individual Somali Diaspora finds himself/herself in.

Another interesting point is that the Arab Islamic literature informs us that in the past, Somalia was a country of emigration where Arabs who had economic, political and social difficulties in the Arabian peninsula settled along the Somali coast (Nasif, 1974). Apart from the Yemeni Diaspora, there

---

[10] al-Majallah, Issues 613-620, al-Sharikah al-Sa'ūdīyah lil-Abḥāth wa-al-Taswīq al-Barīṭānīyah, 1991

were also Italians, Indians, other Asians, Ethiopians and many other Africans that settled in the country. We also need to remember Portuguese settlements in places like Barawe (Abdiwahid, 2001)[11]. The Portuguese seafarer and "discoverer" of the sea route to India (1497-99), Vasco da Gamma, was the first European who in 1499, on his return from India, bombarded Mogadishu, at the time according to Ibn-battuta, who visited the city about 170 years earlier, an urban prosperous stable city (Subrahmanyam; 1998: 121). This confirms that confrontation between western powers and Somalis is not restricted to recent colonial and post-colonial periods. The tendency in media and research is to start the Somali history and development from 1991, the period following the collapse of the Somali military regime, and from 1992 when Americans lost 18 marines in Mogadishu in confrontation with local warlords[12]. Like many other coastal cities across the country, Mogadishu brought diverse peoples from different parts of the world together. Old neighbourhood names such as *Billaajo Carab, Cambo Amxaaro, Beexaani, Shinganis, Casa Populare, or Yaqshiid* confirm such cosmopolitan historic coexistence[13].

Research on Somali Diaspora suffers from essentialist bias, and it is important to bring how the essentialist argues in contrast with non-essentialist. In this research we look the Somali Diaspora phenomenon with open theoretical and empirical perspectives without excluding the range of ways by which the Somali migration has been presented. In this regard western approaches have been contrasted with non-western approaches. It is important to have examined both western and non-western with the purpose of getting deeper and richer understanding of the Diaspora condition. We have therefore applied a multiple methods and analysis in

---

[11] *Brava* (Barawa, Baraawe) Port town located south of Mogadishu on the Indian Ocean coast of *Somalia*. ... In 1503, *Brava's* sea merchants were threatened by *Portuguese* pirates and agreed to pay tribute to them in exchange for safe passage (Encyclopedia of African history and culture: From conquest to colonization (1500 to 1850), Volume 3
Facts on File Library of world history) Willie F. Page, Facts on file, Inc, Facts on File, 2001.

[12] The conflict was profiled in a best seller written, Bowden Mark (2010). Black Hawk Down: A Story of Modern War. Grove press, and Hollywood filmatised.

[13] http://wardheernews.com/articles/Feb/perspective_faisal.htm.

bringing the community at the centre of data collection and analysis. This epistemological approach follows an emancipatory method that engages both essentialist and non-essentialist approaches with the objective of going beyond their weaknesses to generate as much empirically grounding social reality as possible.

CHAPTER 4

METHODOLOGICAL CONSIDERATIONS

The knowledge source

An old saying goes the moment an *Alim* (a scholar) begins to believe his/her own superior knowledge capability then the *Alim* begins to demonstrate ignorance. This implies knowledge accumulation infinity. Reality not exempted from this study focusing on the Somali Diaspora in transnational context, particularly those in Denmark and the UAE. The research process involves the selection of cases, the identification of the respondents, the collection of information and the analysis and interpretation. With regard to the chosen philosophy and methodology, in terms of the researcher's own *habitus* (Bourdieu, 1993), the work reflects the researcher's continuing active membership of the Somali Diaspora community and a decade long professional work as an official at the municipality, working with organizations and governmental institutions dealing with the Somali Diaspora in Denmark. Recognizing the epistemological and methodological research position improves and makes the study more sincere and convincing. In this way the researcher's world view comes to represent the research methodology itself (Neuman, 2000), thus confirming the proposition that our knowledge mainly emerging from human interactions, observations and interpretations.

Whether the knowledge acquired through individual lenses qualify as an acceptable science remains debatable. Positivists emphasize the objectivity of scientific inquiry based on knowledge confirmed by the senses. In contrast, interpretivist proponents contend research should contain practical and applicable wisdom with the aim to capture the subjective *"inner meaning of social action"* (Ballard, & Heshusius, 1996: 79). The assumption is that objects do not exist independently but rather emerge from constant reflection through the process of discourse and conceptualization. Foucault makes a point when he links discourse to power relations and social hierarchy in the society. He argues for the elevation of our experiences and point of views to a useful knowledge making through the application of multiple lenses:

> There are times in life when the question of knowing if one can think differently than one thinks, and perceive differently than one sees, is absolutely necessary if one is to go on looking and reflecting at all. (Foucault, 1990: 8)

Foucault further suggests the prevailing discourse as well as contextual historical background and consciousness impact our social understanding and conceptualization (Foucault, 1982: 209). This implies research taking interaction and discourses seriously appears more inclusive as it stresses a dialogue which represents a *"pragmatic knowledge"* (Bourdieu, 1977).

The privilege of sensing, thinking and reflecting experiences simultaneously characterizes human behaviour. That does not mean we are immune from social or institutional mediation, modification and influences. In this context, discourse and language attain greater significance. There exist different perceptions of pure science contra narrative based and contextually embedded knowledge. Some of us prefer less complex frameworks in taking the world out there for granted. Such perspectives assume a value free approach with researcher relying on sampling scientific methods and testing. The expectation is to construct universally valid theory justifying or confirming presumed assumptions (Turner, 1996: 157).

Other scholars point the complexity of acquiring and verifying the thing we might consider knowledge. They propose the following distinctions: The *cilmulyaqiin* which is knowledge we get through hearing or listening. The *ceynulyaqiin*, which we get through seeing. The *xaqul yaqiin* which is knowledge that we not only see and sense but knowledge that affects us personally (Aldanij, 2003: 185). Advancing this knowledge acquisition framework, the Arab-Islamic scholar and sociologist Ibnu-Khaldun (1332-1406) suggests the measurement and the observation of historical processes and experiences should constitute the core into a scientific inquiry. For him historical observations and reflections can help the researcher to explain the rise and decline of social systems in response to social transformations (in Rosenthal's translation of Muqadimah, 1958: 414).

Research on the Diaspora topic demands openness in knowledge gathering and willingness to incorporate. An opportunity not often visible at dominant social science scholarship mainly focusing on the analysis of states, nations and boundaries (Wagner *et* al., 1991: 8). The traditional state-centred approach subordinates social processes operating below or beyond the mainstream sphere. Diaspora realities challenge the nation-state exclusivity and boundary making. Thus- its multilayered frame and its transnational context call for the consideration of alternative tools. One such option is the so-called simultaneity approach suggesting the close examination of people's transnational experiences and conducts (Levitt and Schiller, 2004).

Thus, this study, focusing on Somali transnational conduct and experience, draws use of the constructionist epistemological and ontological position. The research assumes basic ideas and themes emerging from the collected data and not from a pre-existing, objective category. According to Bryman (2008), the constructivist approach asserts social actors continually form the social phenomenon and attach *"alternative meaning and significance"* to it.

Research influences

If we accept knowledge mainly emanates from human interaction, then it is possible to conclude human perceptions and prioritization influence research conduct. Bryman (2008) described such influences as the researcher's understanding and interpretation on the epistemological and ontological approaches, the theoretical frames, the values and the practical considerations of collecting data.

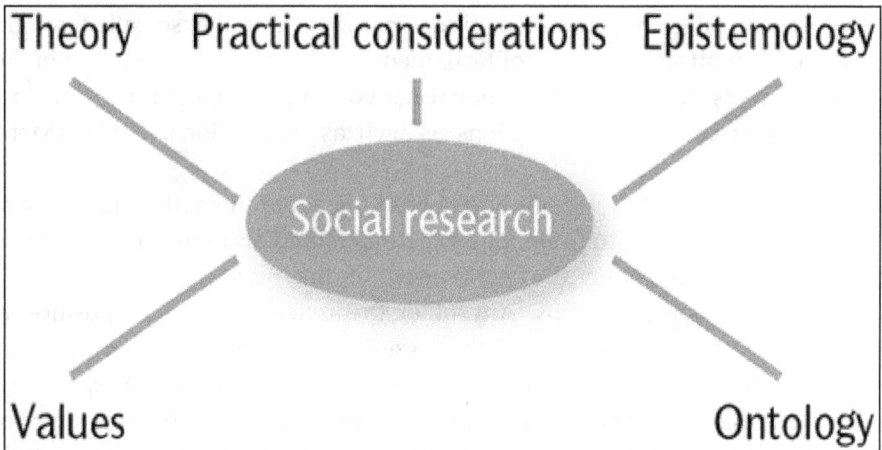

Figure 4.1   Influences in social science

The assumption is that data is often collected in relation to a particular theoretical paradigm, social value or believe on how the world should be analysed and interpreted. This study recognizes unavoidability of influences on research conduct from multiple sources.

As a researcher originating from Somalia and an active member of the Somali Diaspora, the author's position influences the course and the conduct of the research. Obviously this raises objectivity questions and the ability to keep a critical distance in analyzing and interpreting Somali Diaspora conditions. Particularly intriguing is the interpretation of a familiar world one feels attached and fully integrated to. This research does claim neither pure science nor objectivity. Nor do the author intends to create an epistemological inconsistence by asserting *"a monopolistic access"* or *" an exclusive knowledge"* on the concerned community (Merton, 1972). Instead, the project aims at finding and sharing with others what, in Foucaultian terms, is referred to as *"subjugated knowledge"* (Foucault, 1980: 97). This is a knowledge emanating from marginal perspectives often operating or circulating outside the radar of dominant scholarship and society.

Furthermore, the existing scholarship on Diaspora pays significant attention to classical and other powerful Diaspora within the analytical state and nationhood framework (Safran, 1991; Cohen, 2008; Clifford, 1994). The Somali Diaspora is an emerging Diaspora struggling for over two decades within statelessness framework in a fragmented civil war torn nation and country. The recent influx of the Somali migrants, refugees, particularly those reaching the west, the piracy paradox and the so-called religious extremism attracts greater political, media and academic attention. Similarly the Somalis' mobility, transnational networking and continuing link to the homeland confused host nations as well as international NGOs (Mehler, 2009: 355).

By talking to the Somalis and not talking about them, this study takes an inductive approach to listen, observe, understand and interpret the Somalis. This is done through the exploration of the perspectives they hold as individuals and as groups. Any other theoretical existing proposition and characterization build around the core empirical findings from the study. Hence, the gravity of this study centres on what the Somali Diaspora in the two compared/contrasted cases do and have to say about their life situations.

To better grasp the complexity of the Somali Diaspora we need to compare various perspectives including qualitative investigation and interpretation. Particularly residential enclaves in distinctive social spaces in which the Somali Diaspora live contain rich insights on the social biographies and conditions.

Comparative approach and case selection

This study has a comparative design as it compares/contrasts Somali Diaspora communities in Denmark and the UAE. Denmark is an advanced democratic, stable welfare state. The UAE is a traditional conservative, undemocratic, rentier oil state. The two cases also differ on the historical processes of exit and reception with regard to the Somalis and other immigrants. It was comparatively recent, around two decades ago, when Denmark received a large number of Somalis, while the link between the Somalis and the Emirates goes back to centuries. So it is not an exaggeration to claim the UAE hosts old Somali Diaspora while Denmark accommodates an emerging Somali Diaspora, still in its formative stages.

Selecting and comparing/contrasting the two cases is therefore in accordance with the case study method; a research strategy that analyses a single or two cases (Stake, 1995). The decision to include or exclude cases rest on the criteria of critical and better understanding of the situation and the consideration of which cases provide better insights with regard to the research topic (Stake, 2000: 446). The comparative design entails studying two presumably contrasting cases with the application of similar methods. The reasoning of such comparative approach is that we can understand, in this case the Somali Diaspora better, in comparing two dissimilar cases, the Danish and the Emirati contexts. Hantrais (1996) argues for the capability of comparative case studies in examining social phenomenon in two or more countries. The intention is to see and interpret the occurrence of such phenomenon in the different socio-cultural contexts.

Similar to other methodological decisions, the case approach needs validation. The familiar falsification proposition by Karl Popper (2002) helps this endeavour. According to Popper, we should focus on the deviant case and the particular in for instance investigating how, when, where and why this particular case does not fit the conventional scholarship. Then from this perspective we can falsify the dominant discourse or eventually modify and improve it.

Description of Countries	DK	UAE
Type of state	Modern welfare state	Cliental traditional state
Type of economy	Small competitive economy	Reinter economy (except Dubai)
Society	Homogeneous society, protestant, state religion	Multicultural, Islam state religion, (millions of foreigners with multi-cultural and religious background)
Political system	Constitutional monarchy with Consensus coalition democracy, multiple parties	7 Emirates untied into a federal system under conservative monarchy in 1971
Ethnic relation	Restrictive/selective 19.000 Migrants/refugees	Labour, Multi-cultural (Native-foreign difference)
Somalis in the country Migration type		Estimate-200.000 Migrants/refugees

Table 4.1   Contrasting Denmark and the UAE

Participants

Both in Denmark and in the UAE, the enumeration of Somali residents is inaccurate. Comparatively, Denmark provides a statistical overview of Somalis. However, this official data registration relaying on random registration does not necessarily reflect the actual presence of the presumed number of Somalis in the country. Instead of trying to randomly select probability samples, this study applies snowball techniques reflecting a sociological sampling. The approach assumes the contribution of respondents themselves in the sample formation process. In this way, respondents participate in the research effort. The technique also referred to as *"theoretical sampling"* (Glaser & Strauss, 1967) promotes knowledge generated from the members' daily activities. The research method depends on social interaction with and through individuals in an attempt to recruit and reach other relevant respondents (Bearsworth and Keil 1992: 261). The snowball method has nonetheless its limitations. The sample lacks overall representative and generalization beyond the selected respondents (Bryman, 2008: 185).

Research methods

Search for Information (xog doon)

Somalis enjoy talking and transmitting information. In traditional Somali society, verbal ability represents a prime requirement from any person with self-respect. As Afrax (2000) points out, the daily interaction among traditional Somalis is based on oral narratives rich in proverbs and metaphors. Somalis seek information almost all the time. This does not necessarily mean they routinely look for knowledge. The immediate goal is information per say and that could eventually become some sort of knowledge. The primary purpose of knowledge seeking aims at fulfilling and advancing personal gains and ambitions. The more than 14 ways in which the Somalis greet each other reflect the constant search for, and exchange of, information. The most frequent of such a greeting is *iska warran* which roughly translates to "tell me about your condition".

Preoccupied with information seeking conduct, each person expects accessing valuable sources. Then a mutual exchange of give and take becomes apparent. The potential informer is initially concerned in securing *kalsooni* (trust) from the receiver side of the information. This process requires time and patience as most respondents do not provide information unconditionally. People make sure interview sessions bring no risks. One possible way to break the ice entails the interviewer or the researcher providing some useful relevant information for the informant.

In agro-pastoral societies, people need to know about possible rainfalls, grassing areas and potential intercommunity conflicts. For the Somali Diaspora, information seeking has equally a critical role. Many of them frequent Somali political web sites that introduce and analyse developments in the homeland (Salwe, 2008).

We can probably compare the conflicts and hostile environments in the classic agro-pastoral context with the current modern challenges of looking for opportunities and adjustment in host countries. Trust concerns not only respondents and researchers in a research context but also entails as Giddens (1991) suggests in all social relations. Research participants pay critical attention to the researchers and the systems they represent (ibid.). This requires a delicate balance between the researcher's focus on the content and outcome of the research and the possible sympathetic tendencies one might have towards respondents (Reinharz, 1992). The researcher particularly needs to avoid the risk of *"excessive emotional involvement"* in the research process (Lee-Treweek, 2000). In order to create an atmosphere of trust, the researcher needs to overcome the give and take hurdle. The idea of the researcher revealing some of his biographical history might help.

Goffman's analysis of fragmented identities of the existence of simultaneous front and back stage regions of human behaviour is relevant in this regard. In social interaction individuals interchangeably adapt front or back stage performances as identities constantly shift (Goffman, 1959: 106). The researcher, having own front and back stage regions, aims at studying the back stage region of the respondents, meaning their migration history and diasporic personal thoughts and experiences. Here comes the compromise in eventually revealing some kind of back stage aspects on the part of the researcher. Mutual trust between the informant and the researcher might subsequently ease the barriers of front and back stage performances and might at the same time improve understanding and accessibility not only to the individual respondents but also to the network they belong to.

Often Somali group formations appear less fixed and formalised. Leaders and organizers, who remain active in community mobilization, occupy the top of the group. Others, for a variety of reasons, show no interest in involving in community efforts. Reaching such diverse and dynamic groups calls for the application of multiple methods. Approaching these various components, initially the author decided to be informal in, for instance, not openly advertising my researcher background. The aim was to appear less authoritative and more accommodating. The approach informalized the situation in creating a calmer atmosphere for engaging dialogue. Most of the respondents belonged to existing social network. Through this network, the study reached additional respondents for an interview. One of the obvious benefits of being informal was letting respondents speak openly and sincerely assuming the researcher as part of their network. This might raise an ethical dilemma, as the researcher later intends to use the informal information for a formal research context.

The traditional Somali structure placing elders at the top of the social hierarchy and children at the bottom prevails among the Diaspora. Therefore initial contacts to the community started with the elders. Among the Somalis, traditional elder leaders represent the *Huddun* (the umbilical) of the Somali people. From their position, these community leaders engage in a web of links with others. Unlike those with public official positions normally going out and seeking information for professional purposes, any important development in the community reaches the traditional leaders through their routine interactions with the locals.

The problem is that many Somalis, especially elders, do not directly refer to documents. They prefer articulation and oratory rather than written documents. When elders proclaim something as correct others confirm it as reliable and useful. The honour referred to the elders and particularly to their long experiences and wisdom characterizes the tradition. Any person longing for community respect (to become *akhyaar* knowledgeable) should posses some of the following social qualities.

1) *Ha or cadaado* "one's clothes must be clean". The person should avoid dirty not only in the metaphorical sense on one's clothes but also in mind and behaviour. This implies the requirement from a respected community leader to demonstrate patience and avoid corruption.
2) *Ha uus weynaado* "one should have a big stomach" for personal attacks and complaints – implies tolerance and forgiveness for criticism.
3) *Ha ul madoobaado* "one's stick should be black" this metaphor implies a lifelong experience as traditional leaders participate in numerous meetings and social gatherings. In such social events the elders put *subag*- cooking oil from the served food- in their stick making its colour to change from being red or white to black.

Another important employed interview tool was the use of *kaftan*, a popular Somali version of pre-conversing. *Kaftan* functions as an ice breaker and makes the conversational atmosphere more relaxed. Similarly, respondents proposed the interview location in taking place either in their houses or any other preferred location.

In contrast to western societies with apparent demarcation of the boundaries between the individual person and the collective society, among the Somalis, the individual and the common society intermix. This makes selecting an individual for an interview difficult. The surrounding environment, in the form of relatives, friends and community members, usually intervene. For instance, on certain occasions, the plan was to meet an individual for a scheduled interview but the individual arrived, the location with accompanying three additional people. The interview session proceeded with some inputs from the group.

The lack of clear collective-individual distinction hardly surprises an insider researcher. Sharing life stories and experiences one fully identifies with the ideas and complications respondents express. Nonetheless certain differences exist. Not only do the researcher represents a particular professional academic background but also belongs to Somali migrant arrivals that migrated from a relatively well-functioning society, under harsh dictatorship, but a less disintegrated nation and state. Such migration background classifies the researcher belonging to the most privileged Somalis in the Diaspora. Part of the Diaspora blessed with legal status and better education in host countries in comparison to the more traumatised and marginalised recent arrivals. Therefore, for some respondents, the researcher might appear as an elite distant Somali. Similarly, as a Somali with urban background, in the two fieldwork trips, the researcher confronted some minor challenges in reaching Somalis with pastoral background. Interviewing and even understanding an informant with rural background requires expressive oral qualities with particular social tones. In addition, accessing Somali women, particularly in the UAE, represented a challenge. This is not related to the feminist inspired debate on ethnic women suffering from male sanctioned oppression and segregation as gender relations not always contradict but also complement (Al-Salih, 2007: 60). It was rather linked to the Somali women in the UAE having pre-occupied with work and family affairs. Eventually, the study managed to reach some of them through associated networks, their husbands and close relatives. The main challenge was to determine the interview location. Some of the women consented a meeting at their homes, others in their businesses and work places.

Gender remains an issue among the Somalis. Responding to the contextual and social changes in host countries Somali women adjust to new roles and functions. They create their own women specific formal and informal networks, by collecting funds and mobilizing support. Being with other women, provides Somali women with *iskukalsooni* *"self-confidence"*. So in order to normalize and demystify the interview situation with Somali women, the author invited acquaintances to participate in the interview session. The problem was the friends sometimes intervene the conversation.

Location was particularly a critical research point at the UAE. Most people were busy working. In their leisure time, many socialised in cafeterias. Many were therefore interviewed in these crowded and noisy places. This meant not only disturbances but also people became suspicious on note taking and recording.

Among the Somalis, knowledge building is accumulative. People seek identification what others have said and how they interpret events. The historical background is important for assessing what people personally achieved for themselves and for the community. *"Ninka aad kabaha ka tolneyso kabihiisa ayaa la eegaa"* (The one you intend to repair your shoes from must first fix his own shoes).

Acquiring proper information from Somali respondents involves certain engagement with selective groups. For instance, Somali women form their own groups further subdivided into women with families *(xaasas)* and single women or divorced *(un-married or Garoob)*. Men divide themselves into different *qabiils*, class groups, some frequenting *qat*[14] sessions and those active in community organizations. Each group differs on the understanding and interpretation of diasporic conditions. Reaching out of the Somali youth, on the other hand, is less challenging as they are relatively more accessible. They demonstrate flexibility and share their experiences with minimum preconditions. The challenge lies with their limited experiences resulting in not much detailed information.

Interviews (Iswareysi)

For Somalis, oratory is a cultural asset. A Somali saying goes *"Nin aan hadlin hoyadiina wax ma siiso"* Someone who does not talk, meaning articulate, even his mother might ignore. Furthermore, interviewing methods provided by the conventional literature, with emphasis on registering, listing and consenting, will not succeed in a Somali context. Instead, some respondents preferred *iswareysi* "conversing". They first reveal their thoughts when they enter a mutual relaxed conversation. This

---

[14] Qat is classified as a plant Somalis and Yemenis chew or make a tea to obtain stimulant (Jan Dirk Blom (2009). A Dictionary of Hallucinations. Springer, p. 441).

implies the researcher entering dialogue and information exchange in equal terms.

Nonetheless, initially, the study applied a semi-structured interview consisting of three main questions covering the migration history, the adaptation process in the host country and the subsequent link and involvement to the homeland. Under the three main questions, eight major thematic areas emerged capturing Diaspora dynamics between the host country and the home country. Semi-structured interview makes the research open to additional issues and concerns respondents might raise. The plan was to upgrade issues and the topic under investigation as the interview proceeds (Beardsworth and Keil 1992: 261-2). It turned out even the semi-structured interview will not work in the field. When the conversation starts it is difficult to refer and use pre-prepared interview points.

Respondents interviewed in the UAE consist of two main groups. One group the author came into contact with through the names recommended by the network in Denmark. These initial contacts then introduced additional potential respondents from their network. For instance, they told their friends briefly about the author coming from an academic institution in Denmark and wanting to write a book about the Somali Diaspora. Some of the information they provided was not fully correct but there was no need for correction to avoid creating uncertainties.

This study also reached some respondents through distant relatives the author met in the UAE. They introduced their network with an opportunity to interview and discuss. The problem was that certain amount went to chatting about recent developments on a particular region and other minor local developments in Somalia.

The most serious challenge was getting respondents to focus on the research issue and the topics under discussion. Somalis enjoy simultaneously debating on multiple issues. The author was careful not to offend anyone by telling people to concentrate on the relevant issues. Most interviews were recorded immediately. In un-recordable situations, brief notes were taken with regard to the main points raised by the respondents. When respondents rejected recordings and note-taking, the author memorises and wrote down as soon as there was an opportunity to do so. In addition, after listening the interviews, un-understandable areas in the recorded interview was deleted considering it as a *"peace of unclear talk"*. (Gerson and Horowits, 2002: 211).

Participant Observation

The author considers himself an insider and thus did not spend much time on where and when to find places to observe. Research questions deal with how Somalis organize and mobilize and what aspects of their migration history and integration to the host country influence their activities. In this regard, the Diaspora associations/organizations have great impact on the decisions people take to link and contribute to the homeland, as well as their efforts to integrate and adjust into the host society. The study aimed at observing groups and people's activities in social contexts.

This is not a theoretically deductive research approach but a qualitative inductive research expecting data to emerge from interviews and observations. So the author visited Diaspora spaces including residential spaces, cafeterias, restaurants, business and other working spaces. In Denmark, the author knows most Diaspora spaces. In the UAE, the network and their friends assisted to find the locations. The author did not formally tell the Somalis he was a researcher and observing the situation. This was a normal situation, as Somalis do these activities routinely. If one declares the researcher background, relevant information might not emerge, as people would begin speculating an investigator in their midst. To avoid unnecessary tension, the author assumed the role as a Somali visiting the location. On some occasions, the author went to these locations with people interviewed earlier, their network or some other acquaintances. People were obviously relaxed when they saw you accompanied with someone they know.

In the process of conducting observations, the author did not have a pre-formulated idea of what to observe but had in mind an approach resembling a situational analysis focusing on *"Significant local images': Significant people, significant things, or significant observable events"* (Van Valsen, 1967). This is an observation method combining focus on people's everyday life while trying to capture the overall picture (Dresch and James 2000: 2). Emphasis rests on people's activities and their interaction with the surrounding society and its structures. During observation, the study paid attention to important people, important things, important ideas and important events at the location. Similar to the interview recording, the author had some challenges with recording. The circumstances did not allow taking notes in public places. Instead, memorisation of what happened and writing down quickly when opportunity allowed was the best option. In this regard, the study drew use of field notes classification by Lofland and Lofland (1995). They differentiate *mental notes*, a suitable method for the researcher feeling inappropriate taking notes formally, *Jotted notes*, a brief written notes recording main events and ideas, and finally *full field notes* which, detailed observation notes (Lofland and Lofland 1995: 90).

Associations

Identifying Somali Diaspora leadership and their respective organisations is a rather challenging task, as most organizations prefer to remain unofficial. Most have no formal offices and declared leadership, particularly in the UAE. Therefore, we need alternative identifying methods to see how such networks function. Somalis form and dissolve organizations depending on their current needs. The existence of many of these organizations is unknown to the authorities. The author observed some of them in the UAE, a country that prohibits public political organization and manifestations.

This study focuses on organisations established by members of the Somali community and influential members in these organisations. The criteria of observing the Somali associations make use of Lofland's model of organizational activities (Lofland, 1996). The loflands particularly look at the role and the activities of the associations and the outcome.

Reliability and Validity

This study adheres to the qualitative research design approach and tries not to imitate the quantitative research often stressing reliability, hypo research testing and presumed objectivity. Yet as Creswell and Miller (2000) suggest, it recognises the need to validate the study. Claims should be supported with concrete evidence (Seale, 1999: 52). The problem is that what constitutes evidence as such is debatable, depending on our knowledge situation and context. While some consider *"appropriate"* data (Kvale, 1996), others might level it as unreliable as there are no data to discover. Evidence first emerges from the interview situation as respondents acquire and develop knowledge through interaction and exchange (Holstein and Gubrium, 1995: 30). In order to make the study more reliable and valid, we probably need to reflect on the power relations in the research situation, and that itself constitutes what Kvale (1995) referred to as *"pragmatic validity"*.

Thus the above-mentioned multiple methods used in reaching out the diverse Somali respondents in the two comparative cases qualify pragmatic validity. In addition, after the interviews a reality check provided opportunity for some of the respondents to comment the transcripts and the conclusions of the analysis.

Furthermore, the study reflects the suggestions by Lincoln and Guba in checking the reliability and the validity of the research. The first is to achieve *"Credibility"* by checking participant background. The second relates to the process of *"Transferability"* in linking the findings to other relevant studies. The third is *"Dependability"* achieved through peer auditing. And finally *"Conformability"*, involving the reflexivity on the research conducts (Lincoln and Guba, 1985: 247).

Analysis

Preliminary data analysis started while conducting and transcribing interviews. The combination provided an opportunity to structure basic ideas and models presuming the research prospect. The process involves systematic gleaning of themes or basic concepts from transcribed interviews and the observation notes. This early stage of language assessment represents the early stages of inductive concept development, the *'building blocks of theory'* (Strauss and Corbin 1998: 101). The study applied particular transcription techniques inspired by (Kvale, 1997) and the data was transferred to a software data management program QSR Nvivo. It is divided into respondents (the DK cases and the UAE cases), observations (the DK cases and the UAE cases), associations (the DK cases and the UAE cases), external data (main relevant theories and summary of similar studies and research) and finally extracts of relevant Danish and Emirates media and internet outputs dealing with the Somalia Diaspora.

The study draws use of Ryan G. W and Bernard H R (2003) introducing an analytical thematic model with five major theme development aspects. These include *"repetitions topics, indigenous typologies or categories, metaphors and analogies, transitions, and finally similarities and differences"*(ibid., 2003). Advancing this model, Bogdan R. C. & Biklen S. K (1992) proposed an analytical process in finding relevant topics from the context, perspectives held by the respondents, the respondents' ways of thinking about people and objects, process, activities and strategies involving the informant's relationship with social structures.

The combination of these models serves this study as initial thematic development stage concentrated on phenomenon related to activity/action, context/setting, perspectives, strategy, relations and consequences. The multiple applications of complementary or contradicting methods improves the quality and the validation of the analysis. For instance, some interviews are long and in a narrative form in which respondents instead of responding to asked questions start narrating long, personal stories. In order to reduce the text to manageable data and get the proper meaning the study employed alternative models. One such model is Labov's (1972) model of transcription and analysis. This model distinguishes abstract (*What was this about?*) from orientation (*Who, What, When,Where*).

In addition, Geertz (1973) suggests we can improve data quality analysis through *"analytical generalization"* by using analytical findings from the actual study to test or change general ideas. The following table shows how a response from the interview link to social, structure and agency.

Table 4.2   **Dimensions of analysis**

Respondent	Response	Agency	Social Fields	Structure	Core-Concept
Abdalaziz (DK)	I was attracted to Aarhus because the city is home to many Somalis & I wanted to contribute to religious and social empowerment	Wish to empower & change	Social urban dynamic setting	Danish state policies restrict refugee-immigrants mobility in the first	Comm-unity netwo rking

The following chapter introduces some of the ideas presented by major western and eastern social scientists to elucidate social processes and transformations. Particular emphasis rests on whether major conclusions from the ideas presented by the prominent scholars relate to the analysis of Diaspora development, space formation and mobilization. This research aims not to engage a theoretical deductive orientation, but considers linking Diaspora experiences to theoretical concepts advanced by diverse social scientists not only improve the validity of the current empirical research, but also enlighten our attempt to conceptualize the Diaspora phenomenon.

CHAPTER 5

THEORETICAL CONSIDERATION: DEVELOPMENT, CAPITAL TRANSFERABILITY AND HEGEMONIC DISCOURSE

Introduction

Social sciences constitute in general a variety of academic disciplines from sociology to anthropology that are engaged in undertaking specific research on society to build academic scholarship. In this endeavour, a variety of methodologies have been employed. On one hand, there is the dominant positivism which uses methods that emulate the natural sciences in for instance employing falsifiable empirical hypotheses. On the other hand, one finds the interpretivist methodologies that employ the combination of critical and symbolic approaches for the purpose of an inclusive knowledge production.

In addition, the social sciences generate the understanding of human complexities in general and human association, organization and mobilization, in particular, by analyzing factors, that influence and shape social conditions and processes. In this regard, researchers have the crucial simultaneous role of acting social while observing, interpreting and evaluating human interactions and exchanges. Therefore, the concepts and ideas that social scientists eventually construct reflect subjective human concerns and prioritization. This in turn means that, at least in the social sciences, the popular reference to value free scientific inquiry might not succeed.

From this simple reasoning, this research argues that theoretical and conceptual frameworks are socially constructed abstractions. For those of us who utilize relevant theoretical perspectives to understand properly a social phenomenon, we often depend on comparing diverse theoretical propositions with the aim of grasping multiple perspectives. This implies the study and reference to the work of influential scholars from diverse schools with reputed interdisciplinary grasp and insight.

The following sections introduce and compare ideas and concepts formulated by prominent, western and non-western social scientists in using the methodology of

"tearing the theory out of its historical context .., and bringing the logic of all or some of its ideas to bear on a specific situation in perhaps one's own time-the object of the exercise being to determine whether the ideas scattered within the theory help in the under-standing of the situation" (Mazrui, 1963: 121-133).

What do these ideas and concepts tell us about the nature of human association, organization and mobilization? Do these perspectives converge or diverge? Are there epistemological and ontological differences or similarities on the way in which different academic profiles analyse and interpret human relations, organization and mobilization? Could we find similarities and differences between basic ideas developed by major theoretical thinkers from east and west and the theoretical emphasis presented in major Diaspora studies?

Development, Social Solidarity, and Exclusion

Let us first start with a theme we conveniently refer to as a *"Linear contractual hegemonic development"*. This theoretical proposition comes from the classical French social scientist Emile Durkheim who hypothesized human progressive development from a *"mechanical stage"* to *"organic stage"*. Durkheim's theoretical frame resembles the ideas developed by another classical prominent social scientist emphasizing Afro-Islamic perspective. More than 500 years prior to Durkheim Ibn-Khaldun theorized the social progression of human development from *"hadara"* (civilization or modern) to *"badawa"* (primitive or pre-modern). In relation to these classical figures, there is Max Weber, another prominent social scientist who with his widely referred analysis of the instrumentality of rational choice approach contradicts both Durkheim and but nonetheless shared some conceptual frame.

Second, contemporary social researchers such Pierre Bourdieu presented conceptual ideas, developing Karl Marx's original conceptualization on the relationship of labour and capital in *"Das Kaptal"*, to propose the multiplicity of capital acquisition and ownership to include "cultural capital" and "social capital". Bourdieu hypothesized the dynamics and thereby the potential transferability of the three forms of capital, the economic, the social and the cultural. Scholars with Afro-Islamic and Asian backgrounds such as Al-

Qardawi and Amartya Sen have since complemented, and to a certain extent, contradicted such propositions.

Third, under the title of *"Hegemonic and counter-hegemonic exercises"*, this chapter discusses some of the basic concepts proposed by a reputable social scientist, Michael Foucault, who modified the classical approach of arguing an independently existing objective neutral social relation and process. Foucault argued for a subjectively constructed society and societal relations resulting from hegemonic and counter-hegemonic discourses generated by unequal power relations.

Finally, the focus shifts to major Diaspora studies. Based on the analysis and discussion on the above-mentioned perspectives, the research examines whether basic concepts emerging from Diaspora studies link to classical and contemporary theoretical perspectives. Hence, the research complements the critical evaluation of some western and non-western social science ideas with the empirical reality of Somali Diaspora in Denmark and UAE.

Contractual Hegemonic Development

Durkheim and Ibn Khaldun belong to different and, in our contemporary world, competing civilizations, the western and the Islamic. In their specific ways, both scholars appealed for society and state modernization. Durkheim's research concentrated on the dynamics and the consequences of urbanization and industrialization in Europe, studied the rise and the decline of Islamic civilization. Both of them held governmental positions in their respective societies. The two social scientists do not directly deal with the theme of Diaspora, but they comprehensively studied social tra nsformations emanating from migration and Diaspora conditions. For instance though not an orthodox Jew in his adult life, Durkheim experienced anti-Semitism in Europe, where he has published a well-known analysis *"Anti-Semitism and social crises"*, to intellectually deal with xenophobic challenges. On his part Ibn-Khaldun, witnessed the brutality of Arab arrogance and tribal corruption in Northern Africa which caused the ultimate disintegration of the Islamic civilization.

What is interesting is that the work of these scholars from different backgrounds and historical periods, particularly the ideas and the concepts they developed, not just overlap but have also influenced social science research, including migration and Diaspora studies. Durkheim's internationally canonized *"The division of Labour"* and the *"The elementary forms of religion"* and Ibn-Khaldun's *"Muqadimah"* inspire the epistemological and ontological focus of numerous Diaspora studies, particularly those with society and state centric evolutionary approaches to individual, society and institutional organization and mobilization.

Let us start with some persisting concepts in Durkheim's theorization of social and institutional organization. First, Durkheim is a committed enthusiast of a society and state modernization that comply with what we could call *"contractual modernization development"*. To reach this stage, he proposes the diversification of people's occupational roles (Durkheim, 1933: 190). The assumption is that the division of labour will elevate society from primitive forms of social association *"mechanical solidarity"* to advanced level of social organization to *"organic solidarity"*. On the one hand, relationships based on mechanical solidarity characterize underdeveloped rural societies that often engage in ritualized and traditionalized manageable social interactions, while relationships resting on organic solidarity concern modern urban societies with a sophisticated professionalized division of labour. This distinction implies a hierarchically-structured relationship between those who modernize and those who traditionalize. In other words, this is a developmental model that emphasizes the superiority of western, industrial nation states (Castles, 2007).

Second, Durkheim is principally an evolutionist as he believes that state and society need to modernize. This will happen through continuing restructuring and formalization. In this context, individual citizens have to elevate themselves to become socially compatible. For this purpose people abandon or suppress natural egoistic instincts. Even religious sentiments, values and beliefs have to evolve through the secularization of religious attitudes to fit the modern functionalist patterns of life.

Third and finally, Durkheim tells us that the process to consolidate a modern society might confront significant social, economic and political challenges. He theorized this challenge originating from the social dysfunction of *"anomie"* reflecting the weakening of social and state disciplinary regulations[15]. He argues that rapid social and economic changes in the society influence the level of anomie among the different individuals

---

[15] (This is a French word, deriving from Greek, no law) -a state of breakdown and chaos. The term is particularly associated with Durkheim, for whom *anomie* characterizes periods of loosening of social norms, when the loss of authority tends to release moral bonds, produce unlimited desires, and cause increased rates of suicide), The Oxford dictionary of philosophy.

and groups in the society temporarily disrupting modernization and social cohesion. The solution to overcome anomie lies with macro economic, political and regulative solutions (Fish, 2005: 86).

Social science was a personal and professional project for Durkheim. The modernization transition from a *"mechanical society"* to an *"organic society"* with the embedded challenges of *"anomie"* influenced Durkheim both at a personal and professional level. As a member of the Jewish minority in France and a public intellectual employee, Durkheim has written a brief analysis entitled *"Anti-Semitism and social crises"* dealing with the so-called Dreyfus Affair that took place in France between 1894 and 1906[16]. In this work, Durkheim compared the conditions of the Jewish minorities in France and Germany. As a French Jew and official, he was obviously biased towards France. He argued that in Germany the excessive victimization of Jewish reflected existing *"anomie"* in the German society, propagated by powerful constituents in Germany. The German elite, he added, repeatedly profiled the Jewish community as a national threat. Interestingly, he considered the German elite at the time as less sophisticated and traditionally oriented than his French countrymen. Consequently, Germany, he argued, suffered from *"chronic anti-Semitism"* while France with Dreyfus's affair experienced *"acute anti-Semitism"* (Pickering, 1975: 328). The assumption is that the French ethnic intolerance represented brief anomie disturbance, while the German exclusion of the Jewish is more serious and reflected deep traditionalism in the German elite mentality.

For Durkheim, ethnic communities need to integrate and strive to ascend into the modern social hierarchy similar to what the French Jews did by joining and becoming part of the French republic (Strenski, 1997: 41).

---

[16] The affair was precipitated by the wrongful conviction of Captain Alfred Dreyfus, a French army officer of Jewish background, for allegedly selling military secrets to the Germans. The conviction embroiled France for more than a decade before it was eventually reversed, dividing the country into two bitterly opposed blocs. The affair was also accompanied by an ugly and disturbing surge of anti-Semitism in French society (Introduction to Emile Durkheim's "Anti-Semitism and Social Crisis": Chad Alan Goldberg and Emile Durkheim : Sociological Theory, Vol. 26, No. 4 (Dec., 2008), pp. 299-323).

Inevitably, social restructuring and possibly revolution will solve not just the general anomie in the society but also eliminate the problems confronted by religious and ethnic minorities. With proper structural reforms and intervention, minorities will acquire a homeland and the anomic disturbances surrounding them will disappear[17]. In Durkheim's world view there is no trans-national homeland relationship and distinct Diaspora communities with specific social practices and religious values. People regardless of ethnicity should adhere to regulating secular state structures.

Epistemologically Durkheim was empiricist, particularly a social empiricist[18]. Ontologically, he has a dualistic approach to almost all social phenomenon. The individual as *"Natural oriented"* vs. *"Social oriented"*, society as *"mechanic"* vs. *"organic"*, and religion as *"sacred"* vs. *"profane"* (Durkheim, 2005 [1914]: 44). His main focus is on the social and relational and not on the individual as some of his contemporaries. In this regard he insists social origin, cause and explanation to understand social development (Alpert, 1961: 151). The core is the associational, relational and institutional structures.

---

[17] Durkheim wrote: "It seems to me that the Russian Revolution does away with the Jewish problem in Russia. From now on, the Jews are certain to be likened to other religious denominations; they will enjoy the same rights; their martyrdom has come to an end from now on, the Russian Jews will therefore at last have a homeland which they will love as the French Jews love theirs" (Durkheim [1917] 2000, my translation). Durkheim did not live long enough to see the atrocities perpetrated against Russian Jewry between 1918 and 1921. (Cited in the Introduction to Emile Durkheim's "Anti-Semitism and Social Crisis": Chad Alan Goldberg and Emile Durkheim : Sociological Theory, Vol. 26, No. 4 (Dec., 2008), pp. 299-323).

[18] Durkheim's socio-empiricism focuses on a dynamic relation between group members as participants in ritual social processes and the social processes that their participation enacts. While natural forces could only be perceived as particulars, social forces, Durkheim argued, are inherently dynamic and continuous and, when perceived as such by persons assembled to enact practices, provide an empirical source for the categories (Durkheim's Epistemology: The Neglected: Anne Warfield Rawls: The American Journal of Sociology, Vol. 102, No. 2 (Sep., 1996), pp. 430-482).

Durkheim's theoretical proposal for the modernization processes will need some modification if we have to apply them to today's world. First, we have global cities that despite intense urbanization and sophistication contain pockets of multi-ethnic mobile communities with transnational complex networks (Sassen, 2002: 188). Many of them consider traditionalism trendy. In addition, the modernization efforts with focus on occupational differentiation leading to organic solidarity might for instance not fit the Muslim umma and other faith groups which organize around the concept of religious solidarity.

Conflictual hegemonic development

In an increasingly urbanizing and industrializing Europe, Durkheim struggled to study and explain dominant social and organizational complexities at the time. About 500 years earlier, Ibn-Khaldun equally strived to understand the rise and decline of civilizations, particularly the Islamic one. He tells us that this is a progressive intergenerational process, reflecting a social life determined by the relationship between *"badawa"* people (nomads, migrants) and *"Hadara"* people (settled or civilized people)[19]. The relative strength of each group depends on the level of *"assabiya"* (group solidarity). Normally, urbanized settled people have a smaller *assabiya*, whereas people surviving under harsh conditions depend on *assabiya* to survive and defend themselves. Assabiya has dual, sometimes contradicting, functions. Internally, it generates cohesion to cope with the external threat, but externally it brings conflict and hegemonic strive. This *assabiya* regulated *badawa-hadara* relationship proceeds into hegemonic cyclical process (Al-Rashiid, 1997: 240).

Like Durkheim, Ibn-Khaldun argued *hadara* (civilization) brings labour diversification and interdependency and sophistication. While Durkheim proposes total secularization, Ibn-Khaldun argues that civilization can only survive with strong collective *assabiya* combined with religious, moral guidance. Pure *assabiya* appeals to human sentiments while religious

---

[19] For Ibn-Khaldun, the state, like men, also has a natural age. He estimates the life of the state from its rise to youth, old age and downfall with three generations (Maennan, 1975, Life and work of Ibn-Khaldun, p. 118)

morality appeal to rational universal well-being. Unlike Durkheim, Ibn-Khaldun did not experience and study xenophobic outbursts against minorities but he witnessed the antagonism between Arabs and Barbers in Africa and Spain during the Islamic rule (Sand and Lotan, 2010: 202).

Epistemologically, Ibn-Khaldun, similar to Durkheim, was a positivist who considered research work as different from other works as it was scientific and aimed at distinguishing the *"truth"* from falsehood by systematic recordings, presenting proof and causal relationships. He proposes the study of society from its beginning phases to its reach of sophistication and decline with emphasis of weaknesses and strength (Maennam, 1975: 11). Similarly, he is ontologically dualistic and macro-social oriented as Durkheim. Ibn-Khaldun's world is divided into *"badawa"* vs. *"hadara"*, *"truth vs. falsehood"*, *"tribalism"* vs. *"statehood"*, *"halal"* (permissible) vs. *"haram"* (prohibited).

Ibn-Khaldun differentiates bare knowledge which is something in the human mind and the actual knowledge which is the knowledge applied practically in action. He once spoke of a man *"who knows about tailoring but does not know tailoring by not practicing"* (Ibn-Khaldun, 1967: 354). In addition, Ibn-Khaldun differentiates the revealed religious knowledge *"naqliya"* and by the acquired *"aqliya"* which represents intellectual human-processed science and intervention (Cited in Alatas, 1995).

Obviously, Ibn-Khaldun is from another time where coercion often ensured imposed social cohesion. In the world of today, solidarity and social cohesion can be achieved through citizenship and protection of human rights. People can have multiple forms of *assabiya* and simultaneously relate to multiple social contexts. Durkheim proposes formal secular collective social institutions to overcome tribal and particularistic allegiances. This is what Europeans will refer to as the liberal state. Ibn-Khaldun insists that this is not possible as some sort of dissatisfaction from a group will generate particularistic *assabiya,* which will eventually dismantle the collective state *assabiya* (Lacoste, 1984: 111). To avoid fragmentation, we will need, he states, professional organization of the society with religious moral preservation. In contrast to Durkheim, though supportive to state and power hegemony, Ibn-Khaldun indirectly encourages divided loyalty, in the case where the religion of the state is different from that of the citizen. His distinction of two places *bilad al-makhzan* (land of the government treasury and taxation) and the *bilad al-siba* (land of tribal dissidence) is equally strange to today's more complex globalized internet environment. The dilemma of religious Diaspora for instance in Western Europe is the question of who can change who, is it Europe that shape the culture of migrants, or will migrants transform Europe (Tibi, 2007).

Although Durkheim's theory of anomie might partially explain the increased xenophobic focus on some minorities in Europe, it will have difficulty in explaining the increased globalization that particularly after 9/11 has led to *"primordial essence"* and the thickening boundaries of religion, culture and ethnicity (Roy, 2011). In reality, we are indeed witnessing the de-secularization of societies - if not states - contrary to what Durkheim predicted. Here, Ibn-Khaldun's approach demonstrates certain strength in suggesting the superiority of kinship relations and religious belief. In the post modern world, religious affiliation exists alongside and in an ambivalent relationship with the nation-state (Mandaville, 2011). If secularism calls for religious subordination to secular state structures, this has failed in relation to Muslim countries and in the Diaspora, but if secularism entails separation of state and religious affairs, people, at least those in the Diaspora, might live with it (Mazrui, 2004).

Diaspora and hegemonic development

Durkheim appears more influential in Western intellectual discourse than Ibn-Khaldun though the conceptual ideas and research focus of both classics influenced scholars who study modern challenges to social cohesion and development. In relation to Diaspora studies, at least two major Diaspora studies seem to follow the philosophical pattern of the classical social scientists. The first study deals with the theme of Diaspora's engagement in politics (Sheffer, 2003). The second study entitled *"The Sikh Diaspora: the Search for statehood"* deals with the case of the Sikh Diaspora dream to establish an independent homeland state and is conducted by Darshan Singh Talta (Talta, 1999).

In his cross Diaspora analysis, Sheffer defines Diaspora as a community of people with sentimental links to the homeland they originated from (Sheffer, 1986). For him, Diaspora emerges from either voluntary or compulsory migration. In an article entitled *"Modern Diasporas and international politics"* Sheffer proposes a tridiac relationship involving the homeland, Diaspora and the host country (Sheffer, 1986). Later in a book titled Diaspora politics, 2003, he suggests a classification of Diaspora into hierarchical structure of *"classical diasporas"* that are old diasporas from pre-modern times, followed by *"modern diasporas"* that emerged from successive migration waves from the 17th century to the end of the WWII, and finally *"incipient diasporas"* in post WWII world that are in Shaffer's description in *"various evolutionary stages"* (Sheffer, 2003: 148). An interesting Durkhamanian categorization by Sheffer comes with his distinction between *"state-linked"* and *"stateless Diaspora"*. According to Sheffer, state-linked Diaspora such as the Chinese and some parts of the Jewish Diaspora are more institutionalized, stable and formal, whereas stateless Diasporas such as the Palestinians and the Kurdish are more informal, fragmented, communal and traditional oriented (Sheffer, 2003: 31).

Sheffer's Diaspora study assumes an evolutionary process from *"classical"* to *"modern"*. In addition, the study rests on a state-society approach arguing whatever Diaspora does take place within the framework of state and society institutions. Sheffer also emphasizes the significance of historical development as Diaspora needs generations to stabilize and adapt into the host environment. Consequently, Sheffer does not include his analysis Diaspora's *"de-territorialized transnational familial and informal contacts"* (Amersfoort, 2004).

In the second study, Talta compares the conduct of Sikh Diaspora in Britain, Canada and the USA. He argues that the Sikh community in the three countries suffer from racism in their host environments. The exclusion and stigma from their host societies, together with a critical event such as the invasion of the Indian troops in the Sikh Golden Temple in 1984 plus their continuing political efforts in search of an independent state, bringing the Sikh community in different countries together (Talta,1999: 94). In this regard, the Sikh community considers itself marginal as long as it is not linked to its own independent Sikh state. The study focuses on the social, economic and political relationship of the Sikhs in the host environment and with the homeland. It registers the practical, organizational activities that the Sikh communities conduct to achieve their goals. Events are recorded from its initial launch to its advanced stages. The assumption is that proper state institutions will rescue the Sikh community from its current marginal role.

The two Diaspora studies by Sheffer and Talta reflect the epistemological focus pioneered by classical researchers such as Ibn-Khaldun and Durkheim for empiricism and representational. There are certain activities; i.e. rise, decline, crises and events have to take place to register development. They also believe in the existence of independent institutions that people need to create and relate to. They collect data based on membership and organizational history. Ontologically they focus on the social, relational and institutional dimension of Diaspora's interaction with society and state institutions both in the host country and in the homeland.

Capital transferability

What is common about Durkheim and Ibn-Khaldun, despite coming from different traditions, is that they belong to the category of scientists with a state and/or institutional centric world view. They not only see macro-power concentration as the best option for progress in society but also restrict themselves to the dichotomization of social analysis. According to the classics we have the option of choosing fragmentation and   disorganization, or we could pursue institutionalization and consolidation. We should therefore strive to overcome individual and group uncertainty and rivalry to create collective, neutral social and state structures that bring us together by mediating and coercing often competing social components.

Researchers like Bourdieu partially agree with the general framework of maintaining state and national institutions. Nonetheless, they bring new analytical dimensions into the equation. Bourdieu, for instance, suggests that we need to examine critically the interplay between the individual, the community and the surrounding environment. We need to move beyond a restricted macro-lens. What people actually do is not only to adjust into existing social, economic and political institutions, but also to make attempts to achieve less idealistic gaols to get the best out of the practical daily life situations. People are not an empty container to be filled by state structures. Human behaviour is dynamic and creative with an ability not just restricted to the basics of natural and rational creatures but with an ability to enter, embody and transform multiple identities and roles partially independent from macro institutions.

Bourdieu's attempt to modify Durkheim and Ibn-Khaldun's social, linier, hegemonic progression includes the introduction of concepts such as *"habitus"*[20], economic, *"social*[21]*"*,*"cultural*[22]*"* and *"symbolic capital*[23]*"* and *"social fields*[24]*"*

---

[20] Habitus   A set of acquired dispositions of thought, behaviour, and taste, which is said by Pierre Bourdieu (*Outline of Theory and Practice,* 1977) to constitute the link between social <u>structures</u> and social practice

He emphasizes the dynamics between the subjective and the objective worlds by discussing the various capital forms that people as individuals acquire and employ in relation to the wider social interaction. The forms of capital include economic, cultural and the social where the economic capital

---

(or social action). The concept offers a possible basis for a cultural approach to structural inequality and permits a focus on the 'embodiment' of cultural representations in human habits and routines. Although seen as originating in the work of Bourdieu, the concept was first used by Norbert Elias in 1939. Anthony Giddens attempts a similar task with his concept of 'structure'. The best exposition will be found in Richard Jenkins's *Pierre Bourdieu* (1992). *(Cited in A Dictionary of Sociology. John Scott and Gordon Marshall. Oxford University Press 2009. Oxford Reference Online.* Oxford University Pres)

[21] Social capital refers to the social networks, systems of reciprocal relations, sets of norms, or levels of trust that individuals or groups may have, or to the resources arising from them. Its recent popularity can be traced to three authors— Pierre Bourdieu (1930 – 2002), James Coleman , and Robert Putnam— each of whom has a distinctive conception of social capital. (*The Concise Oxford Dictionary of Politics.* Ed Iain McLean and Alistair McMillan. Oxford University Press 2009)

[22] Cultural capital : a term introduced by Pierre Bourdieu to refer to the symbols, ideas, tastes, and preferences that can be strategically used as resources in social action. He sees this cultural capital as a 'habitus', an embodied socialized tendency or disposition to act, think, or feel in a particular way. By analogy with economic capital, such resources can be invested and accumulated and can be converted into other forms (*A Dictionary of Sociology.* John Scott and Gordon Marshall. Oxford University Press 200)

[23] Educational credentials or other resources that an individual controls by virtue of evidencing greater attainment of knowledge, sophisticated taste, or other attributes of culture . As developed by Pierre Bourdieu_, the concept extends Max Weber 's analysis of status and adds a cultural component to Marxist and other economic analysis of social life

[24] The network of social relations, regulations and adaptive possibilities specific to a social group, which may be defined in terms of location (such as a town or village), profession (artists, academics, and so forth), or class (blue collar, white collar, etc.). Developed by French sociologist Pierre Bourdieu, the field is an objectifiable structured space, which means its rules for inclusion and exclusion, as well as the nature of the strategies one may employ while operating within its boundaries, can be identified and articulated (M. Grenfell *Pierre Bourdieu: Key Concepts* (2008)

is the dominant (Bourdieu, 1986: 252). Symbolic capital is a particular capital that *'rescues agents from insignificance, the absence of importance and meaning'* (Bourdieu, 2000: 242). Through obligations and benefits, people acquire social capital (Bourdieu, 1986: 249).

Marx focused on the prominence of economic capital resting on labour force (Marx, 1933: 4). Bourdieu enhances this by proposing not just the existence of social, economic, cultural and political capitals but also their transferability from one capital to another depending on the *habitus* condition in which people find themselves (Bourdieu Pierre and Wacquant Loic, 1998: 288-89).

Bourdieu's experience of French colonial penetration in Algeria might have convinced him that state and society structures and formations are far from neutral. He discovered that the colonized people responded to state society institutions depending on how the state and society macro-institutions treated them. Though Bourdieu brings new analytical insights and appears as a social constructivist philosophically, he remains closer to the institutional structural framework. For instance, he assumes that people have access to some sort of capital readily useable and if needed transferrable.

Another limitation is that Bourdieu's capital transferability depends on approval and recognition from the surrounding environment. One cannot transfer capital that people and institutions do not accept. Regardless of which capital type one apply; one will need some sort of adjustment to benefit from this capital. So what he actually proposes is diversification in the form of not just a one-way relationship with society and state institutions but parallel and transferrable capital opportunities. In other words, Bourdieu is not interested in the actual transformation of people from primitive creatures to modern sophisticated ones but people with an embedded ability to advance and transform their social capabilities. So there is an individual and group-generated continuing change and modification of the society. This is a departure from the classical approach of development from A to B. Bourdieu alters this by suggesting parallel and multiple ways of reaching and not reaching intended goals.

Another significant contribution by Bourdieu is what he refers to as conscious or less conscious *'strategic game'* individuals acquire access to *'social fields and spaces'* by contesting, negotiating and transferring capital

(Bourdieu, 1991: 49). Examples of social fields are education, science, economy or politics. The aggregation of different social fields is social space, which is a place where power relations are contested and conflicts and compromises are negotiated (ibid.). The habitus arises from *"socially qualified sign system"* (Bourdieu, 1984: 172). This makes the individual integrating or segregating from a particular network, leading to the production of *'social capital'*. In the end the process depends on the level of institutionalization and formalization with regard to which particular capital and habitual forms are constructed. Thus, the construction of identities and capital gains depends on the practice and the capacity of the individual in the social fields and spaces.

The above-mentioned concepts relate to Diasporic situations in which individual Diasporas and groups engage and pursue strategies to acquire and transfer the various capital resources that exist in networks in social fields and spaces.

This research argues that Bourdieu's philosophical approach to social reality and development supports the evidence documented in numerous Diaspora studies. These include studies that focus on hybridity[25] and the hybridization dimension of migrant and Diaspora communities. Hybridity provides an opportunity for Diaspora to interchange and transform host country-homeland identities depending on the prevailing condition and habitus. Similarly Diaspora studies, with emphasis on the trans-national dimension of Diaspora communities, also reflect the capital transferability research. With the opportunity of trans-nationalism[26], people transfer nationally-obtained capital to a trans-national one.

---

[25] Homi Bhabha (*The Location of Culture*, 1994) does not consider it as merely fusing existing cultural elements. Rather, hybridity refers to the process of the emergence of a culture, in which its elements are being continually transformed or translated through irrepressible encounters. Hybridity offers the potential to undermine existing forms of cultural authority and representation. Citied in the *Dictionary of Sociology*. John Scott and Gordon Marshall. Oxford University Press 2009. *Oxford Reference Online*. Oxford University Press

[26] Transnationalism refers to activities that cross state boundaries, such as human migration, the flow of ideas and information, and movements of money and credit. The term is often used in preference to "international" to distinguish such phenomenon from interstate political relations (*Dictionary of the Social Sciences*. Craig Calhoun, ed. Oxford University Press 2002. *Oxford Reference Online*. Oxford University Press)

In a study about the Polish Diaspora in Belgium, Mercin (2010) contends that Polish Diaspora have minimum or no social capital. This incapability is linked to their homeland, Poland, where social capital is assumed low. The author argues that this lack of social capital is transferred into the new homeland, where the Polish migrants do not trust Belgium public institutions. Consequently, the Polish Diaspora is inward-looking and relies on homeland-oriented institutions such as relatives and the church.

From his part, Umut (2010) criticizes the conventional literature of treating migrant's cultural capital as ethnic-bounded originating from the homeland. Instead, Umut refers to the dynamics of a Diaspora's cultural capital in building on rather than mirroring on host country and homeland power relations. Similarly, Marpil (2009) shows that through the use of religion in qurbani *(a sacrificial rituals conducted at the end of Hajj)*, by Bangladeshi Diaspora in Lisbon demonstrates cultural capital transferability by reproducing their own place of belonging in a trans-national context.

Ontologically Bourdieu through his dialogical approach opens up for individual and group capability where he focuses not only on structures but also on the agent side at micro and meso levels. Nonetheless, Bourdieu's approach is still nation state centric, as the positioning and strategization of the individual and the group depends on the recognition and approval of the wider dominant society. Unlike Ibn-Khaldun and Durkheim, he takes the subjective side of the social analysis seriously, where he opens up for the dynamics of individual agent and prioritization. However, for Bourdieu, history and institutional evolvement are relevant for the construction of social realities (Bourdieu, 2000: 9).

Central to Bourdieu's conception of habitus is that objective social structures are internalized, though socially restructured at micro and meso levels, by acquiring transformative cultural meaning. He is trying to overcome the Durkheimanian and Ibn-Khaldunian dichotomization but critics suggest he is caught up in the rationality of the dichotomy that he seeks to overcome (de Certeau 1984; Jenkins 2002, 1993; King 2000).

Another criticism comes from Calhoun et al. (1993) who state that Bourdieu's habitus is more applicable to *"undifferentiated societies"*, wherein domination operates through direct interpersonal relations rather than to *"highly differentiated societies"*. In complex societies, Appadurai notes that

65

"As group parts become increasingly parts of museums, exhibits, and collections, both in national and transnational spectacles, culture becomes less what Pierre Bourdieu would have called a habitus ... and more an arena for conscious choice..." (Appadurai, 1996: 44).

Instead of using Bourdieu's concepts randomly, it will be more interesting to link to other related concepts such as hybridity and transnationalism. We should be able to differentiate habitus linked to the body and habitus as Bourdieu suggested linked to the *"field"*. When Bourdie refers to *"field"*, he is talking about a *"social space"*. Post-colonial theorists such as Appadurai who conducted numerous studies on Diaspora proposed the concept of hybridity. The combination of these concepts enables us to capture the social and cultural realities of Diaspora.

Instead of often linking Diaspora to either belonging to homeland or host country, new studies emphasize cultural hybridity (Bhabha, 1994). In this context Diaspora has through hybridity the co-called *"cultural translations"* (Kissau & Hunger, 2010). This contradicts the concept of a community based on national belonging (Chivallon, 2004). People also apply hybridity in different ways. Some adapt temporary hybridity just to achieve some temporary goals of trade, for example the so-called *'partial and short-lived hybridization"* linked to a particular task and period, others prevail much longer (Tarrius, 2001; Mitchell, 1997).

Trans-nationalism refers to *'the process by which immigrants forge and sustain multi-stranded social relations that link together their societies of origin and of settlement'* (Basch, Glick Schiller and Szanton Blanc, 1994: 6). The existence of cheap telecommunication eased the conduct of trans-national activities (Vertovec, 2004b). There is a top down transnationalism involving states, formal institutions and major companies. Trans-nationalism also emerges from below (Smith & Guarnizo, 1998) and creates what Diaspora researchers refer to social spaces (Faist, 2000b). Non-state actors such as Diaspora communities are an integrated part of transnationalism (Portes, 1996).

At practical level trans-nationalism takes place through diverse transnational activities and channels including those based on kinship, national and non-national economic or ideological affiliations (Granovetter, 1973). The *'socio-cultural'* perspective of trans-nationalism refers to the creation of a community based on cultural understandings of belonging and mutual obligation, the formation of a community public space that spans national borders (Itzigsohn & Saucedo, 2002: 767).

Trans-nationalism provides us with a tool to better understand Diaspora's behaviour in a more complex, de-territorialized environment where cultural hybridity, mobility and intense communication are the norm.

Portes et al presented a typology (table 5.1) that differentiates highly institutionalized state linked and informal non-state linked transnational activities. The institutionalized form takes place within more formalized economic, political and socio-cultural frames. Informal transnational social entrepreneurial activities appear less coordinated and regulated (Portes *et al.* 1999).

Obviously Portes et al. follow the classical scholarship pattern of distinguishing modern state centred formalization versus less modern society centred in formalization. In addition Portes's typology underestimates the existence of hierarchy where we can talk of unequal transnationalism based on host country and homeland conditions and interaction. For instance Diasporas in the USA are more transnational due to their citizenship in a country with hegemonic transnational capabilities.

Table 5.1   Typology of transnationalism

		Sector		
		Economic	Political	Socio-cultural
Level of Institutionalization	Low	-Informal crosscountry traders -Small businesses created by returned immigrants in home country -Long-distance circular labour migration	-Hometown civic communities create by immigrants -Alliances of immigrant committee with home country political associations -Fund raisers for home country electoral candidates	-Amateur cross-country sport matches -Folk music groups making presentations in immigrant centres -Priests from hometown visit and organize their parishioners abroad
	High	-Multinational investments in Third World countries -Development for tourist market of locations abroad -Agencies of home country banks in immigrant centres	-Consular officials and representatives of national political parties abroad -Dual nationality granted by home country governments -Immigrant selected to home country legislatures	-International expositions of national arts -Home country major artists perform abroad -Regular cultural events organized by foreign embassies

(Portes *et* al.1999)

From capital transferability to human capability

This research argues that a social theory for stimulating thought and practice to bringing human needs, priorities and social quality at the centre of research instead of merely focusing on social capital will complement Bourdieu's decentralization of capital accumulation. Amartya Sen, an Asian scholar offers such an idea by suggesting that we should redirect our focus from capital and arbitrary institutions constructed to control and structure human behaviour, and instead concentrate on how we could use *"human reason to identify and promote better- or more acceptable societies to eliminate intolerable deprivations of different kinds"* (Sen, 2002: 261). He proposes that instead of debating how modernized or stronger one particular group of people or states are compared to the other we need to unequivocally dismiss intolerance and instead promote tolerance in refraining from exclusion. The tools available to us include reason and reflection on human conditions of well-being. For Amartya,

"It is important for humanity to reclaim the ground that has been taken from it by various arbitrarily narrow formulations of rationality demands" (Sen, 2002, 51).

In the following, he promises that bringing the human dimension into the centre of our understanding the world would eventually enlighten us:

"The bonded labour born in semi-slavery, the subjugated girl child stifled by a repressive society, the helpless landless labourer without substantial means of earning are all deprived not only in terms of well-being, but in terms of the ability to lead responsible lives, which are contingent on having certain basic freedoms. Responsibility requires freedom. The argument for social support in expanding people's freedom can, therefore, be seen as an argument for individual responsibility, not against it" (Sen, 1999: 284,298).

In his analysis of human well-being, Sen distinguishes

"objective and subjective parameters of well-being. The objective parameters include longevity and nutrition, while the subjective dimension includes desire fulfilment that can be influenced by social conditioning and resigned acceptance of misfortune" (Sen, 1987a: 20).

Mammo, commenting on Sen's human well-being theory, suggests that well-being depends on contractive social spaces that constrain social as well as economic opportunities. The assumption is *"all equalities generate companion inequalities"*. If we cannot deal with all inequalities at the same time *"we have to make a choice as to which ones to combat and which ones to tolerate"* (Muchie in eds. Muchie and Xing, 2006: 210).

Discursive hegemonic relationship

Durkheim, Ibn-Khaldun, Bourdieu all three thinkers basically aimed at improving society by concentrating on how structures overtime transform, develop and accommodate social progress. The focus and analyses rested on the inclusion site of social, economic and political conducts. They also believed in the existence of an objective world that human activities should relate to for the purpose of own and societal inclusion and development.

Michel Foucault almost reverses such propositions. First he proposes a departure from the dominant inclusive hegemonic-oriented perspective. He does this by linking power relations to discourse patterns and knowledge manipulation. Through discursive interactions, he suggests, humans not just determine but actually create the structure of the society and state. Herewith he pronounces the prominence of human discourse. This means that what we say about ourselves and about each other is actually what we are and what we see. Through subjective formulations and identification of the so-called objective relations we determine what is truthful and what is not (Foucault, 1985: 10-11). The aim is to establish and maintain a hegemonic social relationship by subjectively constructing a suitable *"social order"* that in the end privileges the most powerful and excludes the marginal components of the society. If the constructed preferred hegemonic world has to succeed, it will, according to Foucault, require sophisticated *"governmentali ty*[27]*"*, aiming to bring social control into coherence. The tools applied include bio-power and systematic surveillance of potential dangers particularly those coming from the so-called outsiders, for instance migrants and the lower classes in the prevailing social hierarchy.

---

[27] Governmentality Introduced in the later work of Michel Foucault as a more refined way of understanding his earlier idea of power/knowledge. Government refers to a complex set of processes through which human behavior is systematically controlled in ever wider areas of social and personal life. For Foucault, such government is not limited to the body of state ministers, or even to the state, but permeates the whole of a society and operates through dispersed mechanisms of power. It comprises both sovereign powers of command, of the kind that figure in traditional political science and political sociology, and disciplinary powers of training and self-control. Sovereign power is coercive and repressive, involving exclusion through external controls and inducements (*A Dictionary of Sociology.* John Scott and Gordon Marshall. Oxford University Press 200)

Second, Foucault alters the classical social science conceptualization of power, normally resting on territorial, and concentrates on presumed objective criteria. Instead, he proposes the biological dimension of power which instead of monopolizing territorial militaristic power fosters and frames the human life and consciousness (Foucault, 1978: 138). Bio-power[28] through bio-politics aims at achieving homogeneity in preventing diversity. Foucault argued that bio-power is a core function of the modern state that uses this type of power to classify people into different competing categories (Foucault 2003: 254). In relation to bio-power, authorities engage discourses promoting and consolidating the *"ethnification"* and *"racilialization"* of the society installing dominant and subordinate categories. In this context, less powerful groups are framed as potential threats to society. In the process, state and society institutions segregate and isolate particular groups that are considered *"deviant"*, *"dangerous"* and *"polluting"* (Foucault, 1977).

Bio-power combined with systematic surveillance and classification concentrates not just on geographical space and place but on a continuous reproduction of relationship (Foucault, 1995: 202). To overcome this, there is a need to disrupt the panoptical[29] gaze of power manipulation. It will require the constructions of relations not detectable by the mainstream panoptical gaze (Foucault, 1986: 26).

---

[28] Biopower is a form of political power that revolves around populations (humans as a species or as productive capacity) rather than individuals (humans as subjects or citizens). The focus of much of his late work, biopower was conceived by Michel Foucault as a distinctively new form of political rationality. Traditionally. Foucault termed this new kind of political rationality biopower because it concerned itself with every aspect of life, right down to its most minute parts, though only in the abstract. It was interested in the health of the people in statistical terms, not existential terms—it cared about how people live and die, but not who lives and dies (*A Dictionary of Critical Theory*. by Ian Buchanan. Oxford University Press 2010).

[29] The Panopticon functions as a kind of laboratory of power. Thanks to its mechanisms of observation, it gains in efficiency and in the ... of hierarchical organization, of disposition of centers and channels of power (Garner, Roberta, 2010:418). Social Theory: Power and Identity in Global era. University of Toronto Press.

This is a process of fabricating the objective world that does not in reality exist through biological domination. The most to suffer in such special discursive segregation are marginal groups found at the margins of the society. Their condition becomes the subject of constant focus in maintaining the dominant society. For instance, through discourse, dominant groups try to link migration with state and society security issues by identifying security spaces and security groups. As powerless groups are not formally members of the producing power, they will have to adjust and accept the dominant moralization, discipline and structure. Consequently, most will seek recognition and acceptance by imitating the dominant discourse.

Empirically, Foucault (1974) analysed the activities of cultural minorities, including what they do and what they say as an act to claim recognition from the macro-society that observes and monitors their actions. Similarly, immigrants are in this regard involved in internal and external claim recognitions. Publicly they will repeatedly have to show and declare that they are not a threat to the security and cohesion of the society.

Though he was a secularist, Foucault considered religion as a political force (Foucault, 1984). This is an opportunity, he suggested, for the excluded to engage counter hegemonic exercises by pursuing *"political spirituality"* that try to acquire alternative social and discursive spaces that might seek immunity from the monitoring, disciplining an structuring of the dominant society. So for Foucault, a structural domination through discursive and power manipulation is obvious but an opportunity to disrupt and contradict this order through Spiritual and biologically unobservable platforms are also a possibility.

Foucault notes that *"political spirituality"* was disappearing from the west. Spirituality, he says, can mobilize people's political will, as it represents an *"additional level of meaning"* (Foucault, 1988). In his analysis, Foucault appeals to marginal groups and voices (Foucault, 1980), and the potential role of agents (Foucault, 1990), who can subjectively construct their lives. He argues that there is always subjective representation of the marginal groups and the task for marginal groups is to disrupt and overcome such representations. Other scholars such as Durkheim, Ibn-Khaldun, and Bourdieu also recognized the force of religion in social organization and mobilization. But they were interested in the inclusion dimension of religious practice. Foucault is interested in analyzing how religion excludes or empowers excluded groups.

According to Foucault, the best way in which marginal groups such as immigrants can interrupt dominant discourses, social and cultural representations is to uncover and promote subjugated knowledge which is the knowledge buried and oppressed by dominant discourses (Foucault, 1980: 81-82). Immigrants are often represented as a deficient problematic group of people who need to change. Sometimes dominant discourse divides immigrants into bad immigrants and good immigrants, urging them to integrate or assimilate in qualifying to be accepted as proper citizens.

The disciplinary power domination though bio-power and systematic surveillance might spatially restrict the body, but it cannot fully control the spiritual dimension that people can use for action and resistance (Foucault, 1986: 25). Foucault does not completely transform structuralism but, unlike other objective-oriented structuralisms', he argues that structure is subjectively and discursively created.

The *"wassadiya"*, the third way approach proposed by Qaradawi and the counter hegemonic approach, suggested by Mazrui, could supplement Foucault's discursive approach to power relations. Thinking of the challenges faced by Muslim minorities in Europe, Qaradawi proposes that Muslims should shift to the centre, a middle position, by balancing the demands from their host societies to assimilate and integrate and their concerns to preserve cultural and religious values (Qaradwi, 1984). Qaradawi suggests Muslims could compromise any issue that does not contradict principal religious values, meaning activities not considered *"haram"* or referred in Quran revelations. This will include the contribution to all progressive social spheres that improve human social life. Qaradawi expands the concept of Umma to include people with common ideology and destiny. For instance the people in Egypt, although practising different religions, consider themselves belonging to the same Umma - the Egyptian Umma with common *wadan* (homeland) and with common livelihood. It is for instance possible to talk a Danish umma consisting of people with diverse religious and cultural backgrounds.

Mazrui (2004) also discusses the possibility of the Islamic civilization challenging western worlds liberal views. He argues that Islam is by nature counter hegemonic to western civilization. Though it sounds a political manifestation, he introduced the concepts of *"Liberatniasm"* vs. *"Dignitarianism"*. The west, he suggests, bases their hegemony on Libertaniasm that includes *"excessive consumerism"*, and *"obsession of freedom of speech"*. He argues that Islamic and other Asian cultures prefer to base

73

their social interaction with dignitarian values, where social respect and preserving of religious values are important.

There are numerous Diaspora studies that apply analytical approach resting on the interpretation of hegemonic discourse approach. For instance, Mavrommatisy applies Foucault's *"archaeology of knowledge"* translating it as *"racial archaeology"* in analysing areas in London called Brixton and Brick Lane in London. The researcher examined how government policy reports profile the two neighbourhoods. The study found that the representations of the neighbourhoods and the people, who live there, depended on the dominant discourse at the time. Sometimes they were represented in a discourse of *"racial pathology"* where race constituted a major problem. In other periods authorities described a mood of *"reflection"* where race is interpreted as cultural difference. Finally, there was a period of *"celebration"* where cultural difference is promoted as *"a multicultural asset to be capitalized"* (Mavrommatisy, 2010).

In another study employing Foucault's' perspective, McPherson argues that this celebration of multi-cultural oriented discourse had almost disappeared in the post-911 world. Instead, antagonism of dividing the world between those who are *"with us"*, the western world, and those who are *"with them"*, the terrorists replaced the earlier discourse of promoting integration (McPherson, 2010). This implies an informal way of unilateral way of claiming *"the end of history"*. Seidul Islam in his study supports this argument, by suggesting that the western-dominated global discourse of 911 was an attempt to remove the last remaining challenge to the *"liberal world order"* by the *"ruthless capitalist expansion to Muslim lands"* (Seidul Islam, 2005).

Engaging counter hegemonic exercise also takes place in non-western societies. Armstead studied a group of female rappers in Cuba, Las Krudas, who through music performances create their own autonomous cultural space that seeks to disrupt the *"gendered, raced and classed disciplining of space"* and instead create a cultural platform that reflects the local Cuban traditions connected to the global black Diaspora (Armstead, 2008).

Foucault's approach on the link between social relations and power manipulation enhances Durkheim, Ibn-Khaldun and Bourdieu's earlier conceptualizations on the relationship between power and development in the society. Though recognizing the dynamics on the agency site, Foucault's analysis is also structural oriented.

The social movement theory[30] can help us overcome the structural concentration in bringing the agency - structure relationship into a much more reasonable way to analyse micro-meso-macro complexities.

In relation to diaspora, Martin Sokefeld studied the Alavis in Germany and published a book entitled *"The struggle for recognition: The Alevi movement in Germany in transnational space"*. Sokefeld also wrote an article in 2006 where he argued how we could use the social movement theory approach to comprehensively understand and analyse Diaspora situation in equally attending the agency and structure dichotomy, by focusing on mobilizing factors such as Diaspora opportunities (resources), supporting structures (institutions & organizations) and framing (ideas and linkages).

The social movement perspective applies a social constructivist approach and considers Diaspora as *"a special case of ethnicity"*. These are mainly imagined *"trans-national communities which unite segments of people in territorially separated locations"*. Diaspora needs *"Opportunity structures"* favourable legal and political environment, *"mobilizing practices"* associations and socio-economic events *"Frames"* ideas that refer to *"roots"* and *"memory"* which then affect the collective imagination of the group and the surrounding environment" (Sokefeld, 2006).

This chapter presented and discussed three different but complementary theoretical perspectives coming or emerging from different approaches in order to explain the conditions of the agency-structure relationship in

---

[30] Social movements. An organized effort by a significant number of people to change (or resist change in) some major aspect or aspects of society. The term was first used by Saint-Simon in France at the turn of the 18th century, to characterize the movements of social protest that emerged there and later elsewhere, and was applied to new political forces opposed to the status quo. Nowadays, it is used most commonly with reference to groups and organizations outside the mainstream of the political system. These movements, often now abbreviated to NSMs (*New Social Movements*), in the latter decades of the 20th century became an increasingly important source of political change. Sociologists have usually been concerned to study the origins of such movements, their sources of recruitment, organizational dynamics, and their impact upon society (*A Dictionary of Sociology*. John Scott and Gordon Marshall. Oxford University Press 2009).

society. The chapter started with the presentation of classical ideas introduced by influential social scientists belonging to different global civilizations, Durkheim and Ibn-Khaldun. The two scholars propose a modern centric development model, advocating for a society based not on *"mechanical solidarity"* (badawa) but on *"organic solidarity"* (hadara) with sophisticated division of labour under the protection of hegemonic state moral regulation. The modernization approach assumes natural human primitiveness and underdevelopment that will require social and institutional-oriented dimensions to move to advanced complex stages of social, economic and political structures. The road ahead, they suggest, is filled with challenges. According to Durkheim, it is possible to overcome such *"disturbances"* through regulative *"disciplinary measures"* and for Ibn-Khaldun, it will need a hegemonic top-down blessed *"prophetic"* power exercise. Apart from the conceptual aspects where the two researchers overlap, they agree on the significance of religion in society. They nonetheless disagree on the role which religious doctrines should play in regulating the society. As a committed secularist, Durkheim calls for the replacement of religious church-based morals with secular institutional religiosity. In this process, religious doctrines are moderated and updated as secular rules and forms. So instead of referring to divine laws, we should refer to constitutional updatable regulations. Ibn-Khaldun maintains the superiority of religious revelations and morals. This is the only way, he considers, humans can avoid corruption and decline (Alazmeh, 2001: 130).

The developmental modernization paradigm inspired numerous Diaspora studies. This is a paradigm that takes an evolutionary and essentialist approach. The assumption is that we develop from primitive stages to advanced stages. In studying Diaspora's political engagement and homeland relations, Sheffer (2003) introduced a model comparable to Durkheim's and Ibn-Khaldun's developmental approach. Sheffer divides diasporas into hierarchical developmental categories depending on how established and state centric each Diaspora group is. For instance established Diasporas are modern, state centric and organizationally oriented. Such Diasporas, he argues, often pursue a constructive relationship with their homelands and their states. In contrast, incipient and fragmented Diasporas are mainly from stateless societies. Similarly Talta studied the Sikh Diaspora and their search for "statehood". The assumption is that Diaspora's main goal is to develop and maintain dominant state and society structures.

With regard to the adjustment in the host society, Diaspora studies focus on how such Diaspora integrates into the host environment. Proper integration means how much people participate in the social, economic and

76

political organization of the host society. Apart from being homeland oriented such Diasporas also operate trans-nationally, but the process follows state parameters.

Such approaches are ontologically socio-state centred. They see states and societies as modern objective neutral criteria. Epistemologically, they propose objective verification, measurement and numbering of categories and histories. This is a structural oriented analysis - agency structure, such as duality of almost everything, for instance natural-social, individual-society etc.

Bourdieu proposes a number of theoretical concepts to improve the state macro centric developmental approach. He introduces the concept of transferability of capital accumulation. With the introduction of concepts such as *"habitus"*, *"social field"*, *"symbolic capital"* and *"social capital"*, Bourdieu focuses on the reflexivity and the duality of agency-structure relations. It is no longer just the dominant structure that we all need to adjust. There exist alternative complementary or competing sub-structures, sub-fields, sub-capital through which their embedded habitus people engage, create and deal with each other and with the structure. So Bourdieu shifts focus from the macro position to a meso and micro - position of social relations. Yet, he is structural oriented as the ultimate aim of social improvement rests on collective society and state formulation. Unlike the classics, however, he argues that we relate to the structure by following multiple sometimes competing paths.

There are numerous Diaspora studies that document the relevance for social fields and the accumulation of different forms of resources and capital by Diaspora communities. They nonetheless disagree on whether such creation of social fields and capital reflect host country environment or homeland environments or if it is trans-national.

Amertya Sen's capability approach complements Bourdieu's de-centralistic approach. Sen proposes a human-centric approach to our analysis. Instead of overemphasizing the structural dimension we need to attend and see the capabilities that humans posses and. The aim is to improve human development but not necessarily through structural dominance and state mechanisms.

The final theoretical suggestion comes from Foucault who argues that structure does not exist in reality but in our discourses and daily practices.

We create the structures by referring to them and by making sense of them to us. Without us talking and referring to them, there will be no structures. Foucault is ontologically closer to Bourdieu but he is more interested in the way in which societies and states exclude and manipulate through the persistence of discourse and hegemony. What we see is a subjectively created world of which all - dominant as well as marginalized groups - are part of it and contribute. Foucault introduces concepts such as *"hegemonic discourse"*, *"governmentality"* and *"bio-power"*. According to Foucault, what we need to do is to conduct a counter hegemonic power exercise by overcoming the obstacles created by powerful groups and institutions. The best way to do this is through disruption and resistance to hegemonic discourses and structures.

Partially complementing Foucault, Qaradawi and Mazrui propose how to express such counter hegemonic discourse. Qardawi proposes that this could be done by occupying the middle position *(Wassadiya)*- ideologically, socially and economically. What is interesting with the *wassadiya* concept is that by taking at the middle ground you will not succumb and condone oppression. Pursuing the middle way will help us avoid aggression and extremism. Mazrui suggests that Islam and Muslims have the potential to resist western hegemonic exercises. This is done by means of maintaining a balance between spirituality and materialism and by maintaining moral religiousness. He provides us with examples of contradiction between western *"libertainiasm"* vs. Islamic *"dignitarianism"*.

Numerous Diaspora studies have utilized Foucault's approach. They analyse how relations between host country and homeland institutions and society with Diaspora changes over time depending on who is in charge and what type of political, social and economic power discourses prevail.

Finally, this research contends that although the above-mentioned theoretical perspectives each have the potential to account for certain dimensions of Diaspora patterns and experiences in host country and homeland relations, we will need a compounded conceptual model bringing the different perspectives and applying it to understand the complex Diaspora practice and relationship with host country and homeland environments. Table 5.2 tries to illustrate the link between theoretical perspectives and with the empirical data.

The chapters 7, 8 and 9 present empirical data collected from an emerging Somali Diaspora in Denmark, which is a modern progressive welfare state, and the United Arab Emirates, UAE, which is a country that on one hand is extremely rich and modern and on the other appears traditional and pre-modern. But before that the research introduces the concept of citizenship and the different forms that prevail in among other countries Denmark, the UAE and Somalia. The research suggests that citizenship is important for Diaspora not just for mobility but also for Diaspora space formation and mobilization.

Table 5.2   **Theories and empirical dimensions**

Theoretical perspectives	Analytical Dimensions
Durkheim's "Contractual hegemonic development "	•Development from traditional "mechanical solidarity" to "organic solidarity". •From traditional Diaspora relations to modern individual oriented relations •Disruption from structural "anomie" that needs contractual moral structural modifications. Diaspora as the victim of lack of macro structural cohesion.
Ibn-Khaldun's "Conflictual hegemonic development"	•Development from "badawa solidarity" to "hadara solidarity". •Diaspora community developing from traditional relationship to modern relations •Disruption from structural moral decline that needs renewed collective "Assabiya"
Bourdieu's "Capital transferability"	•Multiple capital accumulation through physical, social and spiritual fields •The creation of Diaspora social, economic and cultural spaces) •Diaspora's transferability of capital accumulation through structural and individual transformations
Foucault " Subjugated knowledge and counter hegemonic practices"	•Formalization of social exclusion through power manipulation and hegemonic discourse •Counter hegemonic Diaspora positioning and discourse
The Social movement approach " Political, mobilizing and framing opportunities"	•Diaspora exploitation of Citizenship and discursive opportunities to develop, mobilize and frame community mobilizations

Abdulkadir Osman Farah

80

CHAPTER 6

CITIZENSHIP

Introduction

D ifferences in citizenship rights can influence the type of Diaspora organization and mobilization. The first section of this chapter will introduce the various ways citizenship has been conceptualized. The second will expound on how this citizenship perception changed as a result of global wars and decolonization processes in the developing world. The third section looks at the different kinds of citizenship options with which African states including Somalia have experimented. The fourth section discusses how Diaspora, transnationalism and religious movements across national boundaries challenge the national and territorial based citizenship formalization and status.

From a Diaspora research perspective, there is a need for citizenship clarification, as an estimated two million Diaspora with Somali origin, many of them the most resourceful with dual and multiple citizenships, currently reside outside the Somali Republic.

Definition of Citizenship

Citizenship is a formal recognition by a state or a society of an individual's membership of the concerned state or society. It also entails access to equal rights in the governance of the country. In most countries the constitution of the country states the rules of citizenship entitlement. For instance, the American constitution endows citizenship and naturalization to all persons born in the country (Saye,1979). In the past, people also got US citizenship following annexation (Colegrove,1921: 5).

From political and legal perspectives, citizenship includes rights and obligations for members of a sovereign country. This was not always the case, as in pre-modern Greece any person who lives in the city qualified to obtain citizenship with a right to participate in the political debate. Some cities demanded citizenship applicants to demonstrate descent relationship to the city (Dellolio, 2005: 19). This citizenship privilege did not include women and slaves. With the emergence of democratic and more inclusive systems in Europe, the concept of citizenship expanded to include earlier excluded groups such as women, ethnic and other socio-economically marginal groups. In current welfare societies, citizenship signifies the right to access the services provided by various organizations and institutions (Kremer, 2007: 26).

Bottomore (1993) differentiates formal citizenship from a substantive citizenship. The first refers to a person's membership of a nation state, while the latter implies *"the possession of a body of civil, political and especially social rights"*. In many countries, particularly developing countries, the standard citizenship is the formal citizenship allowing people's participation in the political system and the right to obtain national documents such as passports, etc.

From restricted citizenship to expanded citizenship

The establishment of modern European states formally linked state territories with nations. Each nation had its own designated territory. The Westphalian state form[31] considered a citizen a resident person, in a particular territory, who belongs to a particular nation (Babu, 1996: 4). Europeans at the time strived to overcome decades of brutal religious and tribal wars. Hence, they created state and citizenship forms to prevent future religious conflicts.

In the process of citizenship acquisition, it is uncertain what to prioritize, the legal, the economic or the social. It is also unclear whether citizenship entitlement should concentrate on a particular territory or beyond. In the current globalized world, prosperous countries in the North often express concerns on their social citizenship opportunities they assume confronting a threat from migration and *"open borders"*. Another problem relates to the emphasis on the economic dimension of citizenship. Instead of providing service for the citizens, governments encourage and create associations and

---

[31] In the city of Westphalia, Germany, European kings, nations, warlords and many use to fight religious an tribal wars met in 1648 to construct the nation state form that the world knows today.

communities with the aim to let people govern them. Consequently, new territories and relationships emerge making people less dependent on governments and instead increasingly relate to each other. This society restructuring might appear as an attempt by authorities to indirectly rule citizens (Rose, 1996). Furthermore, contemporary democratic practices in the West focus on deliberative democracy building on three main criteria, *"inclusion, deliberation,* and *citizenship"*[32]. But such citizenship roles require formalization and a creation of citizen institutions that in return will need some kind of social capital benefiting powerful constituents rather than marginalized groups (Smith & Wales, 2000).

The industrialization of the West led to global expansion and colonization. European colonial powers had to provide citizenships for non-residents and non-natives in colonial territories (Spinkard, 2005: 8). The post-World War Two order equally transformed citizenship conceptualization. The most significant development came with the introduction of the so-called Marshal paradigm, which introduced the new term of *"social citizenship"* (Isin & Wood, 1999: 26). From this time onwards, citizenship was no longer restricted to political legal rights but also included economic and social components. The state embarked on social and economic development activities to provide and improve welfare services for citizens. Two destructive wars devastated Europe which makes the need for reconstruction and rehabilitation a priority.

In recent years the Marshal paradigm of social citizenship has been in decline due to intense technological and economic transformations. The original citizenship approach idea was not just to provide welfare service for citizens. As Turner (2001) informs us, citizens were required to become *"work citizens, warrior citizens and parent citizens"*, but the world has since changed as people do not need to work to acquire citizenship as well as they do not need to be warriors to maintain citizenship. Instead, governments introduce concepts such as *"social investment"* where the state argues it will invest in citizens' education and health. Opponents say that such future investment arguments are not about the improvement of the citizen's

---

[32] The three terms are somehow connected to each other as through inclusion people will have an opportunity to participate in public deliberations that enhance the role of citizens. It is through inclusion and debates people demonstrate their ability to be part of a society.

education and health as such. The social investment approach aims at creating the future *"citizen worker"*, making citizenship construction a process of rational economic calculation (Lister, 1967). In developed stable democratic countries, citizenship is an integral part of the political system as governmental systems directly and indirectly, creates civil society institutions that not just deal with the state but also go beyond the state. In such constructions the market acquires a dominant role eventually leading to a democratic deficit (Swyngedouw, 2005).

Welfare citizenship came under pressure from two quarters. First, the WWII decolonization processes led to intense transformation including forced and voluntary migration from colonized territories to formerly colonial countries. In addition to that, many subjects from the colonies participated not just in the liberation of Europe but also in its reconstruction. Many of them decided to stay and become citizens of their colonial mother country. Consequently, migration from Asia and Africa to the West increased, additionally complicating and gradually globalizing the acquisition of citizenship.

Secondly, the processes of globalization and technological advancement made the concept of citizenship more fluid and complex (Adams and Carfagna, 2006: 127). Under globalization with intense mobility and transnational connections, it is becoming difficult to maintain traditional welfare citizenship opportunities. We might find a solution to pursue a citizenship status redefinition, taking into account people's particular conditions and requirements.

Recently, a number of interesting citizenship conceptualizations have emerged. In the past, citizenship was considered a direct relationship between the state and the citizen. The state provides rights and designates obligations, and citizens access these rights and comply with the obligations. With the emergence of civil society constellations, an intermediate structure emerged mediating the citizen and the state. The state loses monopoly to provide services and rights, as society plays a significant role in who gets what, when and where. The process leads to civil society proliferation, competition and even intense rivalry.

Citizenship is continuously modified and politically constructed. A case in point is the third way approach aiming to reconstruct the citizen as a morally responsible community member. It is based on the idea of a horizontal society not divided into rulers and the ruled. The problem is that the third way might favour the middle class, as citizens with limited economic and social capabilities might risk falling behind (Rose, 2000). Such processes reflect the government's attempt to construct the unity of the

84

nation and manage the internal diversity of the society, eventually leading to the marginalization of communities (Clarke, 2005).

From colonial citizenship to fragmented qabiil and regional citizenship

Africa is a continent colonized by Europeans. In colonial times, Africans did not have access to similar rights as those exercised by colonialists and their associates. After independence, post-colonial leaders did not change much. Many African countries replicated colonial citizenship rules, with minor symbolic modifications (Chafer, 2002: 48). They have for instance focused on government revenues frequently instigated civil disobedience especially when such resources disappear in government corruption (Roitman, 2007). After obtaining independence, some countries made minor changes moving from a citizenship based on the territorial model, inherited from colonial powers and the colonial division of Africa, to a citizenship resting on patrilinial descent(Cheater & Gaidzanwa, 1996).

African dictatorships have complicated the process of citizenship when they turned their countries as their personal properties. They used to give citizenship to anyone complying with their political dictation and denied citizenship to those opposing them. Later African dictatorships paved the way for devastating ethnic and tribal civil wars leading to the de-nationalization of these countries. Currently, many of them are trying to overcome this grave ethnic tribal framing by reintroducing a national citizenship. The problem is that African people, due to resource scarcity and political disagreements emanating from colonial legacies and natural disasters, compete and unilaterally introduce sub-national and regional citizenships excluding people from a particular region to access resources and citizenship rights. This creates fractured tribal homeland spaces of regional citizenship with sub-national identities and resource competition (Kraxberger, 2005). There are, nonetheless, some African success stories. Rwanda learned from ethnic cleansing that led genocide in 1994 (Mamdana, 2002: 17). Through bottom up reconciliation processes, Rwandans redefined their citizenship status moving beyond the colonial and post- colonial invented citizenship categorizations based on tribal allegiances such as Hutu and Tutsi classifications. Instead, they constructed an identity resting on Rwandese national affiliation (Buckley, 2006).

Another important dimension in the pursue of suitable citizenship frame in Africa is the need to include often marginalized groups such as women, children and immigrants. Women and children are normally not included in the citizenship rights, at least not in the political and legal dimensions (Roche, 1999).

Somali citizenship

The Somali constitution[33] links citizenship to people and not just to territory. This implies that people who comply with the country's obligations qualify to access numerous rights such as political and property ownership rights. In return, citizens will have to contribute to the country's security and prosperity by, for instance, paying taxes and, if requested, by fulfilling national service duties.

Following the independent and the subsequent union of the northern and the Southern parts of Somalia, the country's legislative body adopted laws of citizenship from 1961-1969 that reflected Italian, British and mixed model constitutions for the central government, local administrations and many legal aspects (Zweigert, 1997: 5-69). Qualifications for a Somali citizenship included anyone who was born in the territory of Somaliland and Somalis who renounce other foreign citizenships. What is interesting with the citizenship law of 1961 is that it did not stress ethnicity as it included anyone who was born in the country before June 26 1960 to be qualified to pursuit citizenship (Contini, 1969: 51).

Somali citizenship can be acquired at birth or people can apply directly to relevant authorities in the country or representations of the Somali republic abroad. Somalia had in the past granted citizenship to all ethnic Somalis living in Ethiopia and Kenya (Herbest, 2000: 236). Due to the millions of Somalis in Diaspora, Somali citizenship will have to be revised to accommodate Somali Diaspora's relationship with the homeland and countries of settlement.

---

[33] Since independent Somalis had two formal constitutions (the first from 1960 and the second from 1979) and two transitional charters (the one from 2000 and the updated one from 2004). (www.dastuur.org)

Table 6.1   Citizenship laws: Denmark, UAE and Somalia

Denmark	UAE	Somalia
• Society centred citizenship	• State centred citizenship	• Unsettled citizenship
• Social citizenship (adding to other existing legal and political rights)	• Passive citizenship (The UAE is ruled by one family- citizens have limited access and influence on power and politics)	• Before the collapse in 1991, according to the Somali constitution from 1979 all persons born in the Somali Republic qualified citizenship
• How to obtain Danish citizenship (a) Automatically at birth b) Automatically if the parents marry after the child's birth c) Automatically if a person is adopted as a child under 12 years of age d) By declaration for nationals of another Nordic country e) By	• By decent meaning child of a United Arab Emirates father, regardless of the child's country of birth. Child born out of wedlock will obtain citizenship upon being legally recognized by the father. • Through marriage meaning a	• All persons of Somali origin qualify citizenship • A child adopted by a Somali citizen qualifies citizenship • Children without parents get citizenship

naturalization, that is, by statute • The new active citizenship (In order to qualify for a permanent residence permit, you must have shown yourself to be an active citizen by serving on a board or through active membership of other organizations for at least 12 months. (New legislation from 2010)	foreign woman who marries a United Arab Emirates citizen may obtain citizenship • Through naturalization citizenship may be acquired by various groups of persons under certain conditions	

Diaspora, Trans-Nationalism and Religious Citizenship

Exclusive national citizenship confronts globalization and technological advancement whereby people's citizenship can no longer be limited to a particular territory or nation. This type of citizenship was possible in the past. With the emergence of Diaspora communities, many with homeland-oriented organizations and mobilizations, there is a need to differentiate formal citizenship from ethnic and nation belonging. Diaspora communities operate at transnational level and often link to communities through complex networks both in the homeland and in the host country and beyond. In essence, they routinely engage in multiple relationships that further complicate the core issues of belonging and citizenship.

Diaspora had in the past the option of either assimilating or suffering from citizenship exclusion leading to community victimization and marginalization. In the current world, most Diasporas do not need to assimilate due to the globalization and trans-nationalization of the world (Baubock &Faist 2010: 300-301). Diaspora communities can preserve and reinvent ties with host and homeland societies. On their part, states have also abandoned the idea of forcing and demanding complete loyalty from Diaspora. In the process, new types of citizenship forms such as multiculturalism, dual and trans-national citizenships emerge to better accommodate the Diaspora's multiple priorities and connections (Cohen, 1996). What makes the conditions of Diaspora more complex is the existence of two main citizenship-related paradoxes. These concern the inter-connectedness between rights and identities. It happens through the mobilization of identity and practicing citizenship through which Diaspora tries to combine mobilizing ethnicity and practising citizenship in transnational space (Soysal, 2000). For instance, such communities are interested in acquiring citizenship privileges such as passports of, let us say, a western country. But that does not mean they are interested in the basic national identity of the concerned host country. Their agenda is to instrumentalize citizenship for practical reasons such as mobility and not for identity reasons. A Somali will for example insist on remaining Somali at an identity level, but at a practical level, the individual utilizes the benefits of having an American passport and citizenship. That is why immigrants as well as their homeland and host states are interested in the acquisition of external citizenship (Bauböck, R., 2009). Some countries strategically encourage their Diasporas to obtain foreign citizenships so states through their Diasporas gain extraterritorial power through economic remittance as well as accessing transnational political capacity (Sheffer, 2003: 123).

Similarly, the concept of trans-national citizenship, where people access multiple citizenships, can help us better understand the Diaspora conditions. Under such conditions, immigrants place themselves in an intermediate position and pursue an alternative forms of belonging (Faist, 2000). The link between transnationalism and citizenship involves the instrumentalization of citizenship. Through the strategic use of citizenship and migration, people plan mobility, return, optimizing financial opportunities in many countries (Waters, 2003). Because it is possible to claim citizenship without claiming identity, Diaspora disrupts the assumption that there exists a direct link between citizenship, state and nation. We therefore need to explore new forms of citizenships with multiple identification opportunities that people can negotiate and into which they can place themselves (Nagel & Staeheli, 2004).

Many Somalis in Diaspora enjoy the benefits of citizenship. Actually, there is an indirect hierarchy among the Somalis where having a western citizenship is valued. Somali Diaspora, through their western citizenship acquisition and dispersed family relations in multiple locations, lead a transnational life with the aim of accessing different sources and capabilities (Al-Sharmani, 2010). Somalis with no permanent residence and citizenship status suffer from the lack of labour market participation and access to social and citizenship rights (Bloch, 2000). After committing some offences in the host country, some of them have been deported to volatile Somalia where they are confronted with exclusion and alienation (Peutz, 2006). In some European countries, people also confront religious exclusion, restricting immigrants' rights, especially women, among them the Somalis, to wear hijab and practice Islam (Bassel, 2007). Older Somalis, especially those who migrated to the West, confront numerous challenges including language and cultural barriers making them difficult to adjust and access citizenship rights (Cook, 2010). Community organizations play a significant role in providing services for these marginalized groups. Fangen (2007) informs us that educated young Somali Norwegians who through their contribution to Somali community organization combine integration in the host country with a sense of responsibility and belonging to the homeland culture.

Finally, the issue of religion is relevant for citizenship. In Islam, citizenship concerns membership maintenance in the Ummah (the community of believers). Anyone who is a member of the Ummah should, according to Islamic principles, acquire citizenship and protection in any Islamic territory where Islam rules (Darul-Islam) (Suryadinata, 2000: 134). So in Islam, citizenship rests not on nation and national descent but on religion. The apex of Islamic civilization occurred before the introduction of western European state model that propagated the modern citizenship form based on nation and territory. Islam also gives citizenship rights to non-Muslims if they comply with basic citizenship requirements (Ghannushi, 1993).

Religion is particularly important for the Diaspora. Trans-national Islam gives Diaspora opportunities to operate at global level – by creating transnational public space and contesting the political citizenship (Bowen, 2004). The Muslim community's wish to acquire and pursue transnational citizenship creates tensions, mainly based on stereotypes. In this regard, Diaspora Muslims might contribute to the construction of post-national and multicultural citizenship frames (Werbner, 2000).

Citizenship formulation represents an attempt of identity construction by the state and powerful elites. National identity, Islam and ethnicity are important for Diaspora but Diaspora is not a static phenomenon. There exists a generational difference as the younger generation is more host country oriented and has stronger citizenship attitudes towards the host country rather than to the country of origin (Hussain & Bagguley, 2001).

Denmark and UAE Citizenships

The Danish welfare system provides citizenship rights as an integral part of a universal care system. Apart from welfare services, in Denmark citizenship benefits include voting rights for all including immigrants. This has made Denmark a country with the highest immigrant local electoral participation in Europe, sometimes reaching similar vote turnouts as the native Danes (Togeby, 1999). Unlike many other countries in Europe, Denmark gives local electoral rights to resident migrants even if they don't have formal citizenship.

Though Denmark provides more inclusive citizenship and welfare opportunities for immigrants, the country has in recent years shifted towards more restrictive social policies. First the so-called Scandinavian model *"safety net"* has diminished to a form of a *"Trampoline"* welfare system, as policy makers consider finding alternatives for the expansive universal social citizenship (Cox, 1998; Oorschot &_Abrahamson, 2003). The welfare debate is controversial and takes place at discursive level with language formulations that reflect power relations. In the past, political rhetoric emphasized universalism and equal opportunity while in the 1990s, the debate stressed on economic growth and individual freedom (Siim, 1998). This debate might reflect an internal ideological competition but it could also be recognition of the challenges to maintain a universal welfare system in a globalized, competitive environment.

91

One of the main arguments calling reform for welfare systems is that the generous welfare system attracts migrants from developing countries. Thunø (2003) finds that Europe, particularly Denmark, tried to close its doors to immigrants in particular those from developing countries. But these immigrants keep coming to Denmark not in search for welfare benefits, as politicians claimed, but to pursue economic opportunities.

Obviously, the shift on citizenship and welfare discourse in Denmark, though mainly taking place internally among native Danes, is linked to the issue of migration and ethnic minorities in Denmark. For instance, the naturalization of immigrants have been tightened several times with the requirements of a longer residence period in the country, years of employment, and documentation for extensive language capabilities (Silvia, 2008). Thus, ethnic minorities are at the forefront of the debate when politicians in Denmark try to reform the welfare system. In addition, since 2001, there has been an increase of *"securitization"* (Kinnvall, Nesbitt-Larking, 2010).

A position that is relatively different from other Scandinavian countries with similar cultural and historical traditions. Norway and Sweden differ from Denmark in citizenship rights, especially with regard to ethnic minorities. Denmark prefers a restrictive approach whereas Sweden has one of the most liberal citizenship laws in Europe (Brochmann & Seland, 2010; Midtbøen, 2009). This is mainly to blame the emerging populism in the political system negatively affecting immigrants' citizenship rights in Denmark (Andersen *et* al., 2009). Danish legislators repeatedly modify citizenship and naturalization laws demanding of immigrants to pass *"Danishness test"* and sign *"Declaration of Integration and Active citizenship"* (Ostergaard, K., Sinclair, K., 2007).

The UAE has a restrictive citizenship policy. There are very few people who gain a UAE citizenship. The country does not allow dual citizenship (Bauman, 2007: 402). Certain number of Palestinians and Iranians get citizenship rights through naturalization processes. Millions of Indians and Pakistanis who do the harshest work in the country do not have formal citizenship rights. The general legal status in the UAE is complex and depends on whether immigrants have employment contract or whether they are with families. If and when such contracts expire, individuals and their families might lose their legal status (Nazir & Tomppert, 2005: 314).

A study on the Indian Diaspora shows that the Indians consider the UAE as an extension of India. This happens despite most Indian immigrants not having formal citizenship rights but a permanent status as guest workers. The Indians in the UAE exercise some form of belonging through informal citizenship practice through *"consumer citizenship, participation in civil society and through the production of "Indian socio-cultural spaces"* (Vora N., 2009). India has a historical link with the UAE and the Indian Diaspora continues to link to the homeland. In the UAE the Indians participate in economic entrepreneurship in the host country, continue to link to the homeland and in the process redefine the concept of *"citizen"* and *"foreigner"* in the UAE (Vora N., 2009).

To sum up, this research concludes that Denmark in the past offered expanded citizenship that included welfare opportunities. From 2001, Demark adopted a more restrictive citizenship approach. In comparison, the UAE had since independence restrictive citizenship laws and a state welfare structure that divided people into nationals and non-nationals. Nonetheless, the UAE provides informal citizenship opportunities where immigrants through informal networks, entrepreneurship and continuing link and exchange with the homeland by creating Diaspora spaces where people feel at home.

Perceptions on Somali Diaspora

Perceptions of the Somali Diaspora depend on which country Somalis migrate to and try to settle. The most suitable way to measure such perceptions is talking to the Danes and the Emiratis' directly. This was beyond the scope of this study. However public perception both in Denmark and the UAE exist in different ways. In Denmark it appears that numerous studies have measured Danish attitudes towards immigrants (Togeby, 1995; Andersen, 2002). In addition, in the Danish context, both media and politicians often discuss migration and integration developments. This can also give us an indication on the general perception. One can, nonetheless, question whether mainstream media and politicians actually represent ordinary public perceptions and attitudes in the country. Obviously, both groups exercise significant influence in shaping society perceptions and opinions (OECD report, 2010: 141).

The media in the UAE are not fully independent as they refrain from directly criticizing the government as well as not going into details on controversial socio-political developments. The Gulf, including the UAE, have nonetheless, in recent years, become a media magnet for major semi-independent satellite TV stations such as Al-jazeera, Al-Arabia, MBC and others (Azran, 2010: 12). But they seem to concentrate more on the complexities of Middle East politics.

Perceptions expressed in media and among politicians can give us an impression on the general attitudes towards immigrants. For both, Denmark and the UAE the research examined on how public perception and attitude about Somali Diaspora is represented in the media. For this purpose the methodology employed to analyse the texts and media information dealing with the Somali Diaspora draws on the Foucaultian approach of critical analysis with emphasis on *"problematization"* of asking questions of where, how and by whom and which institution (Foucault, 1991: 79). The study particularly examines the main issues discussed in the media and among the politicians in order to describe the process, the power relations and reactions among the different actors involved.

The analysis concentrates on one to two years of the articles and statements about the Somali Diaspora, mostly editorials. In Denmark, the research selected important newspapers such as *Jyllandsposten* (JP), which in some way is a right wing newspaper, *Politiken,* which could be described as a centre-left oriented paper, and *Information* that might qualify as a leftish newspaper often with critical and intellectual orientation. On the UAE side, the study examined two popular news papers, *Al Itahad* and *Arab-alyoum.*

On the political side, the research focused on what politicians said about the Somali Diaspora. In Denmark, politicians' positions and attitudes are recorded and transcripts are available from the Danish parliament (Folketinget). Particularly debates and question times can tell us about the general attitudes politicians reflect about their representation in the Danish society. Politicians try to express strategic views trying to satisfy constituents as questions asked might come from the party or from the immediate constituency.

In the UAE, it is difficult to explore politician's attitudes and expressions. There are some sort of consultative bodies (*Shura*), but the country is ruled by a family (Al-abed & Hellyer, 2001: 159). The attitudes towards Somalis and other immigrants are not officially expressed.

Perception of the Somali Diaspora in Denmark

In Denmark, the public image and perception of immigrants, especially those profiled in the media and the political system, are generally negative. In recent years, debates on the integration of ethnic minorities circulated around the concept of *"Danishness"* representing historical and cultural link to Danish values and *"un-Danishness"* signifying primitiveness (Schmidt,

2010). Such public perceptions are reflected in statements by senior politicians in the government, among them Bertel Haarder, a powerful Danish politician who have occupied senior ministerial posts since 1980s. Following are some of the statements made by Haarder about Danish culture in comparison with other cultures:

> Danish culture is more important than other cultures.... When I as a Minister of Education stressed Bible stories as central for education in Christianity, it was clear discrimination.... All this talk about equality of cultures and equality of religion is nonsense.. . . Denmark is after all a Danish society. The Danes have the right to make decisions in Denmark. We decide how many immigrants can be let in (weekendavisen, 1 March 2002, cited in Schmidt, 2010) .

On another occasion the minister suggested the following:

> Arranged marriages and honour killings make every Dane shiver and feel pushed back to the middle Ages. There is a massive majority in Denmark who do not want to see [such marriages]. And they are right because the children grow up in Denmark and their parents should not push them back to the Middle Ages by arranging a marriage that frequently has an unhappy ending (cited in Larsen 2002 & in Schmidt, 2010).

For the Somalis, since arrival in Denmark, they have endured a negative media and political focus. Since 2001, emphasis and criticism on Islam were added. Later, the debate included allegations of radicalization, terrorism and piracy.

The issues that dominate the Danish perception on Somalis are joblessness, welfare dependency, cultural difference, radicalization and piracy. The Danes disagree on how to interpret and resolve these challenges. On one hand, there are the populist oriented newspapers such as *Jyllansposten*, blaming the Somali Diaspora, their cultural background and religion for deficiencies. On the other hand, liberal newspapers such as Information and *Politiken*, though recognizing the existence of integration challenges, remain critical to the structural limitations to adjust and pursue multicultural solutions to these problems. Absent from the debate are often immigrants themselves, particularly the Somali Diaspora.

Furthermore, the newspapers disagree on the underlying main causes of the famous cartoon crises. *Jyllandsposten* argue that it was religious extremists among immigrant organizations in Denmark eventually linking religious constituents in the homeland that led to the crises. The newspaper considers the freedom of speech a limitless noble undertaking and the cartoonist depicting the prophet as a symbol for the freedom of speech[34]. In contrast, the newspapers *Information* and *Politiken* state that it was mainly ignorance and the lack of understanding and failure on the part of *JP* and Danish politicians to properly address the issue diplomatically that led to the crises.

The newspapers also differ on the piracy issue. In an article titled *"A Somali solution"*, the newspaper *Information* analyzes the piracy at the Somali coast with critical focus on Denmark and NATO's involvement[35]. The article opposes western efforts, suggesting it is based on economic and strategic interest, and not necessarily a rescue for the Somalis.

"Somalis have a [qabiil] structure and their own way of government the efforts by the western countries to impose a western model state form might fail"[36]

The newspaper considers the piracy as a problem originally created by the Europeans who illegally fish and dumb a toxic waste on the Somali coast.

The article in *Information* seems to support the Somalis, by referring to Somali proverbs and by suggesting that Somalis tradition should be respected. At the same time, the article refers to Somali Diaspora in Denmark and their resources and ability to contribute to Somalia.

In contrast, *JP* accuses immigrants for criminal behaviour and criticizes Danish intellectuals who sometimes defend immigrants[37]. In situations where the newspaper accepts immigrants, it divides them into two categories; those immigrants with humility and a hard work ethic, the Vietnamese and Sri Lankans, and those who the paper considers to have no respect for the Danish society, immigrants from the Middle East.

---

[34] JP 9. June 2010

[35] A Somali solution, , 3 March 2011, Information

[36] Ibid.

[37] JP February 2011, Editorial

When discussing radicalization and terrorism, the newspapers also differ. For *JP* radicalization is a problem brought by immigrants and linked to their homelands and connecting to their cultural background. This means that radicalization is culturally conditioned and there are people who are more radical and extremist than others due to their cultural national heritage. JP suggests that the Somali Diaspora is linked to radicalization and terrorism in the homeland and beyond. Even in cases where there is a success in integration projects, JP remains critical[38] as a Somali woman municipality supported employment promotion shows. In order to improve the participation of Somali women in the employment market, Aarhus municipality compensated Somalis to open a specific day care centre for Somali children. JP interpreted such developments as an indication by the Somalis not wanting to be part of the Danish society. *JP* considered the municipality effort as a reverse discrimination affecting Danish natives. By discussing the case and by criticizing the municipality, *JP* forced the municipality to abandon the day care centre project.

Unlike JP, newspapers such as *Politiken* talk about hate crimes, exclusion and restrictions confronting immigrants[39]. *Information* further argues that the issue of radicalization and the threat of terror are exaggerated[40]. The release of five persons, including Somalis, earlier accused to have threatened the leader of the Danish people's party – for the lack of evidence indicates such tendency.

Politicians in the Danish parliament also discuss developments related to immigrants and the Somali Diaspora. Recently, they focussed the issues of radicalization and piracy in the red sea. Representatives of the ruling party, *Venstre* (The Liberal Party of Denmark), are interested in finding out what has been done to deal with the increasing radicalization of the Somalis. They refer to the alleged Danish-Somali suicide bomber in Mogadishu. Similarly, representatives of the Danish people's party demand Somalis in Denmark be investigated and monitored to prevent radicalization and link to terrorism in the homeland[41].

---

[38] JP, Ynkeligt forløb, November 2010

[39] Politiken Nov. 2010

[40] October 14th 2010, False news and false martyr

[41] Parliamentary debates and questions (Folktinget)

Similar to the newspapers, the perception of politicians is also polarized. Right wing parliamentarians ask questions linking Somali Diaspora to the extremism and civil war in the homeland. They demand the government to scrutinize the Somali Diaspora. Leftist parliamentarians, on the other hand, defend the Somali Diaspora and discuss how to overcome challenges of exclusion and discrimination in the host country, while Denmark internally tries to help efforts to provide development to Somalia.

The attitudes and perceptions articulated in the different newspapers together with the debates of Danish parliamentarians at the Folketinget show that Danes disagree on the perceptions of immigrants in general and the Somali Diaspora in particular. Denmark is generally a consensus-oriented country, but since 2001, the country has experienced a greater polarization in the society especially in relation to the issue of migration and ethnicity.

It would have been nice to have tested the degree to which the attitude of politicians and the media may have influenced the attitude of ordinary citizens in Denmark. The focus on the media and the politicians has shows the way Somali Diaspora have been represented and projected. Clearly what comes out is proudly negative projection of the Somali Diaspora judging by the media and the politicians. Although there are sympathetic voices, the predominant representation appears to be not welcoming to Somali Diaspora to make the integration in Denmark fully successful.

Perception of Somali Diaspora in the UAE

Perception towards migrants and Diasporas in the UAE is more difficult to assess than in Denmark. Immigrants constitute 80% of the population. Without them, the country cannot properly function. Therefore, the attitude from the politicians and the media appears generally positive. The indigenous citizens are minority, even if they have negative attitude it would not have a damaging impact on Diaspora. Like in Denmark the research looks at the media and the politicians and not ordinary people's perceptions. The study monitored Arabic written newspapers *Al-itihad* and *Arab-alyoum* in about two years and what comes out is more general discussion on issues of terrorism, piracy and other political problems that Somalis confront in the homeland. Most articles do not see the Somali Diaspora in the UAE as a major problem despite the expectations that they would.

Emirate newspapers differentiate Somalis in the homeland and those in the UAE. Neither politicians nor the media publically link the Somali

Diaspora with the civil strife and piracy incidents at the coast of Somalia[42]. On rare occasions, the newspapers write about Somalis who have problems with renewing their passport followed by a decision by the transitional government of Somalia to introduce a new, digital passport[43]. Large portions of the Somali Diaspora in the UAE do not recognize the transitional government in Somalia and consider the new passport as an attempt of acquiring support and recognition. The UAE authorities are interested in the new passport as it is considered more immune to forgery compared to the old passport. Articles discussing the passport issue are sympathetic to the Somali Diaspora caught in between decisions taken by the Somali and the UAE authorities.

Similar to the newspapers in Denmark, the UAE newspapers and media do not necessarily represent the general attitude and perceptions towards immigrants. But unlike some Danish newspapers and politicians, the UAE media and politicians do not negatively link, at least in public, the Somali Diaspora to a troublesome and chaotic homeland.

Despite the lack of public media and political campaign against immigrants, the UAE is far from a promised land for immigrants. Over the years, there have been a number of human rights violations and abuses against immigrants in the UAE. These include the cases of exploiting Asian immigrants, and to a lesser extent the Somalis. Recently, there was a case that involved a prince from the ruling family who video-recorded his torturing an Afghan trader[44].

In the UAE it appears that from the media and politicians perceptions it is difficult to assess what the media and the politicians do in relation to the Somalia about the indigenous citizens of the UAE. This is due largely that the media seem not paying attention to the Somali Diaspora and concentrate on what is important for the Somali Diaspora in the UAE. It will therefore be very useful in the future to study the actual public perception of the Somali Diaspora in the UAE. Further study is thus needed to explore how the Somali Diaspora integrates.

---

[42] Al-itihad, 14th of November 2010

[43] Al-itihad, 23 March 2009

[44] http://www.dailymail.co.uk/news/worldnews/article-1176091/UAE-prince-caught-camera-torturing-Afghan-trader.html

Perception of Somali Diaspora in Somalia

Data from a fieldwork conducted in Somalia to assess the perception of the Somali Diaspora among the homeland Somalis shows the existence of both negative and positive perceptions. Most people appear satisfied with the remittance flow into the country. The younger generations, especially young men, consider Diaspora life prestigious and are consequently preoccupied with migration. Many of them see the positive reception of returnees who enjoy higher status just for being from the Diaspora.

Although the Somali Diaspora contributes to the homeland positively, homeland people's perception of people on Diaspora's role and influence varies. Through their continuous interaction and communication with relatives and friends and media exposure, Somalis in Somalia learn about the social, economic and political challenges Somali Diaspora confronts in respective host countries. Such challenges include overcoming the organizational, cultural and religious obstacles that Somalis face adjusting into the host society. Similarly, they know the internal divisions and disagreements among the community. Some homeland people suggest that in order for Diaspora to better coordinate and help the homeland, Diaspora first needs to overcome rivalries. Others admit that Diaspora conflicts might originate from the homeland. Furthermore they propose the idea that contemporary Somali Diaspora can learn from earlier Somali Diaspora that succeeded in community mobilization through specialization and the adaptation of division of labour with regard to funding, media and political tasks:

> There was good work division in the SNM- and many Diaspora today can learn from that. The Diaspora in the Gulf had the role to raise funds, finance the rebellion. Those in the west with democracy organized demonstrations, publications etc. What we could do is decentralize- for instance create local branches in Copenhagen, Denmark – Representative of any Somali government can then organize (Boobe, SOM, 2010).

In general, people in Somalia observe numerous benefits emanating from Diaspora, particularly from Diaspora returnees.

Somalis are divided both in the country and in Diaspora. Some of these divisions concern regions, dialects, food styles and even qabiil. Nonetheless, they are united by their Somali background and the way in which they are treated collectively in host countries:

Somalis need to overcome internal unnecessary division (language and food consumption etc). They need to organize where they are. Actually Somali Diaspora can lead and protect Somaliness (Boobe, SOM, 2010).

Diaspora is not just the communities abroad in host countries. There are also Diaspora returnees. In recent years, many Somalis have returned to the homeland, particularly to more peaceful regions such as in Somaliland and in Puntland (Lindley, 2010: 81). The two regions enjoy relative peace and Somali Diaspora contributes to the development as they return not only with capital but also with social and educational competencies acquired during residence in host countries:

I returned because I feel for my country and for patriotism. I want to help and help myself. I cannot stay and relax in Denmark while my country suffers. When I returned I started working for a firm for a salary of 500 USD. I felt with my experience I have helped people around me- indirectly gave them jobs etc. Through my presence and contribution I felt many of them learnt from me. For instance the way I work and my conduct- I studied business (Salih,SOM,2010).

Homeland Somalis often debate on Diaspora returnees. Some suggest that the returnees consist of Diaspora members who failed to properly integrate into their respective host countries. Others contend returnees largely constituting men who failed to live up to their potentials in the Diaspora. Others again propose Diaspora returnees represent a conservative, religious and possibly nationalistic portion of the Diaspora:

In my opinion Diaspora who returns does so because they are looking for qabiil (clan). There is no difference in the Diaspora- all are suffering. The main problem is culture and religion (Gees, SOM, 2010).

There is evidence that Diaspora returnees contributed to the *"qabiilism"* in the country. Diaspora has also its share of the notorious Somali piracy and Islamic radicalism. Apart from dominance in the economic sector, Somali Diaspora have in recent years dominated Somali politics:

While some members of the Somali Diaspora return to the homeland, many Somali in the homeland often dream of migrating to the west. Once a Somali elder speaking at a Somali social gathering suggested that if Somalis had the opportunity to migrate, most would. This reflects the economic and political hopelessness affecting specially the youth. The lack of education and employment opportunities hampers the younger generations' potentials. Consequently Somalis suffer from *"Buufis"*- a daily psychological obsession to migrate (Horst, 2007:161).

> I believe that Somalis in Diaspora are better off. We are in contact with them. I have also tried to immigrate I left for Addis and stayed there for three years, I could not get education and I returned (Burhaan, SOM, 2010).

To sum up this chapter, the research concludes that Somali Diaspora in Denmark have the privilege of accessing formal and expanded citizenship providing them with an opportunity to be mobile and thereby achieve improved social quality compared to pre-migration times. The Somali Diaspora utilizes this citizenship by participating in political mobilization and electoral processes. Apart from accessing welfare benefits, the Somali Diaspora receives state subsidiary for community organization and mobilization. So far, Somalis, similar to other immigrants in Denmark from developing countries, do not enjoy substantial, informal citizenship in the form of having contacts with natives and their networks (Schmidt & Jacobsen, 2000). Thus, Somalis in Denmark relate to formal institutions and associations.

In contrast, most Somali Diaspora members in the UAE do not access formal citizenship, as the UAE restricts citizenship privileges to the country's minority population. The lack of formal citizenship makes the Somalis engage more informally with individuals, networks and institutions in the UAE. In the process, they create informal social relations helping them to access social, economic and political privileges.

Denmark and the UAE also differ with regard to their respective attitudes towards immigrants. In Denmark, the dominant political rhetoric is negative towards immigrants. There are also in Denmark critical voices opposing the dominant rhetoric. However both politicians and the media, particularly those from the right wing constituents, profile immigrants as representing primitive cultures posing threat to the Danish culture and political system in the long term. The media and politicians in the UAE do not consider immigrants as a threat to their existence; on the contrary they - at least publicly - praise immigrants for keeping the country moving. Thus there is formal citizenship exclusion and an informal citizenship inclusion in the UAE, while in Denmark there is a comparatively a better formal citizenship inclusion and informal citizenship exclusion. The lack of historical link and political manipulation explain why Danes hold such negative attitudes on particularly immigrants from.

Due to colonialism and dictatorship, citizenship was not properly advanced in Somalia. People had formal citizenship to acquire passport and nationality, but no more than that. The country currently suffers from a devastating civil war and an abject chaos. This makes citizenship discussion difficult.

The perception of homeland Somalis towards Somali Diaspora appears mixed. People express gratitude for Diaspora remittance and appreciate Diaspora members who better organize and eventually return to the country to stay for good or to invest. But there is also increasing scepticism towards Diaspora in transmitting alien cultures and creating inflation, brain drain, youth migration and *buufis*.

We have now explored the perception through the media and politicians from the host countries Denmark and the UAE about the Somali Diaspora. The research will now through the primary interviews explore the issues through the Diaspora experience. The following chapters link the theoretical approaches and Diaspora studies presented and discussed in chapter 5 to the empirical data on Diaspora's development, space formation and mobilization collected in the field work among the Somali Diaspora in Denmark and the UAE.

CHAPTER 7

DIASPORIC DEVELOPMENT AND SOCIAL SOLIDARITY

Introduction

Somali migration beyond the Horn of Africa region (HOA) and the Arabian Peninsula in large numbers is a post WWII phenomenon. Colonial powers, particularly the British, recruited young Somalis as soldiers and workers to their overseas operations. Some of them participated in wars in faraway territories[45]. Later the postcolonial dictatorships in the country triggered additional migration. The collapse of the Somali state in 1991 subsequently scattered Somalis all over the world. Somalis migrated for a variety of reasons. Some migrated for economic purposes while others migrated for political reasons. The migration intensity eventually transformed Somalia from a country with no significant international migration in the past to a country exporting refugee and migrant waves all over the world.

While settled in respective host countries, diasporization enabled Somalis to plant one leg in Diaspora while keeping the other in the homeland. Based on empirical data collected among Somali Diaspora communities in Denmark and the UAE, this research contends that Diaspora development follows multiple trajectories.

The chapter first addresses the issue on whether Somali Diaspora conditions reflect the developmental approach (discussed in chapter 5) that assumes a shift from a mechanical social solidarity to organic solidarity. Second, the chapter discusses anomie challenges or (social decline or gap) that might emerge in relation to Diaspora's adjustment into host countries. Third, the chapter examines whether Diaspora's homeland relationship and interaction confirm the developmental paradigm. Finally, it compares and

---

[45] Interview with Jama Mohamed, a war hero from Burma and other Asian wars. Jama is probably 90 years old. He will not tell his exact age or he probably does not know as Somalis normally do not count birthdays. He carries a British honorary medal from WWII giving him particular retirement privileges. He now lives in the UAE.

analyzes the two cases, Denmark and UAE, particularly emphasising the differences and similarities with reference to relevant Diaspora studies.

Balancing Moderation and Tradition: Somali Diaspora in Denmark

The first Somalis in Denmark, most of them men, arrived in the 1960s and 1970s for work and education. Similar to other European countries, Denmark experienced economic growth and invited "gæstearbejdere" (Kureer, Henrik & Lundgren, Svend Erik, 2006: 101). The second group, who included political refugees, came from the mid 1980s onwards. The group constituted diverse opposition groups at the time opposing the military regime. From the 1990s, following the collapse of the military regime and the subsequent mayhem, mostly vulnerable and traumatized Somalis joined the influx.

Table 7.1   Somalis in Denmark

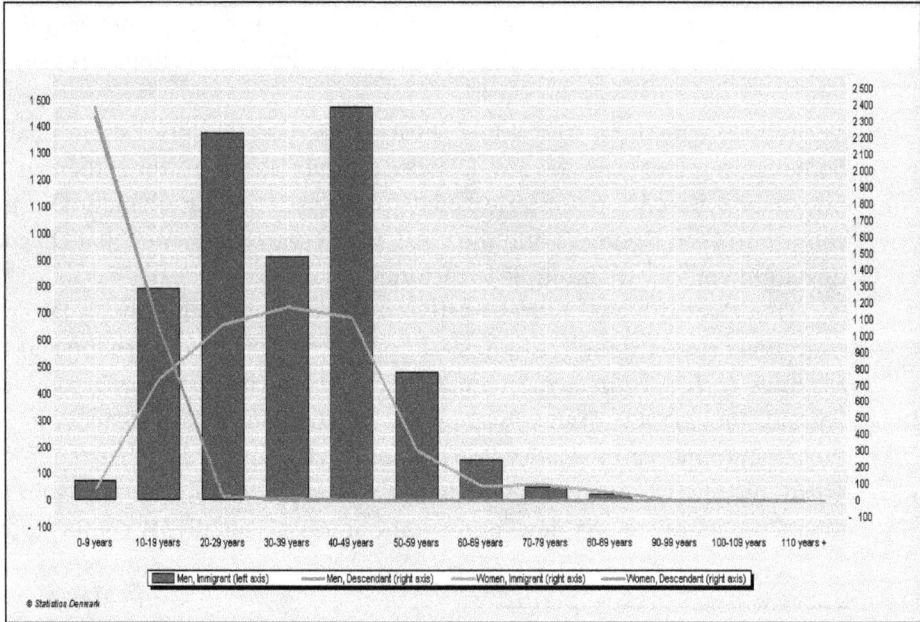

As table 7.1 shows in early 2001 Danish statistics on immigrants there are 16.493 Somalis in Denmark. Out of this number 8.829 are men, whereas 8.114 are women. The number of Somalis in Denmark between 0 up to 19 years is 6.832 , whereas Somalis we could describe as youth between 20 up to 40s constitute 4.431 persons. That means more than 2/3 of the Somalis can be

106

described as young and children. This tells us that many Somalis in Denmark are still children and thereby not available for the job market. When discussing the number of Somalis at work in Denmark this fact is not often included. If one deducts the number of aged people and those sick or traumatised then less Somalis seem ready for taking Jobs. The statistics further indicate that the Somali presence in Denmark is future oriented as most are either born or grown in the country.

However, in recent years job opportunities for the Somalis and many other immigrants improved due to the combination of economic growth and restrictive welfare rules. The following table 7.2 shows that the number of Somalis getting jobs in Denmark has increased. The longer people stay the closer they become of getting a job. This reflects Somalis adjusting into the country by learning the language and getting the training needed to get a job in Denmark.

Table 7.2 Somali employment and years of residence in Denmark

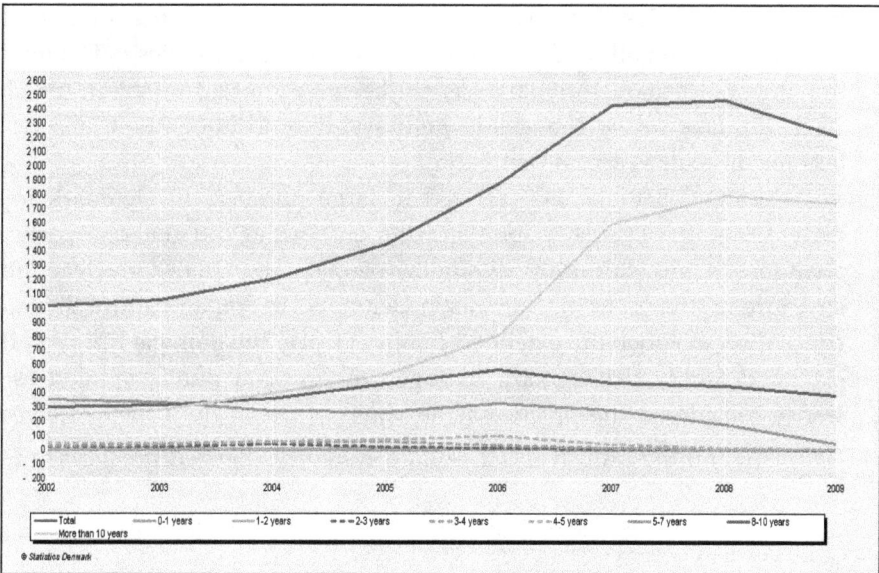

Table 7.3   Somali asylum application in Denmark since 1990

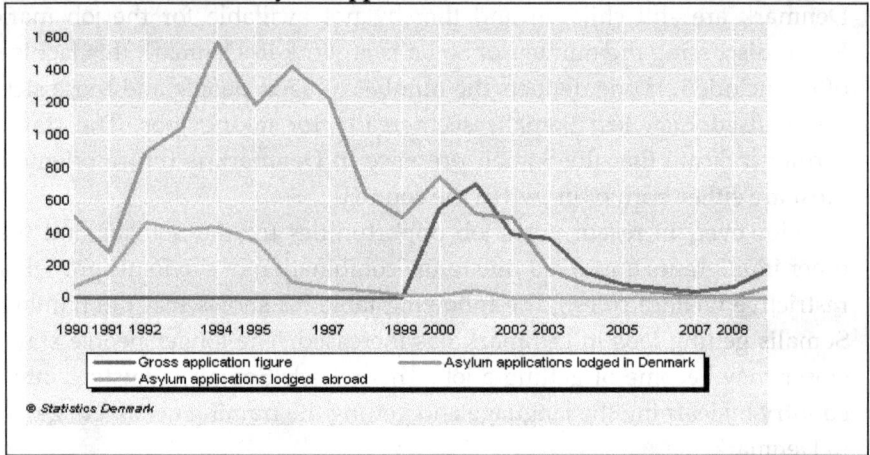

Table 7.3 shows that the number of Somalis applying for asylum in Denmark both from within the country and abroad increased. The number of Somali refugee increased during 1990s following the deteriorating conditions in Somalis and flexible family reunion possibilities in Denmark at the time. Since 2001, Denmark has not been a refugee destination (Stephen, 2005: 25). Due to the changes in both asylum and integration laws, it has become difficult to access Denmark.

Although, Somalis first arrived in large numbers to Denmark in the early 1990s, the Danish public and the authorities did not pay particular attention to this culturally dissimilar people. The Danish nuclear family structure is strange to the Somalis in Denmark. In Somali culture the family conception includes the extended family. Hence, the Somalis bringing their extended family to Denmark outraged the general public opinion as the Danes considered the practice as an abuse of the asylum they received in Denmark and the Danish social welfare system[46]. Alleged practices of FGM

---

[46] 23rd May 1997 Extra bladet a tabloid newspaper in Denmark published an article discussion Ali a Somali from Northern Somalia who was married and had about 11 children. He was on welfare. The article described the Somalis people who are not genuine refugees but came to Denmark to exploit the welfare system. This was the start of negative attitude towards the Somalis that still prevail.

108

(female genital mutilation) further undermined Somali image in Denmark[47]. Consequently, this led to the introduction and implementation of the restrictive Danish immigration laws. DNA tests were introduced to prevent the reunion of extended family members. In part the arrival and the presence of Somalis and other immigrants and refugees from developing countries generated the introduction of restrictive legislation of foreigners in Denmark.

As the following statement suggests in general, despite certain reservations and cultural complaints, Somalis seem enthusiastic about life in Denmark. This is mainly because Somalia belongs to the least developed countries in the world, while Denmark qualifies as one of the most prosperous countries in the world[48]:

> For us, Diaspora is freedom, development, meeting with other people, opportunity to learn and interact with other nations. We left from our country for two main reasons. The poverty of the region where we are from and the security problems due to civil wars and *qabiilsm*, we could not live there. We also want to get education (Abdulrahman, Denmark, 2009)

When Somalis receive formal refugee status and resident permit, Danish authorities offer them housing, education and language training. The so-called integration process starts. Later, people acquire citizenship and create their own individual or group Somali-Danish identity. Since mid 1990s the number of Somalis who got Danish citizenship increased. In the past few years the number of Somalis obtaining Danish citizenship decreased following the introduction of restrictive naturalization laws.

---

[47] 19th November 2002 the Danish newspaper Published an article with a Somali Imam from Aalborg who earlier in the week supported genital female mutilation (FGM) but later dismissed the allegation.

[48] Human development index, 2010, Denmark ranks nr. 19. in global ranking, for Somalia, the index says "information not available", but Somalia belongs to one of the poorest countries in the world.

Table 7.4   Danish nationality for Somalis from 1979-2010

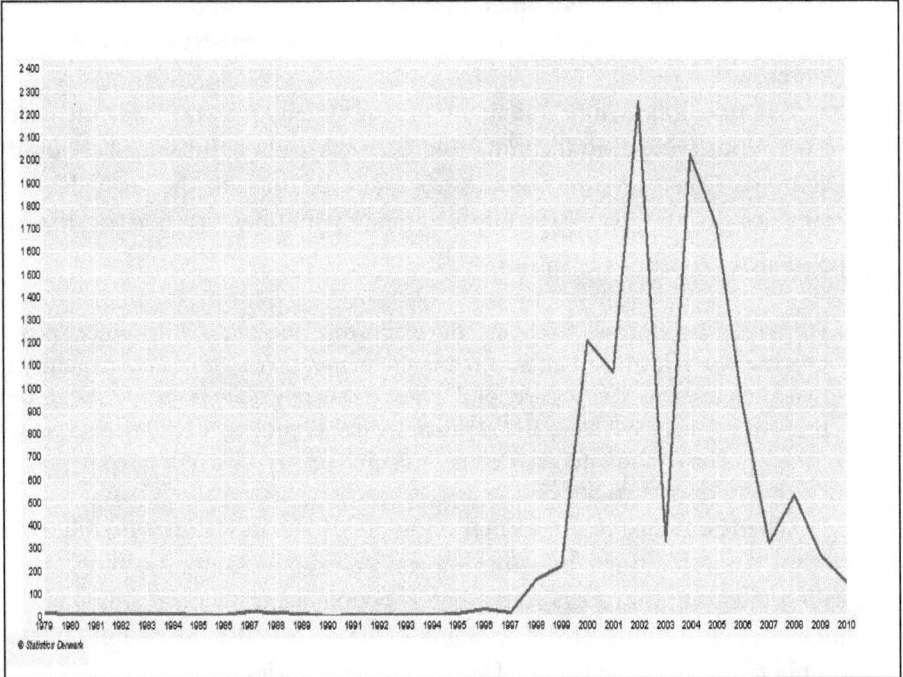

In general, Somalis acquire socio-economic and political benefits, rights and access to a new country that is more prosperous and more enlightened; a country that provides them with education, economic and citizenship opportunities. As table 7.4 these opportunities impact Somali families, the Diaspora community and their relationship with the homeland. Somalis often move to major cities for social, friendship and networking reasons. The city environment provides better network and opportunities and attracts diverse immigrants including the Somalis.

Obviously, the structural, social, economic and political conditions in Denmark influence the Somali community and their internal and external social relations. Post-independent Somali states operated under personal and militaristic rule as their colonial predecessors. Therefore social solidarity among the Somalis mainly rested on mechanical solidarity (*assabiya*). The extended family and the *qabiil* provided basic social solidarity and insurance. Following the arrival of Somalis in Denmark, such relationships might come

110

under pressure as Somalis access new opportunities in a more developed country and state that aim at integrating ethnic minorities into the society. The question is whether Somalis continue to maintain their old social relations based on family centred kinship relations or whether they will adapt new forms of social relations.

To a certain extent, it seems that Somalis in Denmark adjust to the structural opportunities in the country. In the Danish case, the new socio-economic conditions challenge the traditional Somali social solidarity and hierarchy in several ways. First at community level, Somali Diaspora seems to replace kinship (*assabiya*) solidarity with religious (*assabiya*). Instead of organizing through kinship lines, Somalis organize through religious and other neighbourhood and friendship lines. This does not however mean kinship affiliations disappear from the Somali consciousness. Second, following the welfare opportunities in Denmark, Somali Diaspora's family cohesion comes under pressure from gender conflicts and intergenerational gaps. Thirdly remittances to the homeland gradually shift from a relative and family oriented transaction during the initial stages of residence in Denmark to a more institutional and ideological-oriented homeland investment and humanitarian assistance.

Declining Kinship Assabiya and Emerging Religious Assabiya

Kinship relations represent an important social factor among the Somalis both in the homeland and in Diaspora. Community networking often involves kinship dynamics influencing the cohesion and conflict among Somalis. The question is whether this relationship represents the continuity of homeland traditions, or it reflects socio-economic and political conditions, a sort of anomie, that Diaspora confront in the host country.

Financially, Somalis in Denmark depend less on kinship relations. The relative economic independence influences the maintenance of cliental kinship as Somalis modify the practice with nationalistic and religious activities. Thus, kinship loses its major organizing social role among the Somalis in Denmark:

In Denmark Somalis are mixed. Everybody participates weddings and funeral people help each other. There are no obvious qabiils, The qabiils have no monopoly here. If people stayed with their qabiil, so there would have been a problem (Abdi, Denmark, 2010)

111

For Abdi, a 38 year-old community organizer, Somalis abandon *qabiilism* and increasingly organize through religious-inspired community associations rather than kinship-related relationships. According to him, such developments reflect the Danish socio-political context attributing less significance to kinship relations. He predicts the *qabiil* phenomenon gradually losing prominence among the Somalis. In this regard, Somalis seem to adjust. But Abdi sees Somalis instead organizing in religious associations. Abdi's observation might reflect his position and status in the Somali Diaspora. He is not just a respected community leader and organizer, but he is also a member of Pan-ethnic transitional organization that campaigns for Islamic revivalism *akhwan al-muslimiin* (Muslim brotherhood). A study conducted by Lene Kühl from Aarhus University confirms that Somalis are among those ethnic communities that organize themselves around cultural centres or religious institutions. Religious elites often led by Sheikh (religious scholar) dominate structures and decisions in such institutions (Kühl, 2006: 11-17). The tendency to de-traditionalize might also reflect historical grievances. For some members, severing *qabiil* relations means distancing from the homeland civil war. Migration and settlement in a country with no obvious kinship relations provides such opportunity.

In Denmark, religion and being religious play a central role among the Somalis. Somali associations organize and empower youth, women and vulnerable families. Among community activists, there are religious leaders who feel obliged to fill *"the religious & organizational gap"*. A kind of intergenerational religious gap exists. The parent generation feels insecure with the absence of *"proper"* religious upbringing of their children in a secularized Danish society. As the political debate on Islam in the west, including Denmark, intensified, so did the extent of Somali community organization through religious activities. Somali communities conduct common annual religious activities, such as the two *Eid* holidays, with pan Islamic associations. In addition, they organize excursions and participate in religious and cultural festivals[49].

Denmark is different from other Scandinavian countries. In Sweden, for instance, state and religion are two separate entities. The Danish state, however, constitutionally favours Christianity (Clausen and Mikkelsen, 2005: 40). This makes minority groups, including the Muslims, insecure making them pay more attention to religious aspects. For instance, many Somalis express concern about how to maintain and practise their religion.

---

[49] Interview and discussion with community leaders and activists, February,2010

Religion and being religious is important for the Somali Diaspora as the Somali culture mainly reflects Islam. Although some elements of the culture date back to pre-Islamic periods, Somalis consider their cultural identity resting on Islamic values (Houtsma, 1993: 486). Religion also plays an important organizational role in the community. Mosques, cultural centres and the leaders there represent the core leading institutions. The increased attention to religion creates tension among the community. With regard to Danish society, religion plays a limited role in people's daily lives. If Danes practise religion, they do it culturally during national holidays or discretely and individually (Ludvigsen, 2007: 121).

Gender and Intergenerational Challenges

Changes to the Somali family structure represent social transformation process among the Somali Diaspora in Denmark. The first crucial role to change concerns Somali women, who in Denmark occupy the role of the *"family leader"*. In this regard men appear increasingly marginalized. Compared to Somali men, Somali women in Denmark feel integrated into the Danish welfare system, but they experience exclusion in the employment market coupled with recurring negative political campaigns in a country among the most upfront when it comes to gender equality[50].

The second social change is intergenerational. Somali youngsters seem to assimilate more in the Danish society by getting better education and leisure time jobs. This creates tension between the old and younger generations. As the following interviewee proposes, tensions seem to rest on the limitations by the parent generation:

> We Somali parents have no tradition talking to our children. We speak Danish but it is not fluent Danish. Our children speak fluent Danish but they converse in non-fluent Somali. (Iidle, DK, 2010).

As young Somalis grow older, their attitudes to the homeland language change. In Denmark, young Somalis, who have grown up or were born in the country, rediscover their Somali identity while in secondary school or at university. Together with Somali peers, they start communicating in Somali.

---

[50] http://hdr.undp.org/en/statistics/gii/

Initially, statements are mixed with Danish phrases but gradually develop to understandable Somali language.

From Traditional Remittance to Ideological and Social Remittance

The Somali Diaspora relationship with homeland rests on two main interdependent pillars, economic and social relationships. The economic ties include remittances, fundraising and direct investments in the homeland. The social relationship encompasses Diaspora's frequent interactions with relatives, networks and constituencies in the homeland. At the intermediate level, community associations and Diaspora spaces, initiated and coordinated by traditional, religious, business and professional elites, influence the formation and maintenance of the relationship.

Significant portion of the Somali Diaspora constitute refugees who fled their homeland following persecution or the general freedom and economic deterioration under military rule. Many others joined after the collapse of the regime, fleeing from extreme civil war generated perpetual poverty and insecurity. Therefore, Somali Diaspora continues to involve and contribute to homeland developments. Most feel sharing privileges acquired in host countries with the suffering relatives back home. The contribution is not just restricted to economic and humanitarian matters but also involves politics. Such multiple homeland involvements bestow Diaspora members certain status. For instance in returning to the homeland, homeland Somalis receives Diaspora members as heroes, sometimes seem more appreciated and respected than the local leaders.

> When you return, people in the homeland will welcome you better than their rulers and local chiefs (Mohamud, Denmark, 2009).

Mohamud is a prominent activist in the Somali community. He has been in Denmark for the past fifteen years. As a naturalized Danish citizen, he feels privileged to live in Denmark. He believes such privilege provides him income, education and status, which he intends to share with people in the homeland. This can happen through associational and organizational links. Apart from remitting to relatives, together with other religious and associational figures, he mobilizes the community during national disasters and Islamic *eid* holidays *"to not forget their suffering countrymen in the homeland"*. On a recent trip to the homeland, he experienced the local community attributing him greater status and respect. He is convinced that

114

his alleviated status in the homeland reflects his presence in a country like Denmark and his community mobilization efforts and remittance.

Diaspora finds itself in a precarious situation where they have to deal with challenges both from the host country and homeland simultaneously. Homeland remittance remains key to Diaspora status formation and legitimacy. Whether or not the remittance will continue is rather uncertain. For instance, people who abuse *qat* seem lost and distant from the homeland. In addition, the young generation who are born here appear not emotionally linked to the extended family in the homeland, which means they might contribute as they potentially can. Thus, Diaspora needs to shift homeland support from remittance-oriented to development and ideology-oriented.

Ali is a 41 year-old Somali from urban Somalia. He came to Denmark in 1990 and he did not in person experience the civil war tragedies. As naturalized Danish citizen, he feels integrated into the society in e.g. acquiring Danish education and he currently works in the public sector. He is married and has children. For Ali, remittance is an individual family-related effort to provide these families a minimum income to survive. Due to the security challenges on the ground, remittance is the only option:

Remittance is the only support we can give (Ali, Denmark, 2009).

Diaspora also remit on special occasions e.g. during homeland natural droughts and other disasters. In addition the community mobilizes resources during religious Islamic festivities such as the two *Eid* holidays[51]. Such efforts often occur through organized fundraising where community elites play a central role:

We remit and contribute ideas and we have people we share ideas with in the homeland. During Eid holidays we collect money from the community and remit, especially when people suffer from different catastrophes (Abdalaziz, Denmark, 2009).

Other Somalis remain sceptical as they expect financial remittances not to change much in the long term. They refer to remittances as not having any significant impact and the practice mainly representing an escape or excuse

---

[51] Muslims celebrate two major festivities; Eid-alfidr & Eid.aladha that include prayers, sacrifices and presents to family and friends (Winchester, 2000.p. 19).

115

by the Diaspora for not seriously engaging in proper developmental endeavours. Instead, they suggest, Somalis need to concentrate on overcoming the security challenges and the civil war by contributing to ideological development:

> We can remit money, but Somalis are divided into Als and qabiils. They will not get progress in Diaspora and in the country. We need ideological and social remittance instead of financial (Kaarshe, Denmark, 2010).

Kaarshe is a 60 year-old resident in Denmark. Before the civil war, he was a senior official for the Somali state. For him, remittance is a transitional pain relieving process not pain curing procedure. According to him, the homeland needs intensive progressive ideological framework where Diaspora engages in social remittance pursuing peace, security and state-building initiatives.

Others consider efforts to overcome the current remittance dependence more pressing. They do this by providing microcredit for families to invest small income-generating projects. The efforts aim at complementary outcomes. First, to prevent remittances affecting Diaspora in the host country negatively. As remittance is often deducted from Diaspora's limited income its continuation might negatively impact on Diaspora's wellbeing in the host country. Hence, Diaspora members consider the replacement of the monthly monetary remittance:

> We are trying to help Somalia. But in a way where they overcome poverty. We for example invest small projects for about 2000 USD. In this way we will replace dependence on remittance (Mulki, Denmark, 2010).

Mulki, a 39 year-old Somali lady in Denmark, married and has several children also remits to the homeland. Together with other Somali women in a Somali women association in Denmark they intend to change the monthly remittance to Somalia to a long term strategy of empowering women and children in the homeland. Mulki and the other ladies in the organization believe that people in Somalia, particularly women, should receive micro-credits of about 2000 USD to make them independent in the long run. Mulki and her friends believe that the monthly remittance negatively affects the children and families' well-being in Denmark. Despite this, Somali women feel obliged to assist vulnerable people in the homeland. Through the Somali media, such as satellite TVs, Somali Diaspora sees the ongoing suffering of vulnerable Somalis in the homeland[52]. Such emotional fund-raising programs often attract attention and support from Somali women in the Diaspora, including those from Denmark, who make interventions in these programs and donate.

Combining Moderation and Tradition: Somali Diaspora in the UAE

Somali migration pattern to the UAE has a long and complex history. It was originally colonial and imperial driven. Later Somalis flocked to the Gulf for work. Since the 1990s, refugees and large families arrived. The specificity with the UAE is that among the Somalis one finds not just Diaspora and settled migrants but also return migration, transit migration and secondary migration. In addition, in the UAE, the legal residence status continuously shifts as the country offers few permanent residence permits and citizenships. On the other hand, the country remains attractive among the Somalis as it provides modern infrastructure and business opportunities, allowing the community to relatively easily establish private firms. Likewise, the community benefits from historic and cultural linkages between Somalia and the UAE (Lewis, 2008: 132).

Legal residential and social challenges in the UAE amplify kinship relations among Somalis. The first problem to emerge is gender related. Somali women distance themselves from the Somali civil war and consequently refuse to return to the homeland. Somali men, on the other hand, feel obliged to resettle or link the family to Somalia. The second challenge is intergenerational. The younger generation of Somalis integrate and to a certain extent assimilate. Consequently some of the youth, as they got older, particularly those without citizenship, engage more in homeland developments.

With regard to the relationship with the homeland, Somalis contribute to both development and underdevelopment. Somalis contribute to the development positively as they frequently interact due to the geographical proximity to the homeland. They seek alternatives for remittance in replacing this with expanded investment in the business and education

---

[52] Somali satellite TV with headquarters in London organizes weekly humanitarian programs for Diaspora donation to humanitarian challenges in the homeland (http://tvuniversal.tv/NS/).

sectors. On the negative side, many Somalis exploit the homeland and create social, economic and political problems. In this respect, the role of the tycoons is important. The business elite dominate the Diaspora in the UAE and some of them exploit their position to harm the homeland[53].

Consolidating Diasporic Assabiya

Kinship relations are central to Somali social, economic and political organizations in the UAE. Consequently, traditional leaders occupy a crucial role in the community. The closeness and frequent link to Somalia and an Arab host country with rooted kinship traditions itself further consolidate traditionalism[54]. The kinship relationship also affects the relationship between the community and the homeland. Apart from engaging with relatives, Somalis in the UAE often interact with their *qabiils* and sub-qabiils in the homeland. Such associations and links divide the community into traditional and regional lines. The annual national celebrations bringing diverse community constituents disrupt traditional *qabiil* sentiments[55].

One of the main reasons why Somali kinship relationship remains relevant for the Diaspora in the UAE is that the traditional social relationship enables Diaspora members to overcome potential socio-economic hurdles. For instance, if people face economic challenges they refer to their kin relations. This informal system represents a social security net that involves taking resources from the capable, those with jobs and income, and distributing it to the less capable, those without jobs and the sick. In this

---

[53] Some Somali business elites in the UAE are believed to contribute to toxic dumping on the Somali coast and export of charcoal from Somalia to the Gulf causing drought (Horn of Africa bulletin, Volume 15, Issue 3 - Volume 18, Issue 3. Life and Peace Institute, 2003).

[54] Natives in the UAE are divided along kinship lines. Seven powerful families rule the seven Emirates joined in the UAE. Recently qabiils in the country have homepages where they update information of birth, marriage etc.

[55] The Somali Diaspora in the UAE conduct annual national celebrations to commemorate independent day when Somalia gained its independence from British and Italian colonies in 1960 (http://qaranimo.com/2008/july/safaarada_dubai_maalinta_xornimada_july_04_0 8.htm).

regard, the process operates as an insurance mechanism preventing potential social deprivation. Meanwhile, some Diaspora members perceive their contribution to the community as debt payment to a kinship network that helped them to overcome past deficiencies:

"People get help from *qabiils,* they also contribute. It is kind of investment. Men lead the beels [the kinship community]. Their decision is *xeer* [customary law]. After *wadahaldal* [discussion] people accept the verdict" (Jaama, AE, 2010).

The case of Jaama, a 35 year-old man who fled from Somalia's civil war, illustrates this tendency. After a long dangerous journey across Yemen and the Saudi desert, he arrived at the UAE. The young man received assistance from kin relations providing him with accommodation, food and pocket money. The welcome package helped him to overcome the transition period until he found a job. For Somalis like Jaama without incorporating kinship network, life in the UAE entails serious consequences. Instead the traditional structure ensures dignity and community cohesion despite the legal exclusion and uncertainty Somalis confront in the UAE. Though informally organized, the kinship support mechanism builds on Somali customary law *(xeer)* and involves intensive consultation and inclusion (*Wadahadal*) among members (Mohamed-Abdi and Johnson, 2003).

Clearly Jaama benefitted from the strategic economic exchange which characterizes the kinship relations. In difficult periods, he qualifies community assistance in return for allegiance to contribute to the collective well-being during better employment conditions. Within this collective provide and benefit relationship, Jaama aims not to strengthen or maintain homeland-oriented kinship structure, but merely wishes to adjust and pursue a dignified life in the UAE. The alternative is to return to the homeland where he fled from a deteriorating economic and security situation. Though kin relations ensure Jaama an employment and overall economic well-being, it does not preclude him from socializing and interacting with Somali friends and multiethnic colleagues from his work.

Obviously kinship relations provide substantial welfare for the Somalis in the UAE. Nonetheless, the traditional relationship also contains negative dimensions. The network, for instance, can facilitate violence and civil war in the homeland. In addition, within the kinship structure, traditional leaders dominate community organization and mobilization efforts. In this context, kinship relations reflect traditional power structures and social hierarchy:

Somalis failed to acquire citizenship in the UAE due to *qabiil* disagreements (Mohamed, UAE, 2010).

An episode between the late ruler of the UAE, Sheikh Zayid[56], and the Somali community illustrates the rivalry and competition among traditional elites often leading to community disorganization and embezzlement. The late president admired the Somalis for the historical links between the two nations, his good relations with Somali governments and for his exclusive summer residence in the outskirts of Mogadishu[57]. He once invited community traditional leaders to the palace in Abu-Dubai, asking them to elect a community leader, a sort of Somali Sheikh. This was in accordance with other major *qabiils* in the country that similarly appoint their Sheikhs, including the president himself, as Sheikh for his ruling Al-nahyan *qabiil* and for the country. Due to internal division, Somalis failed to propose a common Sheikh. Some Somalis in the UAE believe the failure to gather around one leader mainly emanated from *qabiil* divisions, as well as other nationalism and community composition related factors. In early 1970s, when the UAE was created as an independent state, Somalis in the UAE mainly consisted of men, many of them nationalistic and with strong sentiments towards the homeland. They considered their presence and work at the UAE as temporary and expected to return. For them, acquiring citizenship and becoming part of the UAE was not a priority.

Following the collapse of the Somali state in 1991, Somalis in the UAE became fragmented. Before the collapse, the community interacted with the Somali state, providing sense of common Somaliness. With the state collapse of, *qabiil* relationship and regionalism assumed prominence. The following statement illustrates the difference between state-linked and stateless Diaspora:

---

[56] Sheikh Zayed bin Sultan Al Nahyan (1918-2004) served as President of the United Arab Emirates since the formation of the Federation on 2 December 1971 and as Ruler of the Emirate of Abu Dhabi since 1966.http://www.uae-embassy.org/uae/history/sheikh-zayed.

[57] Sheikh Zayid, former ruler of the UAE built a summer residence in Afgoi, a city 30 km to the South of. The luxury building still stands and houses some of the brutal Somali warlords.

We were better organized in the past. We had a state and a president. When our president visits the UAE, he used to begin his visit by meeting with us and inquired whether we had any problems. Even the UAE government used to invite us at official level before the collapse. And our women here in UAE had a women organization that was connected to the Somali women organization in Somalia (Maryam, UAE, 2010).

Maryam migrated from Somalia to the UAE for about three decades ago to join her husband working in the oil sector. As an experienced community organizer, she witnessed Somali Diaspora formation during, before and after the state collapse. She believes that the current statelessness condition in Somalia promotes kinship relations and makes *qabiil* affiliation more prominent among the Somalis. As a community organizer, Maryam often participated in community events organized at the Somali embassy in the UAE. Before the state collapse, Somalis referred to the embassy not just for passport renewal and obtaining other official documents but also for cultural and national celebrations. In addition, the embassy organized study excursions for community activists like Maryam, and their Diaspora women organization cooperated with the official Somali women organization in Mogadishu. Following the collapse of the Somali state, formal public institutions mediating the Somalis disappeared. Instead, kinship relations fill the vacuum occasionally leading to community fragmentation and increased traditionalism. Through informal kinship associations, coordinated nationally and trans-nationally, Somalis also engage humanitarian and developmental projects both in the host country and in the homeland[58].

Somali Diaspora in the UAE continues to identify, organize and express solidarity to each other through kinship relations, representing the continuity of homeland traditions and cultures. Such multidimensional kinship relations can be divisive but also cooperative and developmental. The lack of permanent legal status, the absence of a welfare state system in the host country, the proximity and the continuous interaction with the homeland make Somalis Diaspora having one leg in the host country while planting the other in the homeland. In this regard, kinship relations provide economic security and social network particularly in the early stages of host country adjustment.

---

[58] Interview with Maryam, a community leader who lived decades in the UAE, February 2010

Somali kinship relations are traditionally patriarchal with the potential to undermine women's position in creating generational and gender tensions in the society and the community. But through marriage and the extended family system, kinship relations become complex.

Traditionalism vs. Moderation

Somali Diaspora in the UAE confront two major challenges, gender and intergenerational. As Somali Diaspora refers to kinship relations in a kinship-organized society, one presupposes women's inferiority to men. But that is not always the case. Sometimes the employment structure in the UAE allows women to enter the medical and domestic branches. Among the Somali women in the UAE, one finds nurses and teachers. Although Somali migration to the Gulf was generated as *"muscle drain"*, many Somalis entered professional sectors in the UAE in early1970s during which the revolutionary regime in Somalia exported professionals to the UAE (Lewis, 2008: 24). Overtime many of them migrated to Western Europe and to North America or returned to the homeland (Lindley, 2010: 32). In the UAE, Somali women sacrifice for their families:

Somali women care for the children and the family. Some work as nurses helping their families and forgetting themselves by not marrying (Khalid, UAE, 2009).

They work in the health sector and conduct businesses and other manual work. They refrain from marrying and instead provide for their parents and younger siblings. This commitment does not, however, translate to recognition in the Somali kinship hierarchical structure. Somali women, especially young recent arrivals, struggle to acquire proper settlement and employment opportunities.

Another controversial group among the Somalis in the UAE, are Somali women married to native Emiratis. These isolated ladies often find themselves caught between the Somalis and the Emiratis. In the case of a divorce, they confront serious challenges. Most divorces occur due to pressure from their Arab in laws, urging the Emirati men to divorce Somali women and instead marry their *ibnatulamma (cousin)*. For the Somali men in the UAE, an Arab divorced woman is referred to as *hambo carab* (Arab leftover):

In the UAE divorced Somali women with citizenship are trapped in between two cultures" Halima, 2010, UAE

The Somali women also include vulnerable young girls who in recent years, due to the civil war, have grown in numbers and in desperation. Many of these women suffer, but those fortunate might access qabiil protection or services from informal women associations. Among the Somalis in the UAE, a terrible story of a daring qabiil rescue mission circulates. An Emirati family detained and enslaved young Somali teenage girl for several years. The promise of lucrative employment for a rich Arab family, international trafficking agents lured the innocent girl's parents to reluctantly consent for her migration to the Gulf[59]. Instead of fortune, the young girl experienced hard work, physical abuse and no payment. When her kin relations in the UAE discovered the incident, they secretly arranged her escape, subsequent repatriation and reunion with her parents in the homeland.

The second major challenge confronting Somalis in the UAE is intergenerational. There exists an intergenerational gap with regard to the ability to speak and preserve the Somali language. At schools, children learn Arabic, which is the language of the Quran and the Islamic religion.

In the UAE, young Somalis also rediscover their homeland in a more practical involuntary way. Those over the age of 18, especially males with non-citizenship status, confront legal restrictions. So although born and grown up in the UAE, they reluctantly connect to the homeland through investment and marriage. In the process, their Somali identity, including their mother tongue, strengthens. The older generation of Somali Diaspora retains the Somali language for community cohesion and homeland development. The younger generations, for instance in the UAE, command the native language. This creates an intergenerational gap and tension which eventually diminish as the youngsters grow older. For the youth in the UAE, the connection and return to the homeland explain their rediscovery of the homeland culture and language.

The cultural closeness between Somalis and Emiratis also contributes to Somali youngster's cultural assimilation in the UAE. However, as they grow up, they confront residence and citizenship challenges, forcing them to establish themselves in the homeland. Frequent holiday travelling to the

---

[59] The Arabian Gulf countries including the UAE trafficking of young girls for domestic work and exploitation are high (Louise Shelley (2010). (Human perspective: *A Global perspectives*. P. 275.).

123

homeland exposes the Somali youth to the homeland realities at first hand. Spiritually transformed on return, the youth organize humanitarian activities to support vulnerable Somalis. With assistance from the business community, they collect and send clothes and medicine to Somalia. For instance African airways, a Somali co-owned airline, sponsored consignment expenses[60].

For the Somalis in the UAE, religious affiliation is not a socially contested issue. They experience no significant, intergenerational, religious gap. In the Emirates, Islamic religion is not politicized and does not constitute an organizational factor among the Somalis. There are mosques everywhere and Somalis, similar to other Muslims, freely access such institutions.

Diaspora Developing and Under-Developing the Homeland

Somalis in the UAE contribute to the homeland in various ways. They subsidize the education and business sectors and remit to relatives in the homeland. The remitted amount increases in periods with natural or humanitarian catastrophe. In recent years, due to remittance fatigue, people think that developmental efforts promoting public education and infrastructure should replace the cash remittance.

Diaspora's role in the homeland is not without trouble. Diaspora actively involves not only in the economic spheres but also in the social and the political spheres. This creates tensions with regard to the people in the homeland. Especially the business elite appear to profit from the vulnerability of the civilian people following the lack of a central governing authority[61]. This is a business community integrated in global networks. Particularly the UAE has an unfavourable, international reputation for hosting warlords and business elites. The assets of the collapsed state and subsequent transitional governments ended up in Dubai. The shipment of scrap metal from Somalia to the UAE is well-documented (Muhamed, 2008: 38). The charcoal business, the investment and smuggle of illegal weapons and goods add to the list of illegitimate businesses destroying Somalia and its people:

---

[60] Interview with Somali youth in Sharjah, UAE, February 2010

[61] Dubai is the centre Somali business elite fouling the conflict in the homeland by supporting diverse warlords (Political, social, and cultural series, Volume 43. Africa research bulletin, p. 43).

There are cases where the business elite offer accommodation, transport and luxury for members of the different transitional government. This is mostly limited to the time when they have a particular interest and objectives. Business tycoons are in general not interested in nation and state building (Elmi, UAE, 2010).

Diaspora returning to the homeland is normal among the Somalis in the UAE. They do this for not only travelling and conducting businesses but also for establishing families and resettling. Most think of returning, others plan their retirement in Somalia. So for the Somalis in the UAE returning is almost certain. This is due to the uncertainty of the residence status. In preparation for a possible return and future insurance, Somalis invest their surplus in homeland businesses.

Somali Diaspora transformation in the UAE and Denmark: Similarities and differences

Table 7.5 Somali Diaspora development: UAE and DK

Host country	From Traditionalism to Moderation	Gender & Intergenerational Challenges	Homeland Relations	From State Linked to Stateless Diaspora
UAE	Traditional *qabiil* consolidation Anomie in the form of legal exclusion	Gender & intergenerational challenge emanating from employment and legal anomie	Expanded homeland involvement due to the closeness and legal anomie in the UAE From remittance to intensified investment and business	From national state orientatin to community *qabiil* and regio nal fragmentation
DK	Decline of *qabiilism* Anomie in the	Gender & interrogational conflict	From remittance to social, ideas	From secular celebrations to religious celebr

125

form of social	emanating from	and political	ations
(contact &	the integration of	remittance	
networking)	the family into		
exclusion	the welfare		
	system		

Diaspora is geographically located outside its homeland but has the capacity to form trans-national identities linking to the homeland. They do so by among other activities constructing psychological and spiritual ties expressed through cultural and kinship practices (Shain and Barth, 2003).

The most obvious form of this constructive ethnicity, the feeling of belonging to a group, is kinship. Ibn-Khaldun introduced the concept of *Nasab-Asabiya* "Kinship solidarity" to describe the essence of kinship relations. Ibn-Khaldun, though recognizing the power of kinship ties, suggested the need to move beyond this basic relationship and instead engage in *wala* (institutionalized loyalty) which is an adaption to non-genealogical relationship (Kassis, 1985). Ibn-Khaldun insisted religious superiority over kinship authorities.

Furthermore, kinship relations facilitate business entrepreneurship. For instance Greek shipping tycoons drew support from their kin relations to reduce transactions costs in their multinational companies (Harlaftis, 2007). People use kinship genealogy to ensure personal identity and link it to wider ethnicity and nationhood. Nonetheless the presumed biological tracing appears racially oriented and gendered while ignoring other forms of social ties (Nash, 2002). Traditional genealogy is biological and patriarchal centred, often subordinating women, though in Diaspora, women manage to overcome such obstacles. Kinship relations can also lead to inter-*qabiil* competitions and resentment (Faist, 2000). In recent years among Diasporas, non-kinship trans-national cooperation based on interest and professional affiliations emerged (Smart & Jinn, 2004).

Transnational kinship relations operating across nation state borders are important for Diaspora communities (Fiast, 2000). For instance, a study on the second and third generation young people of Caribbean descent in Britain finds that Caribbean young people's participation in trans-national family and kinship events and celebrations integrates them into globally dispersed family networks. The connection, combined with other multi-ethnic social relationships, allows younger generations to develop alternative ethnic identity models taking into account local, national and trans-national identities (Raynolds, 2006).

126

Even among much older Diasporas, who assimilated long into their host countries, there are tendencies to retain and rediscover kinship relations. For instance, the Scottish Diaspora in the US often engage *"roots-tourism"* in search for their ancestors by travelling to Scotland to *"recover their own indigenous identity"* (Basu, 2005). Similarly, the Indian Diaspora utilizes transnational Indian kinship relations as *"portable assets"* to articulate Indian identity in a globalized world (Uberoi, 1998).

Furthermore, religion and being religious secure social cohesion among Diaspora. Practising faith ensures a social continuity, despite the community dispersion into different parts of the world, in providing the Diaspora with its own *"intrinsic unity and spatial roots''* (Hovanessian, 1992: 200).

For centuries, Somalis practised traditional social relations e.g. kinship and sub-kinship affiliations. The phenomenon remains particularly prominent in rural parts of the country. When Somalis migrate to other countries such social relationships seem to survive among the Diaspora, but with different purposes and constructions.

This is also the case for Diaspora communities in the UAE and Denmark. This study finds that prevailing social, economic and political conditions in the host country influence Diaspora's behaviour and social relations.

On the surface, the UAE appears a modern and sophisticated society but the Somali Diaspora increasingly traditionalizes in consolidating kinship relations. The lack of a welfare state system that supports immigrants in the UAE creates some sort of anomie, forcing Somali Diaspora to turn to kinship constituents for social and financial insurance. On the positive side, the UAE offers the Somalis cultural similarity, historical link, historic Diaspora and the proximity to Somalia proper.

Apart from the historical link and relationship between the two countries, the UAE have in the past few years become a global contact zone for the Somalis in the Diaspora and the Somalis in the homeland. For those coming from the Diaspora, the UAE provides an opportunity to combine modern technology and infrastructure with traditional Islamic values.

The situation is the opposite in Denmark, where kinship relationship not only loses its core *assabiya* value but also the traditional cultural ties diminish as significant formal economic, social and organizational factor. The main reason is the Danish state system taking over responsibilities formerly belonging to the family sphere by providing welfare opportunities for inhabitants with legal residences. This does not, however, mean that Somalis abandon all forms of *assabiya*. The Diaspora replaces traditional kinship

127

assabiya with religious *assabiya*, in congregating around socio-cultural community centres. While the decline of kinship relations among the Somalis in Denmark is linked to the incorporation efforts from the Danish state, Diaspora's religious inclination is linked to the anomie resulting from exclusion coupled with recent increase in religious discourse and anxiety in the Danish society (Roald, 2004: 342). The permanent settlement status combined with reasonable access to the Danish welfare system and the geographical distance to a troubled homeland reduce kinship relations among the Somalis in Denmark to community informality cyber discourses and homeland humanitarian concerns. Instead, Somalis organize in national and religious platforms.

The Danish welfare system provides social and economic security for all citizens. In its current form, the Danish system can potentially undermine the economic and security legitimacy of kinship relationship. Nonetheless, an informal kinship relationship among the Somalis prevails, though, mainly in Somali Diaspora virtual spaces on the Internet. For instance, Somali Internet media frequently report *aqoonyahan* (intellectuals*)* and *odayaal* (elders*)* gathering in Diaspora locations, including Denmark, in support or opposition to homeland developments[62]. Somalis in Denmark have the option to exploit kinship relations if they run into difficulties, but the state provides more qualified assistance so that people prefer to relate to the system rather than to their kin relations. This is gradually changing, as Danish centre-right government and its allies in the parliament reduced welfare subsidiary for marginal groups, leading many to seek help from relatives (Quraishy, 1999). Thus structural exclusion from the Danish society has the potential to reinvigorate dependence on kinship relations as the UAE context.

Gender Conflict

Normally, the social and economic conditions of Diaspora particularly in the west empower women from Africa and the Middle East. But men in Diaspora do not easily give up their traditional homeland status. A study among the Zimbabwean Diaspora in Britain, discussing Diaspora's public and private space construction, suggests that African women's improved

---

[62] Informal kinship meetings directed to events in Somalia take place in Denmark in support for political developments in homeland constituents (http://kismaayo24.com/?p=4031).

status and financial autonomy challenge patriarchal traditions, causing tensions and conflict within the Diaspora households. In this context, men, in their attempt to reaffirm traditional roles and relations, turn to religious and social spaces to resist structural changes (Pasura, 2008).

Furthermore, a study of the Chinese Diaspora in Central America proposes that Diaspora identity and belonging are negotiated through and alongside gender lines. Community, socio-cultural performances and debates become sites for ethnicity and national difference negotiating Chineseness and Diaspora belonging (Siu, 2005).

Even among Europeans, who supposedly assimilate, gender relations confront challenges in Diaspora. For instance the Greek Diaspora, following more trans-national and globalized world, Greek women negotiate and contest their positions in traditional Greek *"family construction and femininity"* (Rajgopal, 2003).

However, in certain Diaspora communities, women maintain homeland traditions. Indian women in the Caribbean, for instance, choose to build a traditional communitarian space in the host country and thereby strengthen kinship relations (Mintz, 1987). This happens with setting up families and extended kinship networks to recreate the homeland in the host country (Jain, 2009). In addition, the Indian Diaspora constructs trans-national kinship networks through offshore marriage agreements and chain migration processes. A process in which Diaspora women create their own spaces for negotiating their claims not just within their families and kin relations but beyond (Shobhita, 2010).

Both Somali Diasporas in the UAE and in DK confront gender and inter-generational challenges. The gender conflict among the Somalis in DK results from a state intervention that provides economic and sometimes political backing for Somali women (Andersen, 2008: 197-200). It changes the traditional balance of the Somali family, leading to family confusion and fragmentation. In the UAE, the gender conflict among the Somali Diaspora emanates not from state intervention but from disagreement on the possible resettlement to war torn Somalia. It is nonetheless partially linked to the state as men often disagree with their wives, as a consequence of unemployment and uncertainty regarding their legal residence status in the country.

Intergenerational Conflict

The Diaspora platform also creates inter-generational tensions, linguistically and culturally. Younger generations are different from the parent generations in behaviour and priorities. The older generation creates institutions mostly linked to the homeland traditions. For instances, mosques as religious teaching institutions and centres for Diaspora coordination and mobilization. But over time, new generations with diverse linguistic and cultural capabilities join these institutions and demand modification if not transformation. Consequently, urban cultural centres and mosques grow to inter-generational community institutions *"decorated with indigenous and Diaspora legacies"* (Kahera, 2002). Eventually, host country born or grown up generations take over such homeland-oriented institutions and apply it as a platform to challenge homeland traditions and host country exclusions. That is why e.g. the younger generations of British born Muslims *"self-identify simultaneously with Britain and homeland traditions in an effort to balance "cosmopolitanism and tradition"* (Bhimji F, 2008).

Somali Diaspora both in the UAE and in DK confronts intergenerational challenges. In the UAE, the younger generations integrate/assimilate in the host country. They learn the language, dress and behave like native Emiratis. This leads to a widening cultural gap between parents and children. Eventually, the youngsters link to the homeland and learn more about the homeland culture. Ironically, the exclusion, in the form of not obtaining permanent legal citizenship status, in the host country, makes most of these otherwise assimilated youth re-link to their homeland and cultural origin.

The Somali Diaspora in Denmark also confronts interrogational challenges emanating from the youngsters' better integrating into the host society and utilizing host country opportunities. Consequently, the gap increases between the homeland-oriented parents and the host country-oriented youth. Similar to the UAE, the Somali-Danish youth eventually re-embrace their culture. Interestingly this return to tradition is linked to anomie in the host country where negative media and political campaigns target immigrants, particularly Muslims.

Both in Denmark and in the UAE, Somalis experience an intergenerational language gap. Often children command the host language, while parents struggle to learn and speak. This does not create serious challenges in the UAE where parental support for children's homework is not widespread. In Denmark, on the other hand, most parents tend to support their child's homework. In this context, Somali parents confront communicational challenges with their children. Parents insist their children to preserve and speak the Somali language, while some children ridicule their parents for not commanding the Danish language. In worst case, the conflict not just undermines the youngsters' prospect to learn but also the Somali parent's authority[63].

Homeland Link

Diaspora's homeland link is the most significant classification of Diaspora. There exists no consensus on how, when and where Diaspora engages in such a relationship. For instance the Lebanese Diasporas in three major cities Montreal, New York City and Paris construct solidarities that include their homeland, host societies, and the larger Diaspora community in various parts of the world, thereby incorporating multiple identities and loyalties (Abdalhady, 2005). Similarly, the Sikh Diaspora combines political activities with religious identity construction to strengthen their support for Sikh homeland (Shani, 2000). With regard to politics, Diaspora supports and involves homeland politics through *"long-distance nationalism"* (Anderson 1992, 1994). In recent years, such efforts have become easier as, with the help of global media, technological advancement and communication, Diaspora not just engages and pursues resource generation but also *"communal, religious and traditional mobilization through social frames"* (Werbner, 2004).

The data collected both in Denmark and the UAE indicate that Diaspora homeland relations build on cultural, social and economic ties, particularly in the form of continuing remittance from Diaspora members transferring certain amount, often monthly, to relatives in the homeland.

Figure 7.1   Diaspora and homeland relations

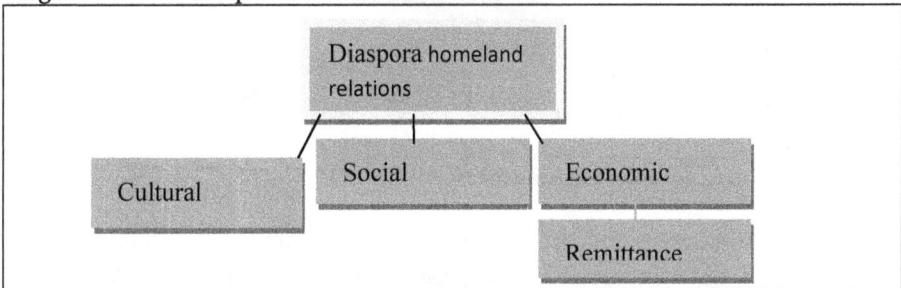

---

[63] Discussion from a Somali-Danish Diaspora seminar held on 22nd to 23rd October 2010 in Klovig, Denmark.

131

Remittance

Remittance is one of the main developmental categories linking Diaspora with the homeland. Studies show that remittances reduce income inequality between developed and developing countries. Such financial transfers from richer countries to poorer ones seem to balance global, economic disequilibrium (Kapuri & Mchale, 2009). However, these studies underestimate the history of underdevelopment and the actual mechanisms of pursuing alternative developmental strategies. The approach fails to explain the current developmental leap of China and India, not directly emanating from outgoing migration and remittance gains. In contrast, Asian countries benefited from return migration of professional migrants bringing needed skills and investment capacities back to the homeland (Saxenian, 2002).

Certainly host country economic conditions determine Diaspora's remittance. For instance in rural Mexico, wealth accumulated mainly from migrants in the US, brings development to rural Mexico. In this regard, Diaspora acts as financial intermediary to counter homeland credit and risk constraints (Stark , 1991; Taylor & Martin, 2001). Similarly, in Egypt, the number of poor households decline by 9.8% when household income includes remittances (Adams, 1991: 9). In 33 sub-Saharan African countries, remittances reduced poverty and between 2000 and 2007 increased from US$11.2 billion to nearly US$27 billion (Anyanwu & Erhijakpor, 2010).

Table 7.6   Remittance flows to developing countries

INFLOWS	2002	2003	2004	2005	2006	2007
Developing countries	116	144	161	191	221	240
East Asia and the Pacific	29	35	39	47	53	58
Middle East and North Africa	15	20	23	24	27	28
Sub-Saharan Africa	5	6	8	9	10	11

($240 billion in 2007-US $ billions).

The problem is that the dominant global economic discourse portrays remittance as a financial miracle for developing countries (World Bank, 2006), but closer comparative analysis suggests the opposite. The following table shows that among the top ten, most remittance recipient countries include the UK, France, Belgium, Spain and Germany. Most of these countries belong to or are on their way to the core.

Table 7.7   Remittance recipient countries

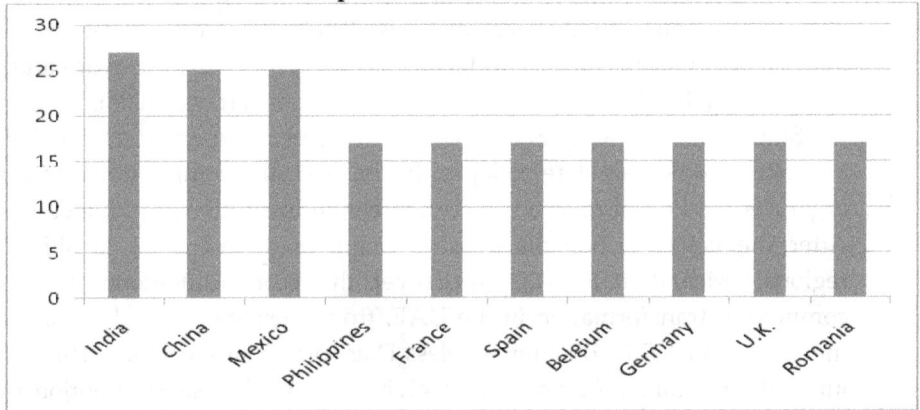

(World Bank.org)

With regard to homeland relationship and contribution, Somalis in the UAE engage more towards the homeland due to the uncertainty in the host country and the closeness to Somalia proper. They provide financial support for remitting to relatives and increasingly invest in developmental sectors such as businesses and infrastructure. There are, however, both negative and positive sides to this involvement. The business elite exploit the opportunities in this mainly uncontrolled stateless country.

Diaspora in Denmark also are involved in homeland development. In recent years, Diaspora's aim was to minimize financial remittances and instead increase social and political remittance. Such trend is probably linked to the stable, mainly legal, situation in which the Somalis find themselves in Denmark.

State-Linked and Stateless Diaspora

There is a difference between state-linked and stateless Diaspora. The weakening nation state following transnational Diaspora enhances Diaspora's scope and opportunities (Sheffer, 2005). Over time, some Diasporas shift from a period under stateless to a situation where they acquire a state or a host country citizenship. Diaspora behaviour differs under such distinct legal conditions. For instance, the status of Tibetan exiles changes from a stateless Diaspora in India to state-linked Diaspora in the US with citizenship rights. The Tibetan Diaspora behaves differently depending on their status as stateless situation in India or whether they are American citizens. As American Diaspora activists, Tibetans protest against decisions by US authorities to consider India as the Tibetans exiles' birth-place and not Tibet, which the US officially considers part of China (Hess, 2006).

Similarly, in the UAE Somali Diaspora behave differently during, before and after the Somali state collapse. In the past, the community was better organized and often referred to governmental institutions e.g. the embassy. After the collapse, Somalis became fragmented and more kinship and regional orientated. Somalis have over the years undergone significant community transformation in the UAE, from been state-linked Diaspora in the 1960s and 1970s to being stateless Diaspora from the 1990s. This led to internal community fragmentation giving rise to decreased attention from UAE authorities.

In Denmark, Somali Diaspora, though few in numbers, also behaved differently before the Somali state collapse. They were less traditional and occasionally celebrated national holidays.

This chapter explored the differences of the Somali Diaspora development situation in the UAE and DK. Empirically through the interviews the research found the two countries differ on immigrant reception and integration. Denmark is a western secular democratic welfare state, while the UAE is a traditional, non-democratic, rentier oil state. Despite this structural difference, in certain aspects Somali Diaspora in the two countries confront similar challenges. Both Diasporas confront gender and intergenerational challenges more or less directly linked to host states and societies. In general, there is no evidence that kinship affiliation and sentiment diminish when people move to modern democratic societies. Current conflicts raging in Somalia/Somaliland, the participation of military and qabiil leaders in the civil war carry American, British and Canadian citizenships, confirm that moving to another country does not fully transform Diaspora[64].

The two cases further illustrate that it is not just structures that modify the behaviour and conduct of communities, but also the way in which communities interact and react to state and society contexts and environment they find themselves in. From the way interviewees responded, they seem to say their ability to respond to emerging challenges poses the

---

64
http://wardheernews.com/Articles_11/March/Jowhar/02_lessons_from_the_SSC_wars.html

extent of modifying assabiya. This indicates that we need to deal and respond to the new environment they find themselves by employing some relative agent they seem to have not lost. There the Diaspora seems to construct their own destiny rather than passively see their lives been constructed by others.

The following chapter continues to explore within the interviews between the two countries with regard to the following on Diaspora spaces and the diverse forms of capital, habitus, hybrid and trans-national links that can help us better understand the dynamics and the conduct of Diaspora communities.

CHAPTER 8

DIASPORA'S CAPITAL, SPACE CONSTRUCTION AND HOMELAND RELATION

Introduction

The existence of Diaspora communities invariably suggests new social interactions, but it is not easy to bring about these new interactions. There are two important dimensions to the problem. The first is the degree to which host environment is prepared to accommodate Diaspora communities from a different culture and background. The second is the ability of the Diaspora to adjust into the unfamiliar host environment. It is likely that the host can see the problem of adjustment in considering the immigrant culture they don't easily understand as an obstacle. To go beyond these challenges, there is a need to address the welcome overcome dilemma, meaning the host country and the Diaspora has to overcome possible assumptions and obstacles. Thus there is welcome overcome dilemma. It is more important for the Diaspora to be resourceful and in surmount ways to overcome potentially emerging obstacles through cultural, economic and political means. According to Edward Said Diaspora faces homeland related obstructions, as past experiences and credentials not always count in the host context, where Diaspora tries to relieve a *"literal banishment"* (Said, 1993: 113-117). Arriving in respective host countries, most immigrants aspire for a better life. However, contradictions between the actual realities on the ground and pre-formed expectations often disappoint many. Consequently, Diaspora relates to a double consciousness in the form of habitus, reflecting both the homeland norms, livelihoods and circumstances and host society's social, economic and political conditions. Diaspora's main concern is, therefore, to balance the positive and negative complexities in navigating between the two worlds.

In discussing Somali migration pattern and Diaspora formation in Denmark and UAE, this chapter presents the empirical data on Diaspora hierarchy, capital transferability and the dynamics of Diaspora space constructions in the two cases. The analysis section compares similarities and differences in the two cases and explains the reasons for such differences.

Based on the empirical data collected among the Somali Diaspora in Denmark and UAE, the research argues that the following main points elucidate the dynamics of Diaspora's space formation:

- The migration history, the way in which people arrived and what they brought with them from their homeland
- The reception in the host country and what opportunities they are offered
- The opportunities Diaspora has to structure particular social space in the host country and try to link both to homeland and trans-national networks

The Construction of Entrepreneurship Space: Somali Diaspora in the UAE

From Colonial Migration to Cosmopolitan Migration

Somalis in the UAE are not a homogeneous group. Some have been in the region for generations, working with the colonial system[65]. Others arrived in the post-independent and post-Somali state collapse periods. Initially, most were men who got employment in the then booming oil sector and other public institutions? The British colony recruited employees and soldiers from colonized territories, often balancing one native group against the other[66]. Somali migrants who had some basic school education got employment as translators and office employees.

The second wave of Somalis arrived after independence. They were relatively urbanized and better educated and came to fill positions in the

---

[65] Somalis have been settling Arabia for centuries. But large Somali diasporas first emerged from the end of the nineteenth century mainly linked to colonialism and colonial related wars. The opening of the Suez Canal in 1869 created jobs in Aden where the Somalis were employed as stokers and firemen on passing ships. By the end of the nineteenth century there were Somali enclaves in and around ports as far apart as Perth and New York (Turton E. R. (1974), The Isaq Somali Diaspora and Poll-Tax Agitation in Kenya, 1936-41, *African Affairs*, Vol. 73, No. 292 (Jul., 1974), pp. 325-346)

[66] Vassallo, C. (2006)The Indians, for example, served bureaucracy below senior British civil servants, where the Maltese exceptionally represented part of the Royal Navy (*Journal of Mediterranean Studies* 16 (1-2), pp. 273-289).

expanding oil and construction sectors in the UAE. Compared to other expatriates, the Emiratis do not consider Somalis distant foreigners. Apart from sharing common religion, Islam, Somalia joined the Arab league in 1972, giving Somali passport holders certain privileges. As referred to in the preceding chapter, Somalis had a particular relationship with the late Sheikh Zayed, who ruled the Emirates from 1971-2004.

In the past decades, the UAE, particularly Dubai, acquired an international trading and investment Zone (Romano, 2004: 59). Somalis also shifted their employment focus to these sectors by engaging business entrepreneurship. Many invested their *xaq* (pensions) from long time public employment to start business activities dealing with the homeland.

Recently, Somalis from different places, including some from the west, arrived, joining the booming business opportunities in the country. These recent arrivals are complex and include people with cultural, education and legal citizenship capital. This Diaspora group exploit their status as western citizens in combination with their Somali origin. In situations where they find their Somali background useful, especially when dealing with Somalis, they use their cultural and linguistic ties. In periods where they confront legal challenges from UAE authorities, they appeal to their western embassies. In the UAE, a western citizenship particularly British, American and Canadian, gives the Somali Diaspora a higher status in the social hierarchy[67].

The younger generation of Somalis in the UAE is another group not easily classifiable as migrants or as natives. The youth have acquired cultural capital, by attending public schools and socializing with the natives. Nevertheless, they confront legal challenges as they grow up, especially

---

[67] Some Somalis with western citizenship report that when the police and other representatives of the authority and even ordinary emirates find out about their citizenship they retreat and show respect. There was once an episode where two Somali women with Canadian citizenship had an accident on one of the highways in Dubai. Police and others rushed to them and shouted at them. The girls spoke English and told the crowd they were Canadian citizens. The police helped an escorted them free. If the ladies had been speaking Somali and had shown some African or third world documents, they would have had more trouble. Many Africans were deported by just making a simple traffic accident.

those without citizenship status[68]. Some young people get help from their parents and relatives, who save money to let them travel and study abroad. The aim is to improve the young generation's cultural capital and the overall family well-being. Such efforts include attending universities in the West or in Asia, from where they soon after graduation return to the UAE to attain professional positions the parent generation never dreamed of. Another method to improve the social capital of the youth and thereby the family status is the migration of the young to the west to get citizenship and education, with the purpose of returning to the UAE to start businesses or pursue lucrative careers[69].

Illegal Somali refugee women comprise the most vulnerable among the Somalis in the UAE. They have no proper housing, jobs and protection. Both the natives and the Somali Diaspora exploit these underprivileged women for, among other tasks, conducting harsh domestic work. Occasionally, their Somali kinship network assistance.

---

[68] The law in the UAE requires of children when they reach the age of 18 to be independent from their parents. This means that they will have a job by themselves and they need a separate residence. Interestingly, this does not apply to women. The authorities leave girls to stay with their parents. This is probably related to Arab Islamic culture, considering females more vulnerable than men. Or it could be that the Authorities consider foreign men as a threat, if they just stay unemployed.

[69] In a discussion with a young man who now runs an IT company tells us that his father invested migration to Britain when he reached 18 and had the option to return Somalia or get a job. After over a decade residence in Britain, he has not only helped his father and other relatives to join him in Britain, but has since resettled in the UAE establishing a successful IT business, culturally in terms of social and language he is similar to the natives. He reconnected to his wider network of classmates and childhood friends. He also used his Somali and British background to pursue transnational business.

Table 8.1   Somali migration to the UAE

Migration Type	Migration Period	Migrant Resource
Colonial related migration	1940s- 1960	Nomadic young men recruited fill posts under the British empire. Some of them were trained later.
Oil boom migration	1960-	Educated young men women
Business related	1980-	Business activities
Refugees	1991-	Civil war victims
Cosmopolitan migration	1999-	Transnational migration from the west and east

Somali Diaspora Spaces in the UAE

In an effort to reorganize and establish a separate community, Somali Diaspora in the UAE creates and maintains distinctive social and economic spaces that reflect homeland cultures and traditions as well as influences from the host society and beyond.

Table 8.2   Somali Diaspora and entrepreneurship in the UAE

	Context	Space Character	Owners/Actors	Services/Activities
Somali owned hotels		Jubba hotel & restaurant Open for 6 years	Somali-British citizens With mainly Asian staff	Accommodation Somali & international dish Contact & social gathering place for Somalis
Karama Cafeteria		Coffee shop with food Open for 5 years	Somali citizen With mainly Asian staff	Somali and Yemeni refreshments and food Contact & social gathering place for Somalis

			With big TV screen showing football tournaments
Gold market (Suuq)	Large gold market with Somali sections Expanded the past 20 years	Somali women many from North America and Europe Open market, individual & group ownership	Selling gold and other good for transnational Somali, African and other customers
Hararyaale	Market for clothes, small Somali coffees and restaurants at own town Dubai Open since 1970s but expanded	Somali & Asian staff Somali an Asian staff Somali, Arab an Asian owned big boats	Homeland contacts and business exporting and importing almost everything Social gathering and interacting space Employment, community empowering mobilization space
The Sharjah Harbour	Harbour in down town Sharjah		Commercial link to & from Somalia Export of electronic goods, food and cars Import of livestock and goods from Somalia Social gathering, employment and Diaspora interaction space

Entrepreneurship Space

The UAE has an open economy conductive to business entrepreneurship [70]. Such conditions help Somali Diaspora to start small businesses and pursue international trade. Soon after their arrival, most Somalis start their careers with non skilled, manual jobs from which they save enough capital to start or join existing small businesses and trade related entrepreneurships , mostly linked to the homeland. Gradually, they replace the initial monthly remittance to relatives with activities to buy minor shares in important and export businesses or sending goods to the family in the homeland for further marketing.

The Gold Market

Somali sections in the notorious Dubai Gold Market reflect the business opportunities in the UAE. What is particularly interesting about this market is that it is Somali women who dominate this entrepreneurship Diaspora space, where Somali women deal and distribute jewellery and clothes to business relations in the homeland, to Africa and to the global Somali Diaspora[71]. Similar to many other peoples in the world, gold is a source of prosperity and capital for the Somalis. They use gold as potential saving assets. This is particularly crucial considering the stateless environment in Somalia and the legal uncertainty in the host country.

The now established gold market Somali sections in Dubai functioned as trans-mobile gold market. Somali business women, mostly middle class urban inhabitants, used to come to Dubai in 1970s and 1980s to buy goods

---

[70] The UAE is a federation of seven emirates, each with its own ruling family, where they share power for the federal government. The UAE's oil wealth is mostly in Abu Dhabi. It is Dubai that leads the way in economic development and diversification away from oil. It is here, employment opportunities in trade and businesses are concentrated with almost no income tax (Herb, Michael (20099, <u>International Journal of Middle East Studies</u>, 41: 375-395)

[71] Among the major players include Farhiya Jewelry that distribute gold and other jewelry to global customers. She was one of the first to open large shops at the Gold market. She resettled from Canada to the UAE in 1997 (Discussion with business representatives, July 2011)
(http://www.authorsden.com/visit/viewArticle.asp?id=22745)

such as gold partially for personal consumption and to resell in Somalia. During the civil war, some of these women, together with the gold they saved, re-settled in the UAE. Later, Somali women from the west joined to expand the gold market. Now the Somali section gold market is a trans-national business space, distributing diverse jewellery and other products to Diaspora and non-Diaspora communities as far as South Africa and North America[72].

Apart from its prime function as Somali Diaspora entrepreneurship business space, with daily brokering, selling and buying activities, the area constitutes a social and political space where people meet and exchange ideas and socialize. In addition, the space functions as an informal reception and departure space where people stop by in search for information, contact and networking.

Jobs by the Diaspora for the Diaspora

Just a couple of minutes' walk from the Gold Market, there are Somali-owned cafeterias and restaurants. Diaspora members sit and discuss in groups. Others walk towards the mosque close by for *salatul maghrib* (sunset prayers). If it was not in another county with another system, it could have been *Xamarweyne* (once a popular now destroyed down town Mogadishu market). Nearby one finds a place popularly referred to as *Hararyaalle*. This is a Somali Diaspora space with multiple functions. A young man in his early twenties sits in a Somali restaurant not far from Gold Town. Somalis refer to this section of the town as *Hararyaalle*. That is the name of a town in South Central Somalia. In the past, people originating from that region used to gather around the place. Now it is a pan-Somali business enclave.

The young man was born in Mogadishu in 1989, just two years before the collapse of the Somali state and the outbreak of the civil war. He works for a cargo company owned by his relatives. On Fridays, when businesses close, he plays football for his company. Somali business companies sponsor weekend football tournaments. In this way, the business elite show social responsibility with regard to the Somali community. Hoping the sponsorships to strengthen the business community's image in promoting businesses and creating networks.

---

[72] Space observation and discussion with business women in Dubai, February 2010

It is easy to get a job in the UAE, if one is not lazy. I came to the UAE through Kenya where I lived a while and learnt the English language that now helps me work for the cargo company. Apart from the residence permit that should be renewed every three years, there are no problems living in the UAE (Hassan, UAE, 2010).

As a product of the Somali civil war and a former resident of devastated Mogadishu, The young man witnessed destruction and death. For him, a secure environment and a job in the UAE represent great achievements. The Somali enclave in the UAE resembles Somalia in some aspects but is also a contradiction due to the terrible experience this young man and many other Somalis had in Mogadishu. It is not only with regard to the security and job opportunities, but also the way in which Somalis interact. The young man appreciates that in the UAE, Somalis compete, not in violence, but in sports and capital accumulation[73].

Obviously, the case of this young man illustrates that Somalis have better opportunities in the UAE compared to the destructive circumstances in their homeland. Jobs and potential careers nonetheless depend on whether the individual can link to existing networks and relations. Those who are not able to link to business companies will have difficulties in finding jobs and thereby a residence permits. In the UAE, a residence permit is conditioned by the employment (Terterov, 2006: 218). Therefore, with their ability to provide jobs and opportunities for the people, the business elite represent economic elite with considerable influence in the community.

Employment Space and Homeland Corridor

Another important Somali Diaspora space in the UAE is the Sharjah port at down town Sharjah[74]. The port harbours Indian, Iranian and Somali-owned boats exporting goods to and from Somalia. Somali-owned cranes load cars and electronic materials destined for the Red Sea port cities of Boosaaso and Barbara. During high seasons, business activities around the port employ thousands of Somalis, mainly recently arrived young men and women. Some of them entered the country through the same port from

---

[73] Space observation and discussion with Hassan, February 2010

[74] Sharjah is the 3rd largest emirate in the UAE and ancient port and business activities (Noack, 2007:14).

which they now earn their income and remit to relatives back home or save it for further migration or settlement opportunities in the UAE. Apart from being an employment centre for the less fortunate community members, the port functions as a corridor and life line for Somalia.

Ahmed Dilal (nicknamed the broker), a man in his 40s, coordinates the shipment activities from the ground. With a mobile phone, he is connected to *hawaala* (remittance) businesses, traditional leaders, homeland-host country business elites, ordinary employees as well as marketing agents in China, India, Japan and Diaspora contacts from different parts of the world[75]:

> I have thousands of mobile phones and contacts stored in my cell phone. All of them, one way or the other, link to homeland trade (Ahmed Dilal, UAE, 2010).

In Somali *Dilal* literally means a broker. His connections and the business deals illustrate the character of a dynamic space connected to diverse business groups within the UAE and beyond. Among the cargo destined for Somalia, there is a brand new armoured land cruiser heading for the autonomous region in North East Somalia, Puntland. According to Ahmed, the special shipment belongs to the Puntland Security Authorities (PSA). They have paid one million USD in cash, which is an extreme amount for a car to a country struggling to feed its own population. In this regard, entrepreneurship linked to the homeland is not just positive but also includes negative businesses such as toxic waste, charcoal marketing and smuggling activities.

Somali Diaspora spaces in the UAE are less gendered, as the Somali women actively demand equal opportunities. Though having fewer opportunities, they participate in the port businesses activities. They take part in the long working hours at the port, while they at the same time invest in homeland- linked import and export businesses[76].

The Diaspora spaces have regional and kinship characteristics as the different groups in the Diaspora focus and provide services for diverse regions. Following the collapse of the Somali state, Puntland in the North East announced a unilateral autonomy, whereas Somaliland in the North West declared secession from Somalia. The Sharjah port facilitates business

---

[75] Space observation and discussion with port employees, February 2010.

[76] Discussion with employees with Sharjah port, UAE.

activities largely aimed at the Puntland region. Consequently, business elites often recruit employees originating from the target region. In this context, Diaspora creates not just a space that reflects and links to the homeland in general, but also to a particular ancestral region in the homeland. There are also other ports in the UAE that provide services for Somaliland and Mogadishu. This suggests that kinship and regional dynamics contribute to Diaspora space formation.

Regional, National and Trans-national Spaces

Apart from providing employment and entrepreneurship opportunities for the community, Somali Diaspora spaces in the UAE also function as meeting and contact places for the increasingly trans-nationalized Somali community. The Karaama neighbourhood qualifies to the entitlement of a trans-national contact zone. This is a vibrant enclave where many Somalis both live and run small businesses. The neighbourhood is located in Ajman, one of the minor emirates at the UAE union. In the past, native Emirates lived there, but recently, Somalis and other immigrants moved into the neighbourhood for accessing affordable housing.

In the enclave, there is a Somali cafeteria-restaurant owned by a Somali nickname Hindi Baba. He is married to a Yemeni and they have children. Similar to other Somali business owners in the country, he employs Asians. Reasons for employing foreigners rather than Somalis, as other Somali business owners suggest, include the Somali's "instability and unpredictability of leaving work without excuse and notice". Or the problem with the Somalis "sitting in the Cafeteria along regional and kinship lines".

Outside the Baba cafeteria, a father and a son sit together and drink tea. The young man travelled from Texas in the US to meet his father. The father came to the UAE for health reasons and to meet his son. They have not seen each other since the outbreak of the civil war[77]:

> I came to the UAE for a health check and for meeting with relatives . I also met my son who is not willing to come to Somalia for security reasons (Hadji Ali, UAE, 2010).

The young man from Texas rediscovers his religion in the UAE:

---

[77] Observation at Karaama neighbourhood, February 2010

In these days I have prayed many times. In Taxes there are days and months that I don't pray. There is a big difference (The son from Texas, USA, 25.02.2010).

Somali Diaspora spaces in the UAE do not just function as entrepreneurship spaces but also as interlinked social, cultural and political platforms where Somalis meet, debate and exchange political opinions. The following conversation took place between small groups of Somalis on their way to the mosque.

A man of about 40 says:

You are creating a lot of problems in the country (referring to Somalia)" The accused individual responded "You are reer qansax" (a Somali qabiil) and you are controlling all of the sea (the piracy), you have taken everything, what more do you want?

Apparently, one of them supported the current transitional government in Mogadishu[78], while the other supported the rebels fighting the government. A third man of about the same age interrupts:

Many different peoples create trouble in Somalia. Some came with guns; many others came with foreign passports.

Guns are not the only fuelling source for the civil war. Passports often carried by Diaspora members also contribute to the worsening security and politics in the country. The passport is metaphoric for Somali Diaspora who often joins the Somali conflict. So the issue is not just a dominant, aggressive unruly *qabiils* in the country, but also conscious trans-national political engagement from diverse Diaspora communities with foreign passports, citizenships and ideologies that complicate and prolong the Somali conflict[79].

---

[78] Since the collapse of the Somali state in 1991, Somali had three trans-national governments. None of them succeeded to control the country.

[79] 'Political opportunities for rebellion are not entirely determined by domestic factors, …. social actors—including migrant Diasporas and opposition groups— often organize transnationally' (Salehyan, Idean (Jan 2007), Transnational rebels: Neighboring states as Sanctuary for Rebel Groups, *World Politics*, Vol. 59, Issue 2; pg. 217, 27)

Somali men often engage in intense political debates at café level popularly referred to as *"fadhi ku dirir"* roughly translated as *"fighting verbally while sitting"*. At the Gold Market, Somalis discuss kinship related controversies, particularly who is to blame for the increasing lawlessness and piracy in the country. According to an individual participant, particular Somali *qabiils* create havoc and misery for the rest of the Somalis. These are *qabiils* originating from semi-desert regions in the country with a chronic drought and food shortage. In search of a better life, people from these regions migrate to prosperous areas in the country particularly in urban environments[80].

Heibe is a boat owner about 60 years old. He is an Emirati citizen, business man and belongs to the Somali Diaspora groups who stayed the longest in the UAE. The increased piracy along the Somali coast threatens his business. But he has his own solution to the problem:

> The piracy crisis is very serious. The pirates board large ships using sophisticated techniques. Once they boarded my vessel heading with goods for Somalia. About three o'clock in the morning the captain called and informed me a dangerous piracy incident. I asked the captain and the employees to ask the pirates who they were and which kinship relations they belonged to. They told me two were from the Dashiishle *qabiil*, two from the *Owbeeneeye qabiil* and the rest were from *Majeerteen qabiil*. Then I took the phone and called my contacts in Boosaaso and their *qabiils* and the problem was solved immediately. If the problem was not solved I would also have stopped some Majeerteens in Burco (a region where the ship owner's kinship relation live). Piracy is a kind of high seas *"Isbaaro"* (road block). We should not accept it.

Somali piracy initially began as desperate attempts by fishermen to protect the country's waters and their fishery businesses from environmental apocalypse caused by overfishing and toxic waste. Over time, many other criminals joined making the conduct more lucrative. Recent studies put the cost of annual piracy activities in the world *"reaching more than 16 billion USD, including losses of ships and cargoes"* (Bragdon, 2008: 153).

Somali Diaspora spaces in the UAE confirm the transitional political involvement of the Somalis. Somalis involve in the homeland through travels, family relations, economic and political participation. In addition,

---

[80] Ibn-Khaldun considered rural-urban dialectics as the basics for political processes (Finer, 1999: p. 681-82)

the spaces display a multicultural trend. The food, the social interaction and the behaviour resemble spaces in the homeland. But the served meals also include Arab and Asian dishes. Some Somalis dress in the Arab *khamiis* (Traditional male Arab-dress), which is not a normal dress for Somali men. People communicate in a mixture of languages, Somali, Arabic and English. Thus, Somali Diaspora in the UAE created social and economic spaces reflecting homeland traditions and host country practices.

Apart from the gold and the clothes markets together with the port export-import activities, women seem invisible in open Diaspora spaces. In conservative Arab societies, men and women often live almost in separate environments. Interestingly, the restrictions do not include business and other employment sectors. While Somali men gather in cafes and restaurants, Somali women have their private Diaspora spheres in homes and wedding festivities.

In recent years, Somalis expanded their businesses to include hotels and restaurants providing services for an increasing tourism from the global Diaspora and from the homeland. Such businesses came into being after cooperation between the business elite in the UAE and Diaspora communities from Europe and North America. One such Somali-owned hotel and restaurant is Jubba hotel. Local Somali businessmen and Somali-British investors own the hotel that has been open for business in the past six years. The guests include Somalis, Arabs and other nationalities. Interestingly, the staff is exclusively Asian, mainly Indians. This is almost the standard in the Gulf region. Employers favour Asians, mainly for their supposed efficiency and underpaid labour status throughout the Arab Gulf states. One of the employers claimed they prefer the Asians for "discipline and work ethic"[81].

Finally, Somali Diaspora spaces in the UAE convey historical diversity. The business neighbourhood, the contact Zone in down town Dubai popularly referred to by the Somalis Diaspora as *Hararyaalle* and the port in Sharjah are the oldest spaces that Somalis have occupied for decades. The Somali sections of the Gold Market, the restaurant business and the hotels are the most recent. The development from port-concentrated businesses and employment to more diverse business trans-national conducts tells us that Somalis are gaining more capital as they move to service businesses. They are also becoming more trans-national as they provide services for the homeland, the host country and trans-national Diaspora. Table 8.2 show

---

[81] Diaspora space observation and discussion, 20th February 2010.

that the Somali Diaspora in the UAE is homeland, host country and transnational oriented.

Table 8.3   Diaspora orientation in the UAE

	Homeland orientation	Host country orientation	Trans-national oriented
Somali hotels	Homeland food, homeland customers	Host country business network	Multi-ethnic staff Owned by Somalis with western citizens Transnational space
Karama coffee and restaurant	Homeland food & homeland customers	Host country business network and customers	Somali transnational space Multi-ethnic staff
The Gold Market	Homeland oriented business	Host country business network	Transnational marketing and contacts Somali women with western citizenships
Hararyaalle	Homeland oriented social, economic and political space	Host country business and community networks	Transnational business and network connections
Sharjah port	Homeland business link	Host country business and community network	Transnational business links

Diaspora Hierarchy in the UAE: Who Lights the "bonfire"?

Both the quantity and the quality of the Somali Diaspora in the UAE have changed since Somalis began to arrive in the Gulf country during British colonial times. During the early years of oil and construction boom, Somalis mainly consisted of men. Most of them originated from the Northern parts of Somalia and some even belonged to the old Somali

Diaspora in Aden, Yemen. The UAE, Yemen and Somaliland were once British protectorates, so migrants moved between the territories in search for better opportunities. Somalis who arrived in 1970s and 1980s were relatively better educated. Many of them went to school and migrated from urban areas both in the south and in the north of the country. Some of them graduated from higher institutes and national universities.

Later, following the outbreak of the civil war in the 1990s, the composition of the Somali Diaspora and class structure became more diverse and complex. On certain occasions, you had warlords and people who made money from the collapse of the Somali state and the prolonged civil war at the top of the community. There were also some legal Somali businesses that relocated to Dubai after the state collapse.

Among the new elite, there were women who started business at the Gold Market. Lately, the Somali Diaspora have become more globalized consisting of people with diverse citizenships and social capital. So we can conclude that Somalis in the UAE are currently less homogenous than in the past.

Obviously, the business class is the most dominant among the Somalis in the UAE. The group includes both men and women. The most subordinate are those with no jobs and no legal residence. Second in the hierarchy are the educated class, some of them also involved in business, which get well-paid jobs in the private and public sectors. A Somali education or cultural background is not an obstacle in the UAE. On the contrary, it is an asset. The following statement illustrates the different social classes and how these are linked:

> Somalis in the UAE are divided into classes. At the top you have those (dabku u shidan yahay[82]) the tycoons involved in international business deals with big ships importing sugar and other goods from Brazil. At the bottom you have the newly arrived civil war victims with no resources. Some of them are young girls. There is no direct link between the classes, but sometimes if interest approaches they might come into contact. In addition festivities and celebrations might bring them together. But it is usually brief gathering and do not result much (Elmi, UAE, 2010).

---

[82] The metaphor refers to the Somali nomadic encampment where they prepare an evening bonfire to socialize, eat and exchange ideas. There are those that prepare the bonfire and there are those who enjoy it.

Common challenges and interests seem to convince the different classes to cooperate. This happens during mobilization towards significant events in the homeland[83]. Cultural festivities also function as a bridge between the different parts of the community. Traditional leaders in the form of *beel* (*qabiil* leaders) also occupy the top of the hierarchy. They are obviously influential traditional leaders who through dialogue and consultations coordinate Diaspora affairs. Members respect the agreed decisions. The Somali *beels (Qabiils)* are organized in the UAE, as the leaders know their constituents, for instance who works and who needs help. Due to the fairly short distance to Somalia, homeland traditional leaders also visit the Diaspora, strengthening the trans-national dimension and the continuity of kinship relationship:

> Not long time ago the Dhulbahante garaad (*qabiil* elder) was here. He mobilized and he was welcomed and supported by his group (Abdirahman, UAE, 2010).

Homeland traditional leaders participate in host country community mobilization. Sometimes it is difficult to find out who is mobilizing who. Diaspora invites homeland traditional leaders for the purpose of structural gains in the host country and homeland, while homeland leaders, due to Diaspora's economic power try to reach the community.

Among those at the bottom of Somali Diaspora hierarchy in the UAE, one finds young women who entered the country illegally or found their residence permit expired:

> They are less educated and they don't get jobs. There is some *beel* network that can help initially but many of them do not have support (Kiin, UAE, 2010).

It is the *Qabiil* system and voluntary Somali women that help the vulnerable girls and women. Human trafficking networks recruit these young women who are recruited for domestic work in the UAE. But many find themselves living in slavery conditions.

---

[83] On December the 3rd suicide bomber attacked a ceremony of graduating students from a medical school in Mogadishu. Among those killed were four senior ministers and many students and their parents. A member of the Somali elite in UAE tells that despite differences and disagreements Somali Diaspora organized a major condemning terrorism and the civil war, and remembers the ministers who died in the incident. Some of the ministers returned from Diaspora to help Somalia recover.

Table 8.4   Somali Diaspora in the UAE and class

	Those with resources that can turn the bonfire on (the dominant class)	Those who contribute or benefit from bonfire (lower classes)
The business elite (men and women)	Business activities leadership role to invest, organize and mobilize community	
Traditional leaders	Traditional legitimacy, leadership position to coordinate and mobilize	
Returnees from the west (men & women)	Mobility, citizenship and resource to invest, advance and coordinate	
Young people (men and women)		Less economic resources and job opportunities
Refugees and illegal migrants		Confront legal and economic challenges

Capital Transferability among Diaspora in the UAE

The legal constraints in the UAE pressure many Somalis in the UAE to live uncertainty with continuous planning and strategizing[84]. They undertake preventive measures including investing in a family member to immigrate for education and for work in Europe or North America. This is not a project designed for the concerned individual but for a collective strategy for the whole family. The expected return is citizenship, better education, employment and family reunion.

---

[84] Foreigners need to renew their residence permit every three years. In order to get such residence permit to need to have *kafaala*h (sponsorship by a native).

154

We are investing in the children and their education so they can take care of themselves and the family (Shankanoole, UAE, 2010).

Many Somali parents invest in their children's education, mainly to secure the future of their children but also for their own retirement. In addition, as many of these parents did not have educational opportunities themselves, they are eager to realize their dreams through their children. But providing education for kids in a country where one has to pay for everything is very difficult. Instead, parents begin to invest in their children getting education in less expensive but equally competitive universities in India and Malaysia.

On the surface, the legal exclusion of the Somali Diaspora in the UAE appears negative. But the temporal uncertainty makes the Somalis actively searching for opportunities, e.g. becoming entrepreneurs and establishing businesses that not only trade and interact with the homeland but also improve the position of the Somalis in the host country. Somalis acquire and transfer diverse capital from the homeland, host country and trans-nationally to overcome the structural challenges they face. Their trans-national engagement and capability and their capacity to create business confirm their capabilities. In addition, the Diaspora in the UAE becomes the driving force of the Somali economy, as they diversify and gradually develop to a trans-national contact space for the globally dispersed Somalis.

With regard to social quality of life, Somalis in the UAE live a reasonable life. There are numerous challenges, the legal uncertainty, the lack of free education and welfare but for many, life in the UAE is better than that in Somalia and many other parts in the Middle East and Africa. The kind of businesses Somalis conduct change and become more sophisticated, depending on the capital available to the Somalis, the possibilities to transfer and the constraints that Somalis confront.

Somalis have recently expanded to service sectors such as the hotel and restaurant branches. This has resulted in an increase in the number of Somalis with cultural and legal (citizenship) resources. There is an increasing number of Somalis from the west and the richer parts of the world. Many Somalis from Europe and North America transit the UAE on their way to Somalia. The business elite discovered this opportunity to provide service for the global Diaspora.

Table 8.5   Somali Diaspora in the UAE and capital transferability

Capital	Transferred to
Traditional *qabiil* relations	• Social capital to coordinate and provide welfare for vulnerable Diaspora members • Link to host country and homeland • To claim and demand support
Education	• Employment and social capital to organize, mobilize and run business efficiently
Citizenship	• To access opportunities and to sponsor people • Mobility and acceptance
Employment	• To invest and buy share in businesses • Invest migration of relatives and children • Prepare and invest for secondary migration

Somalis have lived in the UAE for decades, some since colonial times. This is a community that has been continuously developing. Although they confront a number of challenges, including legal and citizen status, the community manages to reinvent itself. Currently, the spaces which the community occupies include entrepreneurship and economic spaces. The class division among the Diaspora reflects this reality. The most dominant is the business elite who creates and provides jobs. Vulnerable men and women who arrived in the country without official papers or who lost their permission to stay and cannot leave in the country are at the bottom of the hierarchy.

The Construction of Socio-Cultural Space: Somali Diaspora in Denmark

From Guest Workers to Refugees

The first Somalis, though their numbers were few, arrived Denmark in 1960s. They came here to join the country's post war reconstruction. The second group arrived in the 1980s and they were mainly students. The largest group arrived in 1990's and most of them were refugees and relied on the Danish state for support. But the situation is gradually improving and Somalis are increasingly becoming assertive:

> They got education and the booming economy helped them. In the past Somalis were marginal, now they are improving (Yusuf, DK, 2009).

The Somali Diaspora in Denmark is, in contrast to those in the past, better educated and therefore find jobs more easily. The Danish job market really opened for the community in the booming years from the late 1990s to 2007. Most were employed in areas where the Danes would not work in e.g. low paid hard jobs.

Some of the early refugees who came to Denmark fled from urban areas in Somalia and thereby better educated. In the early 1990s, Denmark did not readily recognize degrees obtained from non-western educational institutions and most certainly not those obtained in developing countries. Consequently, many ended up either receiving welfare support or accepting jobs for which they were overqualified. Gradually, Somalis acquired cultural capabilities in for instance learning the Danish language, getting an education and creating cultural associations to overcome social, economic and political challenges in the host environment.

Depending on the welfare system has created tensions in the Somali family, where women and children received greater social and even economic independence. The Somali culture in Denmark has always been under pressure, since the first large group of Somalis came to this country. Media and political manipulations focusing on Somalis, especially during elections, contributed to the gap between Danes and the Somalis. Somalis used this cultural exclusion to transform it to a cultural asset in creating cultural institutions, allying with friendly Danish constituents and other Diaspora communities, such as the wider Muslim community, confronting similar challenges.

Table 8.6   Migration to Denmark

Migration Type	Migration Period	Migrant Resource
Guest worker migration	1960-1970s	Young men got jobs in industry and construction sectors
Political refugees	1980-	Political activists and students
Civil war refugees	1990-	Mixture of political elites and civil war victims
Secondary migration	2001-	Educated Somalis and their families migrating to UK for jobs and for fleeing from negative focus on Muslims

Somali Diaspora Spaces in Denmark

Table 8.7 Somali Diaspora spaces in Aarhus-Denmark

Context	Space Character	Owners/Actors	Services/Activities
Somali Family Association	2-3 rented apartments Established in 1994	Somali migrant association led by elected board with agreed rules	Community gathering Free time language courses
Somali Culture and Educational association	Rented old industrial building Established 2001	Somali migrant association with elected board	Somali Refreshments Discussion (*Fadhi ku dirir* rooms) Advice and support on

		integration and employment issues Quran teaching for the children Friday and other prayers
Established by Danish entrepreneur 4-5 Somali owned food & clothes business		Focus on Somali an religious upbringing Prayers and religious sessions for the community, especially for children & women
Bazaar West	Somali business men and women	Sell clothes and Somali an Asian food Provide Hawaala an contact space for the community

Somali Diaspora in Denmark do not own their specific spaces and enclaves. Instead, in accordance with Danish association culture and regulations, the community establishes formal organizations. In order to run these associations, the community applies for public funds, where they will have to comply with municipality and state supervision procedures. Following the 9-11 attacks, authorities introduced restrictions on associational life. The new rules demand associations to register annually on a government administered public web page[85].

Once, a municipality supervisor paid an unannounced visit to a Somali association in Aarhus. He saw a large Somali congregation in the middle of Friday prayers at the basement. The Danish media and politicians often focus on such events and eventually municipality politicians decided to reduce public subsidiary for semi-religious associations[86]. In Denmark, only the Danish church enjoys institutional privileges and state subsidiary (Andersen, 2006: 75). Other religious institutions have no claim for state funding. Somalis use association centres for multiple social and leisure activities in which praying is an integrated part:

> We Somalis are relatively new. In this country communal associations are very important. As relatively new we need associations. These could be improved. For example the Somalis we don't have one organization. There are small associations that conduct a range of social activities- the mosques they do a lot of religious and social activities. There are associations that were established here, some have roots in the homeland. They solve and address issues in the host environment (Abdalaziz, DK, 2010).

As new immigrants, Somalis need associations. Now they have established cultural centres and small makeshift mosques used for religious and social activities. Somali associations solve multiple tasks. The aim is to gain access to resources and recognition as well as reconciling homeland and host country engagements:

> At that time there was no organization. There were no people to go to. Now there are places where you can ask. If you want to go to the university there are people you can ask. We have associations. We have people who graduated and learnt a lot. If you want to change job there are people you can talk to. If you need further education there are people you can talk to (Mowlana, DK, 2009).

---

[85] All associations in Denmark are required to register (www.webreg.dk). This was not the case in the past but was introduced recently due to security reasons.

[86] Somali protested the accusation of been religious but eventually lost some of the public support they use to get http://politiken.dk/indland/ECE983092/somalisk-forening-mister-stilskud/

Somalis were not integrated and organized at the beginning. Now there exists different types of work specialization among the Somalis[87]. The condition of the Somalis is far better now as they beginning to employment, education and other forms of organization.

Socio-Cultural Associations

There are two principal associations in Aarhus, the second largest town in Denmark[88]. The associations have similar structures. They have an elected board and they often try to recruit, and sometimes compete, to attract new members from the community. On one hand, Somali women are part of these main associations, on the other, they have their own separate activities. The youth also join the associations but also conduct their own activities. Large community gatherings take place in the two Eid holidays or when a religious figure, a politician or other significant individual, visits Aarhus from the homeland or from the global Diaspora[89]. Similarly, the associations function as a social space after work and school hours, mainly for men involved in intense political debates *"fadhi ku dirir"*[90].

On weekends, there are weekend sessions for the youth, women and others studying language and religion. Children also attend Quran sessions on weekends. Both associations send delegates to Pan-ethnic organizations bringing Arab, Turkey and other communities together. The associations are also active in mobilizing the community during Danish municipality and

---

[87] Somalis now work in numerous branches such as the transport, service, engineering and medical sectors .

[88] The number of Somali association are much higher but here we present major associations that conduct concrete activities influencing the Diaspora community.

[89] Abdulkadir, Osman Farah, and Ali Abdi Yusuf. "Hadraawi's Peace Journey (*Socdaalka nabadda*) Reaches Aarhus, Denmark." 30 March 2004. Accessed online on 30 November 2004 at http://www.hiiraan.ca/2003/nov03/hadrawi_den.htm?ID=46923.

[90] Fadhi ku dirir is increasingly becoming a relevant social and political phenomenon: http://www.mcgillreport.org/fadhikudirir2006.htm.

national elections[91]. There is no formal joint activity for homeland politics, but the associations organize humanitarian support efforts for the homeland, especially during natural disasters.

Table 8.8 Somali associations in Denmark

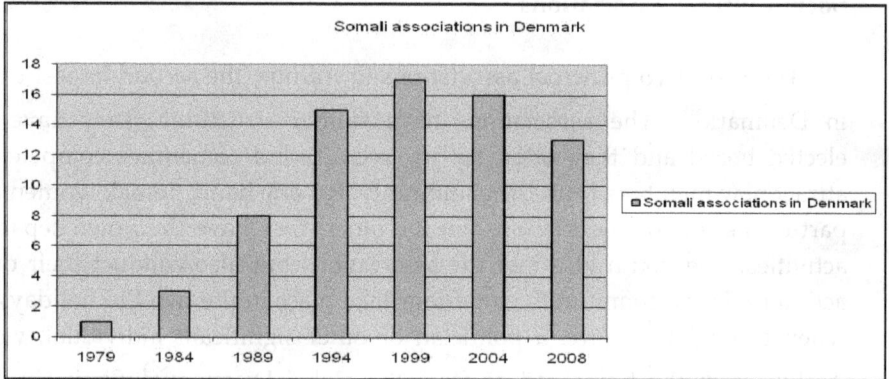

Source: DIIS, Denmark[92]

The table 8.8, shows that the number of Somali associations in Denmark has increased since 1979. It has again fallen from 2004. Most of this association promote socio-cultural activities to empower Diaspora members to cope with the challenges in the host country. There are many reasons for the increased number of Somali associations. Diaspora members have different opinions on how to address the integration and community empowerment issues in Denmark. Organizational disagreements often lead to the creation of more associations leading to the competition of limited resources and community membership. Changes in subsidiary for

---

[91] Somali associations are members of pan-ethnic organization advocating for the building of mosque and more rights for minority communities http://jp.dk/aarhus/kultur/article2231076.ece.

[92]http://siteresources.worldbank.org/INTPROSPECTS/Resources/334934-1110315015165/Trans_Vammen.pdf (This part of a larger study of the African Diaspora. The study also finds that the number of religious cultural associations among the Somalis have also increased, but most do community activities and homeland humanitarian tasks. The number is part of the associations that actually exist as there are many that exist but might not register. The government have in the past few years made registration of associations compulsory. This is mainly for security reasons as it is suggested.

community associations in the past years might have led to the decrease of the number of Somali associations in Denmark (Rasmussen & Boggild, 2008).

Since 2000, the Somali Diaspora in Denmark has entered and expanded to new Diaspora spaces. The need for employment and imported Somali goods among the community led many to start their own businesses. Currently, there are about seven to ten Somali businesses in the big ethnic market in Aarhus called Bazaar West. The media describe the centre in Aarhus as the largest, multicultural market in Scandinavia. The Somali business, apart from the *hawaala* system, includes trade on Somali food, clothes and furniture. Customers and the staff are exclusively Somali.

Although Somalis are slowly beginning to establish businesses, as the following statement suggests, there are fundamental barriers for expanded community business entrepreneurship in Denmark:

It is difficult to have a business and to be an entrepreneur in Denmark. They come and ask you everything. They want you to fill out this form and that form, and ask a whole range of questions and conditions that people cannot answer. In addition, we Muslims we cannot sell everything. Then we will be like Galal[93] sell alcohol (Mohamed, DK, 2010).

Table 8.9   Somali Diaspora orientation-Denmark

	Homeland Orientation	Host country Orientation	Trans-national Oriented
Somali Family association	Cultural and religious activities Language Humanitarian activities and remittance Receiving profiles from the homeland	Community mobilization Political participation Language Education Interaction with authorities	Informal cooperation with European Somali associations in socio-cultural affairs
Somali culture and	Cultural and religious activities	Community mobilization	Informal cooperation with

---

[93] Galal is an Egyptian born Danish hotel tycoon who started his life in Denmark as an immigrant dish washer and is now an internationally respected business giant: http://www.enangalaly.com/Story/

social upbringing	Language Humanitarian activities and remittance Receiving profiles from the homeland	Political participation Language Education Interaction with authorities	transnational Somali associations in socio-cultural affairs

Diaspora Hierarchy in Denmark: Coordinators and Cultural Entrepreneurs

With regard to class differences, Somalis in Denmark appear more homogenous although they, despite improvement in the past years, still suffer from unemployment and state dependence. With regard to community hierarchy based on resources and ability to organize and mobilize the community, we can refer to several interlinked groups, though it is difficult to describe them as a class.

The first are those Somalis who came here with an education from the homeland. The social capital they brought with them could not automatically be used in the country. Some of them succeeded in upgrading their qualifications with some Danish training, while others could not use their resources to empower community associations by participating in the social activities:

I have studied religion. I felt that I should contribute to the enlightenment of the people. I feel more obliged as there in Somalia there are a lot of scholars. I teach young people. We established associations we want to empower students and our goal is to develop and produce a lot of students (Abdalaziz, UAE, 2010).

The educated class created associations and now empowers the youth by filling religious, cultural and organizational gaps.

The second group are the elders who are not necessarily educated but enjoy respect among the community, especially in times when the community needs to mobilize, and they play an essential role in contacting and talking to people. As they are retired, many of them have time to visit and talk to community members. The third group are Somali women who, due the economic conditions in Denmark, have acquired a new status as the leaders of the family. The fourth and the final group are the younger Somalis who are either born or have grown up in this country. They are better integrated, they speak the language fluently and they attend Danish schools.

Due to the significance of cultural association, religious groups and the elders play a significant role. Their role was further consolidated after 2001, when a restrictive government took power in Denmark. The current government considers Islamic values to be a threat to the Danish culture and society (Kühle, 2006).

Because there is emphasis on socio-cultural aspects, Somalis classify themselves on those that assimilate or advocate for assimilation and those that contribute to the consolidation of Somali identity and community empowerment. Those who campaign for assimilation are often in politics, married to natives and are not involved and not aware of ordinary community activities.

Table 8.10   Diaspora in Denmark and class

	Coordinators & Cultural Preservers (the dominant class)	Contributors and Critics of the Socio-Cultural Space
Traditional and religious leaders	-Their role is to guide and educate the economy- responsible of the community's moral economy -Ensure continuity and link to the homeland	
Somalis with education from the homeland or from Denmark	-Knowledge for both the homeland and host country -Capital to organize and mobilize mobilize	
Women	-Mobilizing capacity	
Young people		-Better understanding of the Danish society and contribution to community activities
Men and women that support assimilation		-Adjusted into the Danish society, but isolated from the Somali community

Strategy and Capital Transferability among Somalis in Denmark

Somalis in Denmark also strategize and transfer capital. For instance men have in recent years sent their families to Muslim countries where children can get an education that preserve cultural values. While they remit part of the economic resources gained in Denmark, they also spend resources to straighten and educate their children who they plan for returning to Denmark. In this way, cultural, economic and citizenship capitals obtained in Denmark are transferred to improve the family's socio-economic condition not just in Denmark but also in the homeland and trans-nationally.

Table 8.11 Somali Diaspora in Denmark and capital transferability

Capital	Transferred to
Traditional *qabiil* relations	• Social capital to coordinate and provide welfare for vulnerable Diaspora • Link to host country and homeland • To claim and demand support
Education	• Employment and social capital to organize, mobilize and run business efficiently
Citizenship	• To access opportunities • Mobility and acceptance • To resettle in a third country UK or North America
Employment	• Invest migration of relatives and children • Prepare and invest secondary migration

Somalis in DK are homogenous as most of those who work perform unskilled labour. Significant numbers of the Somalis also receive welfare. There is no significant difference between men and women, as women are

166

also increasingly entering the job market[94]. But due to the gain from the welfare system, women have an advantage to challenge their husbands.

In Denmark, Somalis confront no significant legal challenges as most have citizenships or permanent residence status. They are nonetheless confronted with a cultural stigma with regard to their religion and coming from a poor country. Ironically, the negative focus has somehow empowered the community internally as the members create socio-cultural associations utilizing and feeling proud of their cultural background often ridiculed in the public debate[95]. The associations also give them a platform to link to other networks in the society. In this way, Somalis transform their Somali identity into a space designed to gain and interact with the Danish society. Obviously, such culturally-framed space has its positive and negative aspects, but it is undoubtedly a place of capital generation and human empowerment. Although being Somali appears the prime focus, such spaces appear more hybrid and trans-national in activities and scope. Though linked to the homeland, these cultural activities reflect practical experiences gained in the host country. Somalis daily experience and mix it with habitus both in relation to the host country and homeland. For instance, the associational life in which Somalis engage formally reflects the Danish associational life, informally and in content it reflects Somali habitus.

In recent years, the capability of the Somali people in Denmark has increased, due to younger generations accessing better education and employment opportunities. They have also entered the employment market and are increasingly becoming part of the Danish society.

With regard to the quality of life, Somalis are integrated into the Danish society at the social, economic and democratic levels. They live in a country with one of the highest incomes in the world. Definitely, Somali life in Denmark is better off compared to the socio-economic conditions in the Middle East and Africa.

---

[94] Ressourcemobiliserende beskaeftigelsespolitik strategier og erfaringer fra udsatte byområder
By John Andersen (red.), 2008, p. 220

[95] Islamdebat - om terrorisme, blasfemi og ytringsfrihed
By Allan Poulsen, 2008, p. 64

Diaspora spaces in the UAE and Denmark: Similarities and differences

Somali diasporas in Denmark and the UAE differ in numerous ways. First, Somalis in the UAE acquire status as economic entrepreneurs or as individuals and groups incorporated into Diaspora created socio-economic spaces. In contrast, Somali Diaspora in Denmark obtain the status of socio-cultural entrepreneurs or people incorporated into Diaspora established socio-cultural spaces. Their space lies within the third sector with civil society associations but not in the public and the private sectors.

Second, Somali Diaspora hierarchy in the UAE follows economic class parameters. The dominant classes emerge from those that monopolize financial and cultural resources, while those at the bottom are those with limited economic and cultural capabilities. In contrast, the social hierarchy among the Somali Diaspora in Denmark does not rest on economic monopoly but rather on cultural monopoly. The Somali-Danish elite stresses their position as advocates for cultural and religious preservation.

In general class distinctions are not prominent among the Somalis. Religion and family relations play more significant roles. Nonetheless, it seems that due to the structural challenges that Somali Diaspora confront in the UAE, class solidarity merges with ethnic solidarity, while among the Somali Diaspora in Denmark, class consciousness is not prominent and retain a hybrid situation drawing aspects from the host environment and the homeland.

Among the Somali economic elite in the UAE, one finds women who overcome their traditional gendered position. In addition, class upward mobility is possible in the UAE.

Third, the economic and traditional class-structured spaces influence the conduct of Somali Diaspora in the UAE. They engage in business and politics not just in relation to the host and home countries but also at trans-national level. Consequently, the UAE gained the status as a global business and contact zone for Somali Global Diaspora. The situation is different in Denmark. The socio-cultural space strengthens the Somali Diaspora's cultural consciousness more and appears to provide Somalis to retain homeland traditions.

Somali Diaspora in the UAE become economic entrepreneurs because of three main reasons. First, there exist entrepreneurship opportunities in the UAE, where immigrants can invest and start small businesses in a favourable atmosphere in terms of legislation and institutionalization of economic activities. Second, the proximity to Somalia encourages frequent mobility and economic exchange. Third, there is the legal uncertainty among most Diaspora members who do not access formal citizenship rights in the UAE. Immigrants in the Gulf do not enjoy political and social rights as most cannot obtain citizenship and join trade unions (Weiner, 1982: 4).

Paradoxically, the legal uncertainty leads to ethnic entrepreneurship of establishing *"Ethnic economic niches and enclaves"* with trans-national scope (Ram & Jones 1998:35). In addition, Diaspora's linguistic and cultural advantages transnationalize the economic entrepreneurship linking it to the homeland beyond (Wong, 1998; Light, 2001).

Somali Diaspora in Denmark pursue socio-cultural entrepreneurship because of three main reasons. First the social entrepreneurship opportunities in the form of civil liberties of association and cultural preference support Somali socio-cultural articulation. Second, the legal residential and citizenship rights remove temporal residential concerns. The third and last reason is the long proximity to the homeland, which makes interaction more complex and less frequent. The composition of the social hierarchy reflects the socio-economic conditions in the host country. In the UAE, the dominant classes are those with entrepreneurship business capabilities and their close network, whereas in Denmark, the dominant classes are not directly linked to economic status but to cultural and religious privileges .

Somali Diaspora navigates within the structural dispositions given to them. They are able to employ and transfer the diverse form of capital available to them. Subsequently, group differences, capabilities and opportunities emerge. Those who are able to accumulate different forms of capital are those who benefit the most and exercise power within the community and in relation to the surrounding society. The least fortunate are those who have few capital resources.

In the UAE, the ones to benefit the most are the business elite. They are favoured by the structure and exploit the social space in mobilizing the *qabiil* and their *qabiil* networks in the homeland to promote their businesses. Kinship networks assume a critical role in Diaspora economies among the diasporas in more political unstable countries in the Gulf, whereas in politically stable countries, individual entrepreneurship is prominent (Hanafi, 2000).

Another important dimension is the employment of foreigners in Somali businesses in the UAE. There could be two main reasons. The Asians, especially the Indians and Pakistanis provide cheap labour that businesses exploit. It also reflects the expansion of Somali businesses that increasingly require qualified staff. The status as a trans-national contact Zone for global Somali Diaspora also puts pressure on the business elite to change. The UAE is an international meeting place for people from the Diaspora and the homeland. This is a country that offers a modern infrastructure, cultural opportunities and accessibility both to the homeland and to the wider Diaspora.

In Denmark, Somalis with an education from the homeland and those with training from Denmark are the most dominant. It is particularly the religious elite and the elders who benefit from the socio-cultural dominated space. The traditional elite emphasise the protection of Somali ethnicity and cultural values. Evidence shows that social entrepreneurs can strengthen ethnic communities against racism and family challenges (Mark B. Durieux, Robert Stebbins, 2010: 98). The combination of financial support from the Danish authorities that subsidise all associations and monthly donation collections from particularly women sustain such construction. Diaspora women become cultural preservers, as they prepare and serve food for social events at socio-cultural spaces as well as attending mobilizing and study events (Chafetz, 1999). The socio-cultural space interacts with other related spaces in Europe, the homeland and beyond. This happens when other cultural elites stop for mobilization and fundraising.

Women and the young generation might have some problems with this focus on the socio-cultural dimension, as it prioritizes and sustains homeland traditions. Although in recent years the practice changed, as these associations adapted to more inclusive approaches in the form of inviting some youth to improve the activities so now it reflects both host country and homeland realities. Consequently, the existence of economic entrepreneurship opportunities and activities leads to the construction of economic entrepreneurship spaces whereas socio-cultural entrepreneurship opportunities and activities help the construction of socio-cultural paces.

The two communities further differ on homeland orientation. Diaspora in the UAE are more involved in economic terms, remittance, investment, travel and business deals, while the Diaspora in Denmark also remit but are less involved in economic and political matters. They are nonetheless trying to engage in social remittance activities online. Recent research has shown that Diaspora can alter the development trajectory of developing through the diffusion of knowhow and technology transfers (Audretsch *et.* Al., 2011: 106).

The fact that Somali Diaspora in the UAE are predominantly socio-economic oriented does not mean they are not interested in socio-cultural

170

aspects. The Emiratis share common religion with the Somalis. In addition, religion is not a political issue in the UAE. Somalis in Denmark are also interested in entrepreneurship but institutional and economic barriers make that difficult to establish. Furthermore, culture and religion are major politically contested issues in the country. Finally we should note that both diasporas utilize virtual formal and informal spaces online to communicate, link and advance their positions.

To sum up this chapter presented empirical data that proposes Diaspora formation and conduct are determined by several factors. First, the historical relationship with the host country and the historical background of Diaspora in the form of social and cultural relations originating from the homeland. Secondly, the institutional (legal and economic) opportunities that Diaspora receive in the host country are vital. Thirdly, how these opportunities are utilized, negotiated and transferred by the Diaspora is essential.

The economically friendly, but legally restrictive environment in the UAE produces a Somali Diaspora concentrating on socio-economic entrepreneurship. This leads to the formation of economic Diaspora spaces with host country dynamics and homeland relations. Consequently, the Diaspora in the UAE continuously reinvents itself, always adjusting to the prevailing circumstances. Currently, this Diaspora succeeded to establish a global contact zone for economic entrepreneurship involving the homeland and the other Diaspora.

The welfare system in Denmark, with expanded citizenship rights but with more restriction on economic entrepreneurship, leads to a Somali Diaspora emphasizing cultural and religious dimensions together with interest in homeland ideological development and social remittance. The differences between the Somali Diaspora in the UAE and Denmark call for the re-evaluation several myths.

First with reference to the presented cases, we need to re-evaluate the perception that some immigrants are culturally not interested to work, enjoy receiving welfare and often lack the imaginative and strategic ability to develop and construct independent socio-economic spaces (Kurthen et al, 1999: 25) . Second, we can modify the arguments that Diaspora is purely host country oriented or exclusively homeland oriented. The presented data shows Diaspora operating and linking trans-nationally. Thirdly, we can reject the dominant discourse on women automatically becoming subordinate to their men and cannot pursue independent employment opportunities. The case in the UAE stipulates the opposite. Fourth, the finding suggests that in Diaspora studies we need to reassess the conceptualization on class solidarity often contradicts ethnic or *qabiil* solidarity. The UAE case shows that class identity and ethnic identity might merge. Finally, the data questions the modernization paradigm postulating the longer Diaspora stays in a modern democratic host country the lesser Diaspora involves in the homeland affairs. The approach assumes the conducts and attitudes of the younger generations will overtime reflect more on host country conditions rather than homeland relations.

The following chapter presents and discusses on how the two Diaspora cases respond to the hegemonic constraints the communities confront within the host country and the mobilization, framing and structural strategies and how they pursue.

CHAPTER 9

MOBILIZATION: SOMALI DIASPORA BETWEEN FORMAL AND INFORMAL COMMUNITY MOBILIZATION

INTRODUCTION

We have so far explored two key features to frame an explanatory structure for the Somali Diaspora condition. This was first social transformation and development arising from the Diaspora habitus of hybrid host and homeland environments. The second the Diaspora space formation emerging from the settlement and stability of the Diaspora and the accommodation and welcoming of the host environment. The third aspect to frame conceptually the Somali Diaspora condition is the observation related to community organization and mobilization identifying and capturing both the opportunities and constraints.

Community organization and mobilization relate to the aspects on whether the community is able to organize to exploit diverse resources cultural, social, economic and political in the host environment. The Somali Diaspora can pursue a hybrid strategy combining its own cultural and traditional, cultural values with an open learning attitude towards the host environment In addition, Diaspora organization and mobilization depend on three locational orientations. The first is the host country, where Diaspora has settled. The second is the homeland from which most of Diaspora's values, norms and cultural background. The third is the transnational network that Diaspora might be able to organize and mobilize.

In studying Diaspora organization mobilization complexities, Sokefeld (2006) applied social movement approaches, which he describes as *"collective challenges based on common purposes and social solidarities, in sustained interaction with elites, opponents, and authorities"* (Tarrow cited in Sokefeld, 2006). The success of social mobilization depends on three main opportunity structures. The first is the political opportunity structures enabling such movements to mobilize and allowing them to operate at society level. The second is the mobilizing opportunity structures including the *"collective vehicles, informal as well as formal, through which people mobilize and engage in collective action"*, i.e. networks and associations that movements create (McCarthy and Zald 1996: 3). The third is the projection of ideas, the so-called framing, in strengthening and keeping the movement and its mobilization together (Snow *et* al., 1986).

This study focusing on Somali Diaspora cases in the UAE and Denmark draws use of the social movement framework. First the Somali Diaspora needs political opportunities, particularly the institutional citizenship support to pursue proper community mobilization. Second, Somali Diaspora mobilization requires mobilizing structures and practices in the form of networks and association's people create and join to articulate and express their wishes. Such associations and networks could be host country oriented as well as associations based on kinship trans-national oriented relations. Third, Somali Diaspora needs framing ideas to define Somalis as a distinct group in the process of structuring community cohesion. In this process, the community might create *"master frames"* that construct the identity of the community. According to Sokefeld (2006), such frames not just aim to establish and sustain community but also refer to concrete, significant events *"reflecting collective memoires, grievances, identity and history"* (ibid.) shaping and consolidating community consciousness.

Furthermore, the Foucault's discourse approach guides the analyses of interviews, discussions and texts dealing with Somali Diaspora mobilization. Foucault is one of the first social scientists who linked discourse in the society with the emergence of structures and power relations. For him, discourse is not just utterances but a representation of competing and often unequal, subjective worlds (Neubauer, 1999: 165). The discourse tells us about the subjects under study and the world these subjects construct as well as the one surrounding them. This means the statements of ordinary people contain history and complex power relations and institutions influencing the individual and the collective behaviour. In addition, the meso-domain approach is also relevant in this context. The approach focuses on the dynamics of micro, meso and macro domains, their interaction and relations (Hall, 1995). In the analysis, the research pays attention to the actions of *"significant people, events and institutions"* in focusing on people, institutions and activities to better understand and interpret community dynamics (Jenkins, 2006).

This chapter presents community organization and mobilization with the following categories. The first is how host country opportunity structures influence Somali Diaspora organization and mobilization. The

174

second is how the community exploit both formal and informal channels and resources to access opportunities both with regard to the host environment and homeland. Third what kind of frames ideas and proclamation the community employs to reach and sustain the aims of community organization and mobilization.

Diaspora organization and mobilization: Somali Diaspora in the UAE

Informal mobilization to relieve host country exclusion

The Somali community in the UAE mobilizes to respond to both host country and homeland challenges. In the host country, the community struggles to overcome socio-economic and citizenship constraints such work and residence permits. Most Somalis have residence permit with non-citizenship status. Thus community mobilization takes place through informal organizations. The Somalis as foreigners, individually or collectively, dare not formally and publicly criticize the authorities in the UAE. Instead, the community restricts its activities on providing relief for vulnerable members of the community.

The UAE government controls but does not provide welfare services for non-citizens. The country officially divides people into *"Muwadiniin"* (citizens) accessing institutional benefits and *"Muwafidiin"* non-citizens excluded from social assistance (Peck, 1986: 68). The institutional limitations include the prohibition of collective, formal, political or religious mobilizations.

Despite such restrictions, Somalis in the UAE mobilize both at national and trans-national levels. They do this through mobilizing structures such as gender associations, youth groups, professional networks and business elites. The community mobilizes by utilizing kinship relations and master frames that include references to Somali statehood and nationalism.

Mobilizing traditional and economic structures

Organizationally, the Somali Diaspora in the UAE, community mobilization rests on the kinship network system through which the business community, professionals, associations and pan-Somali mobilization groups interact. Particularly, the traditional leaders and business entrepreneurs play a significant role in leading the organization and mobilization of the community. In periods with major homeland activities, Diaspora's traditional leaders receive reinforcement from the homeland:

Such visits from the homeland attract the business community as well as women and youth groups. They show their solidarity to the visiting traditional leader and in this way, reaffirm their relationship with the homeland as well as the importance of community cohesion in the host country. Although it is an informal social activity, there exists a division of labour. Each sub-group is responsible for the mobilization and the collection of resources from that particular group:

> If politicians and traditional leaders come here or if somebody needs help, people are *waa la abaabulaa* (mobilized) and organized properly. For instance the business people are sent to business persons, the young people to young persons, the women to the women (Faarax, UAE, 2010).

The Somali business community in the UAE is a rather controversial group. Some of them engage in legal businesses while others pursue illegal, economic activities. The support of the business elite is indispensible for community mobilization. They have particularly sponsored high profile visits from the homeland and national celebration events in the host country. This is obviously a strategic action from their side, as they depend on community legitimacy and support both in the host environment and in the homeland.

The *qaraan* (Charity collection) plays a significant role in the community organization and mobilization. Through the collection of *qaaraan* the community shares potential economic burden. Each member of the qabiilah with a job and income contributes to the *qaraan*. In return, the individual qualifies receiving support during recession.

The Diaspora also mobilizes to provide charity and humanitarian support for the poor both in the host country and in the homeland. In a country like the UAE with no universal welfare system, people depend on the Diaspora for survival. So the community mobilizes financial resources in order to reach such vulnerable groups. Though kinship mobilization is dominant when it comes to community structuring, there are also non-*qabiilah* based Qaraan collections. These include networks of friends and professionals who collect and provide support for people in need.

Empowering the community in the host country

At sub-group level, the community mobilizes its resource to reach those who confront major obstacles. These include Somali women, some of them young, who due to unemployment and problems with legal residence suffer in the country. To help them, the community collects resources. The community also mobilizes to empower the unemployed youth to get an education. The aim is to remedy structural barriers that often lead young men losing their legal residence at the age of 18, when they are no longer considered children with their parents. If they do not get jobs, they risk expulsion to the homeland. Individual groups and associations collect money and invite the embassy to support young people with obtaining minor skills and computer training[96]. Normally, it is a governmental task to provide welfare services, but in this context the civil society fills the gap.

Empowering homeland regional alliances

Somalis in the UAE mobilize economic resources to help vulnerable community members such as women, the sick and youngsters in the homeland. In addition, they organize fundraising events for the development of their ancestral homeland region. This includes both humanitarian and political events aimed at supporting homeland constituents. Mobility and the proximity to Somalia make such trans-national engagements more frequent. Again a significant contribution comes from the traditional leaders and the business elite.

Over the past two decades, the community experienced intense mobilization focusing on regional and constituent support. This is mainly to do with the lack of a centralized government in Somalia. The absence of

---

[96] Discussion with young Somali UAE Diaspora members in Abu-Dhabi, UEA (14th, February 2010).

properly functioning Somali embassy exacerbates such community fragmentation. Prior to the civil war, the embassy played significant role in community organization and mobilization. Although kinship network mobilization provides a certain relief for many people in the host country, the system also indirectly undermines the collective, general mobilization of the Somalis.

Organizing national holiday celebrations

The devastating civil war in the homeland in1991 affected the Somali Diaspora in the UAE negatively. Organizationally, they increasingly became regional and *qabiilah* oriented. Each *qabiil* mobilized to openly support its *qabiilah* and regional constituents. Initially, the first to start was communities from northern Somalia (current Somaliland). When the military regime persecuted northerners and later bombarded major cities in the North, Somali Diaspora from the region mobilized to support Somali National Movement, which was one of the main insurgent movements opposing the regime (Mohamoud, 2006: 129). As the hope of reconfiguring the Somali state faded, these constituencies transferred their decisive backing to the current regional authorities in Puntland and Somaliland. Dissatisfied with such secessionist tendencies, an increasing number of the younger generations among the Somali Diaspora in the UAE tried to mobilize across regional and kinship cleavages. They have particularly expressed their vision to organize commemoration and celebration events for national holidays. The youth belong to the age groups between 18 to 35, many of them born or raised in the UAE. They receive assistance from the business community agreeing to sponsor national holiday events. Interestingly, the government of Sharjah subsidizes the event. It is said the support has been a tradition even before the collapse of the Somali state. The UAE, particularly Sharjah, had long historical relationship with Somalia[97].

---

[97] There is a general perception among the Somalis that during the colonial rule, ancestors of Al-qasimi tribe, whose descendents currently rule Sharjah opposed the British empirical rule. Somali tribal leader in Puntland region sent massage to the Arab tribal chief informing that he is ready to send 5000 Somalis with horses to fight the British alongside their follow Muslims in Sharjah. The Sharjah ruler visited Boosaaso in Puntland, which was named after him as "Bandar Qasim". The Letter sent by the Somali *qabiilah* leader is said to be in a Museum in Sharjah, but it was not possible during the research to confirm its existence.

Responding to pressing issues

Apart from the community mobilization aimed to prevent the social exclusion among vulnerable community members, the Somali Diaspora in the UAE, due to a lack of state protection, confront periodical political challenges. Two cases are worth mentioning. The first is the decision by the UAE authorities to ban issuing visas for Somali passport holders. The second is the UN representative in Nairobi who, with the approval of the UN system, accused the Somali community in Dubai, particularly the business community, for their connection and cooperation with Somali pirates.

The two issues were mainly externally generated. For security reasons, western countries put pressure on the UAE authorities to restrict movements form civil war torn Somalia[98]. The current transitional Somali government in Mogadishu also indirectly propagated such ban as an attempt to strengthen its legitimacy. They urged people to change their passports, asking them to abandon old passports and use the new one they provided. At official level, the Somali community approached the UAE authorities for help. The Diaspora also appealed to the transitional government. Interestingl y, the embassy in Abu-Dhabi announced the visa issue concerned only Dubai and not the entire UAE. Underlining the lack of state legitimacy in Somalia.

Unofficially, Somalis tried to help the situation as much as they could. The only formally registered organization in the UAE is the Somali chamber of commerce. Community statements in the local newspapers illustrate desperation and helplessness in their appeal to the authorities both in the UAE and in Somalia. Eventually, the business community, in a mixture of

---

[98] Al-shabaab , a terrorist accused and Alqaida allied Somali organization that control most of Southern Somalia, vowed to wage jihad against western countries and their allies. The organization is registered as terrorist organization both in the US and Europe. They have also recruited young Somali Diaspora members from   western   countries. Some of them have allegedly committed suicide.

threat to withdraw their investment and negotiations, managed to convince authorities that a visa ban is unsustainable[99].

The second major case was the piracy issue. This has brought accusation and suspicion to the Somali businesses elite in Dubai. The Somali community also dismissed this accusation. The UAE authorities also denied such accusations, complaining it was a conspiracy against the image of the UAE [100]. It is interesting to note that there has not been a direct organized official communication between the UAE authorities and the Somali Diaspora. Furthermore, Somalis do not organize formally, not in their interaction with the UAE authorities. The Somali chamber of commerce might in the future at least organize and represent the business community.

Table 9.1   Mobilization and Somali Diaspora in the UAE

	Opportunity Structures	Mobilizing Structures	Framing Structures
Local level			
National Level	Trying to overcome lack of supporting institutional structures in the host country	Kinship networks, associations, business networks	Kinship relations
Transnational level	Trying to contribute to opportunity structures in the homeland	Kinship relations Regional alliances	Kinship affiliations Regional frames Nationalist frames

---

[99] The largest Somali businesses are located in the UAE most Somali *hawaala* (remittance companies) and IT have their headquarters in the UAE (Regulatory frameworks for *hawaala* and other remittance systems, Volume 2004 (International Monetary Fund. Monetary and Financial Systems Dept).

[100] The UAE made statement dismissing any piracy cooperation taking place in their country. They blamed external enemies targeting the UAE reputation (Al-bayan, 14th February 2009).

Diaspora Mobilization: Somali Diaspora in Denmark

Formal organization to resist host country exclusion

The Somali community, as members of the Muslim Diaspora in Denmark, joined the mobilization against the Danish cartoons depicting the prophet[101]. The protest against the cartoons brought Ethnic Danes, Pakistanis, Syrians, Iraqis, Palestinians, Somalis and many other Muslims and non-Muslims together. Ironically, both the 9-11 attacks and the cartoon crises helped to shift the narrative from the Somalis as a distinct deviant ethnic group in Denmark. With emphasis on religiosity, Somalis shared public and political scrutiny with the large Muslim Umma (community). From a mobilization perspective, the Muslim community is not much different from the Somalis. Despite the existence of common grievances that especially intensified after September 11ᵗʰ 2001, Muslims in Denmark appear disorganized and divided into conservative and less conservative groups. Particularly the Turks, the largest and the first ethnic group to arrive, and other Muslims have often been less organized than the recent more politically conscious Muslim refugees (Dassetto, 2000).

Five years after the cartoon crises in January 2010, a young man with a Somali origin attacked the principal *Jylandsposten* (*JP*) cartoonist, Kurt Westergaard. The young man tried to kill the aging cartoonist who luckily survived. The incident affected the Muslim community in Denmark,

---

[101] In September 2005 one of Denmark's main conservative newspapers, the *Jutlandsposten*, published a dozen cartoons caricaturing the Prophet of Islam. The Muslim community in Denmark initially protested to the government and requested a meeting to discuss the issue. Similar steps were taken by diplomatic representatives of several Islamic countries in Copenhagen. The government ignored this call apparently giving for pressure from their parliamentarian coalition partner, the Danish Peoples Party. After months of diasporic consultations, imams travelling to and from the Middle East, community mobilization and diplomatic manoeuvring, the case shifted to transitional level. Angry protesters attacked the Danish embassies in Syria and Beirut. Widespread international demonstrations and counter demonstrations erupted. Over hundred people died worldwide and many more were wounded.

particularly the Somalis. The frustrated young man came to Denmark as a child with his parents. Acquaintances and neighbours described him as an integrated, calm individual. What prompted this young man to act impulsively remains unclear. Obviously it could be the so-called war on terror and the subsequent invasion of Ethiopian troops in Somalia in 2007 that might have radicalized young Somali men from marginalized groups (Eichstaedt, 2010: 46). Apart from the general exclusion in the society, the negative discourse against Islam might also explain the radicalization tendency among the youth (Malik, 2009: 130-6). The angry reaction could also result from the generational gap between the first and second migrant generations for differences in religious interpretation. The parent generation appears more conservative, and kinship oriented, and link to the homeland, while the younger generations prefer universalistic, ideological global orientation (Nayar, 2004: 139).

One month after the axe attack incident, a former Danish councillor from Aarhus with a Somali origin called for the need to focus and deal with an increasing radicalization tendency among the Somali youth in Denmark[102]. He claimed that Somali youngsters from Denmark have become victims of radicalization and recruitment for the conflict in the Horn of Africa. The Aarhus mayor, Nikolai Wammen, supported the initiative. Together they proposed a major conference specifically targeting the Somali community in an attempt to prevent youth radicalization.

In response, Somali associations held an urgent meeting and agreed to condemn the proposed selective conference with special focus on the Somalis. Instead, they suggested an inclusive conference with the participation of other ethnic communities to discuss radicalization and exclusion in general. The mayor dismissed the proposal and together with the Somali politician Ali Nuur decided to hold the conference on the 27th of May 2010[103]. The Mayor had for some time also a good working relationship with Ayaan Hersi Ali, another member of the Somali Diaspora, globally re-known for her harsh Islam critique[104]. The next few months witnessed intense debate, disagreement and mobilization in both camps. The Mayor and Ali Nuur supported by the political network, the bureaucratic

---

[102] Jyllandsposten, 8. February 2010 " Ali Nuur sent a letter to the Mayor warning that Denmark can be a target for terrorism if the authorities do not do more.

[103] Jyllandsposten, 9. February 2010

[104] Jyllandsposten, 29. April 2010

apparatus and the media confronting the Somali associations and leading community activists working on voluntary basis and in their leisure time.

The following sections present and discuss the community mobilization mechanisms and the dynamics, particularly the mobilizing and framing structures Diaspora utilized to negotiate, promote and defend its position. The case illustrates the essence of trans-national Diaspora organization and mobilization.

Political and Institutional Support for Community Mobilization

Similar to other immigrants, Somalis in Denmark access political, economic and social opportunities. This includes the partial economic support for their associational activities (Anderson, 2008: 92). However, immigrants often do not exploit the benefits to actively participate in the political process (Siim, 2004: 76).

To counter the municipality sponsored radicalization conference the Somali Diaspora used local and national opportunities in Denmark and combined it with homeland resources and transnational networks.

For instance four major political parties backed the Somali position in opposing the conference[105]. The parties had probably their own oppositional political agenda to criticize the Mayor for his narrow-minded conference. But intense networking campaign and alliance building from the Somali community succeeded to divide the political parties[106]. The Somali community's proposal for inclusive conference supplemented with political lobbying convinced opposing parties at Aarhus municipality to boycott the Mayor's conference.

The second political support was trans-national and partially homeland oriented. Somalis invited the Somali ambassador in Genève to make the opening speech at their alternative conference at Aarhus Theatre. This move transformed the Somali-Danish local issue to a trans-national level. At the same time, Somalis signalled, despite the state collapse in their homeland, they still had homeland related, international, diplomatic institutions to refer to. The presence of a Somali ambassador elevated the community's status.

---

[105] Jyllandspost, 22. May 2010

[106] Jyllandsposten 9. April 2010

The Somali state does not exist but the transitional Somali government enjoys international recognition and Somali government officials attend international forums in making their case (Shay, 2010: 87). In addition, the ambassadors' presence and the case received coverage in Somali transnational media[107]. From his side the ambassador did not see the issue as a sign of division between the Somali Diaspora in Denmark and the Danish society. He interpreted the case as an evidence for the Somali integration and ability to combine utilizing democratic opportunities Somali s access in the host country with the relationship Somalis maintain with the homeland:

> What you are doing is in accordance with the Islamic, the Somali and Danish values. You should not forget that many Danish support your position (Ambassador Yusuf Bari-bari , 27th May 2010).

In a seminar held for Somali Diaspora activists, participants expressed the following ideas on positive opportunities promoting community development in Denmark and the negative aspects influencing the communi ty.

---

[107] www.Somalitalk.com , serious Somali news internet with branches and news reporters globally

Table 9.2 Opportunities and challenges in Denmark

Opportunities	Challenges
• **Economic opportunities** (Access to economic support from the authorities , We live in a prosperous Scandinavian country, We can establish businesses, Fund raising and investment • **Social and political liberty** (We have political liberty and opportunities , Religious freedom where we can invite an Imam from abroad , We can articulate and protest, Political, social and economic rights • **Peace and stability** (Peace and stability • **Welfare and education opportunities** (Access to education both for elders and for youth, Employment opportunities and voluntary work, Live long learning opportunity, Health care, We can have own educational institutions	• **Racism and exclusion** (Media manipulation and lies ,The police stigmatizing our youth, Undocumented terror and radicalization accusation , Politicians who divide the community for moderates and radicals, Marginalization of the youth • **Internal division** (People who spy for the police and discredit the community, Lack of embassy and lack of government, Using Somali opportunists as Somali experts) • **Segregation** (threat to end at the bottom of the society, inferiority complex • **Assimilation**

Mobilizing traditional and cultural structures

Somalis consider religion as a strength and significant for their presence in Denmark. Their ability to maintain their religion and practice proves their strength and conviction[108]. The community performs prayers in small makeshift mosques in the basement of Somali association premises. Such places do not qualify as proper mosques but function as such. Together with other Muslim communities in Denmark Somalis have for years campaigned to build a proper mosque, but due to economic challenges and political obstacles they have yet to succeed (Gartner, 2007: 21). These temporary mosques together with the religious leaders play an important role in community mobilization and cohesion (Kühle, Lene, 2006: 39-47). Following the 911 events, mosque activities came under surveillance from security agencies (Deflem, 2008: 283).

With regard to associational life, Somalis establish associations mobilizing and defending the community from external political and media challenges. In recent years Somalis mobilized to participate in local and national elections[109]. Consequently, Somalis consider themselves as established Diaspora, overcoming the early stages of refugee life in Denmark[110]. Obviously speaking the language, acquiring citizenship and the younger generations born and grown up in this country suggest certain Diaspora consolidation. Finally, Somalis consider the homeland relation as positive. In difficult times, they mobilize resources, raise funds and remit money to relatives and friends.

With regard to community weaknesses, Somalis recognize numerous, internal community challenges inflicting certain setbacks. These include the community's suspicion on community activists whom they accuse of exploiting their positions. In addition, the frequent inter-community quarrelling and disagreements often paralyze community efforts and cohesion. More seriously, the issue of which Danish political parties and candidates to support divide the Somali Diaspora. For instance, during the latest municipality elections, the community introduced four candidates from four different political parties. This led to intense community mobilization, but none of the candidates made to the municipality council[111].

Another long-term challenge the community confronts is the widening gap between older generations, not born in Denmark and with considerable

---

[108] Discussion at the weekend seminar in Kaløvig

[109] Denmark's statistics (www.stat.org)

[110] Jyllandsposten, March 2010

[111] Discussion in the weekend seminar in Kaløvig

relationships and contacts with the homeland, and younger Somalis born or grown up in Denmark. Although the two groups belong to the same Diaspora, they have diverging world views. The first generation, many of them traumatized, had initially difficulties to adjust to Denmark. Thus the youth complain about the lack of proper role models[112].

Somali associations also recognise their invisibility in relation to the Danish society. They do numerous activities promoting integration not often visible for the wider society in Denmark. More importantly, the community does not own properties but utilizes temporarily rented facilities. Consequently, there are no community managed private institutions such as private schools. Other immigrant communities such as the Turks and the Arabs own and administer independent educational institutions[113]. The lack of community properties and institutions often force Somalis to depend on other Diaspora communities. For instance, Somali pupils constitute more than 50% of students of Arab and Turkish owned schools in the city[114].

On the 5th of April 2010 the Somali community in Aarhus held a meeting to counter the Aarhus municipality and Mayor-sponsored conference. The conduct of the meeting illustrates the dynamics of community mobilization. The gathering appointed an elder to chair the meeting. Although Somalis met to talk about the current developments with regard to the upcoming conference, a gentleman who had just returned from the homeland was the first to speak. For the elder generation challenges confronting Diaspora can only be solved if Somalis manage to reconcile in the homeland. For them, host country challenges are linked to homeland deficiencies:

> We could not reconcile in Somalia. That we will reconcile and make peace in Diaspora is therefore not possible (Kaarshe, 5. April 2010).

---

[112] Discussion with Somali youth group (November 2010).

[113] The Turks community in Denmark run many private schools, one of them is Salam school. Almost 50% of the pupils are Somalis. Lykkeskolen is another school located in Aarhus, here the share of Somali students are also high, prompting mangers of these schools urging Somali associations to establish their own schools.

[114] http://www.lykkeskolen.dk/

After a long debate, the meeting agreed on mobilization strategies. The participants considered reaching out women and young people vital as the two groups are the most difficult to mobilize. Women are busy at home and the youth are busy with their studies and spare time jobs. They concluded the need for outreach activities to disseminate information about the upcoming conferences:

> The problem of the debate on radicalization we are now facing is serious. We need to understand and explain to the Somalis. Those who are the most difficult to explain it to are the youth and the women. There must be publications, home visits, dialogue and contacts (Hassan, 5. April 2010).

Participants also agreed to a division of labour in terms of who will do what and when. The elders will do community mobilization by visiting different constituents. People who are integrated in the Danish society and who hold a certain amount of knowledge of the Danish language and system will have to attend the technicalities:

> With regard to the work the community will do countering the accusations we need to leave the work to the leaders and the educated group. Others need to support (Abdi, 5 April 2010).

Finally the mosque centres, and the associations utilizing the centres, become principal institutions organizing the protest. The meeting agreed to arrange several community activities countering the official conference on the same day on the 27th of May 2010. Financial donations came from women, youth and elder groups. Two major events were held. One at the Music House in down town Aarhus. The other in the ethnic-dominated neighbourhood Gellerup, also in Aarhus. Close to 400 people with diverse ethnic background attended the first event while the second attracted 700 Somalis.

> The issue must be addressed in the mosques and people there must be informed. We need to go to the neighbourhoods (Guuleed, 5. April 2010).

As the time scheduled for the competing conferences approached, a traditional leader (he has the title of Imam- not the religious but the customary one) enters the scene. The community mobilization balance immediately changed. Support by the wider community is considered important by both the authorities coordinating the municipality conference and the Somali community's protest conference. The municipality organizers targeted and invited Somalis to attend[115]. If the Somalis did not participate in the conference, then the conference would be worthless. With the defection from a traditional community leader, the municipality conference organizers could not fully count on community support.

Kinship relations have no political and economic significance in Denmark, but in this mobilization context it represented an important informal mobilization and organization factor. The focus in this regard was not on the kinship itself but on being Somali and the Somali Diaspora's attempt to integrate into the Danish society. In an exclusive interview with Jyllandsposten, the traditional leader boycotted the conference and announc ed his solidarity with political parties and the Somali associations[116]. He dismissed the radicalization of the Somalis and their alleged cooperation with Al-shabaab (a radical Islamist organization in Somalia). The traditional leader admitted Somalis might have supported radical organizations in Somalia during the Ethiopian invasion of the country, but also said that belonged to the past and had therefore nothing to do with the present situation. Similarly, the way in which some political parties changed sides and the move from the traditional leaders followed after determined lobbying and campaign from Diaspora activists who convinced traditional leaders and other important personalities on the importance of opposing the municipality conference.

On the municipality side, another significant person entered the scene supporting the conference organizer's side. Ayaan Hersi Ali[117] aligned with the Mayor and his supporters. Miss Ali visited Aarhus and gave a lecture at *Jyllandsposten* headquarters. Aarhus Mayor attended this lecture. She declared her support to the municipality's conference, by saying:

"It is fine to organize such a conference. It is good to see why the Somalis are radicalized[118]"

---

[115] Jyllandsposten, May 2010

[116] Jyllandsposten, 19. April 2010

[117] http://news.bbc.co.uk/2/hi/europe/4985636.stm, profile of Ayaan Hersi

[118] Jyllandsposten 29 April 2010

With Miss Ali's contribution to the conflict, now the Somali Diaspora became divided into assimilation oriented Somalis and integration inclined Somalis. With the earlier support by four political parties together with traditional leaders supporting the community mobilization, the Somali Diaspora associations eventually gained ground.

Somalis held a cultural festival called *"AarhuSomali"*. Critics called it an act of provocation against the radicalization conference. The Somali commun ity had at the same time established a Danish language homepage (www.aar husomali.dk), with the aim of directly communicating with the Danish society. Danish media often profile ethnic minorities negatively and with prejudice (Nikunen, 2011: 163). The homepage is professionally run by the Somalis and administrated by journalists. In this regard, Somalis managed to bypass mainstream media and transmit their message directly to the Danish public. The community also succeeded in having the Danish media citing and referring to the homepage.

With an offensive strategy in introducing a professional homepage together with the cultural festival, Somalis managed to transform a negative focus on them to a positive one. Apart from protesting, Somalis also demons -trated their active formal participation in society affairs.

Hybrid framing of Danish and Somali Values

The attack of the Danish cartoonist by a Somali Diaspora member triggered a political demonization and subsequent community mobilization. A number of significant people, locally, nationally and globally condemned the attack of the Danish cartoonist. The Mayor of Aarhus was one of them. He described the attack as a cowardly act and in opposition to democracy[119] Somali associations called the attack tragic[120]. In the following days, the Mayor upgraded the incident from being an attack by a frustrated, possibly psychologically disturbed young man to a clash between civilisations, with the democratic, civilised world confronting the uncivilised. The case no longer remained a criminal police case but a mainstream socio-political discourse. Apart from the rhetorical division of the world into good and evil, the Mayor insisted upon the global implications of this event. This was a war, he said, we should fight all the way through[121]. Denmark recently

---

[119] Jyllandsposten, 3. January 2010

[120] Jyllandsposten, 3. January 2010

[121] Jyllandsposten, 3. January 2010

pursued what was referred to as an offensive foreign policy by participating in the *"coalitions of willing"* in Iraqi and Afghanistan (Singh, 2006: 35).

The Mayor and those opposing the Somalis wanted to link the Somalis to the homeland and consider them as people with tremendous challenges to integrate. The Somali associations saw the case from a different perspective. They framed their activities as a process of combining Danish and Somali values.

The issue of belonging is also clear, as Somalis see themselves belonging to both the Danish society and the Somali society. They do not consider this an obstacle to the integration in this country. The presence and performance of the Somali-Danish cultural band at the Music House illustrated the attempt by the Somalis to profile themselves as hybrid and trans-national:

> If we decide to demonstrate, we need to use our flag but also to use the Danish flag, so we could attract Danish participants. This is our second country (Elmi, 5. April 2010).

The Somali community condemned the attack against the cartoonist and described it as a terrorist act. At the same time the community warned politicians and the media not to exploit the tragic event to scrutinize a community already struggling from stigma and marginalization[122]. In their response Somalis referred to the general anti-immigrant atmosphere in Denmark. They stressed that most Somalis are normal citizens, busy with their daily routines. Therefore the action of an individual should not victimize the majority, especially the young and children.

Another important point is the way in which Somalis invited and included historical and cultural figures both from Denmark and beyond. Halima Sofe[123], a resident in Aarhus, anti colonialist and freedom fighter, was invited as a prominent guest in the festival. Amin Amir - Somali artist,

---

[122] Politiken & Berlingske 8th January 2010

[123] Halima Soofe, former freedom fighter is a history for herself. Member of SYL (Somali Youth Legue) an organization that mobilized resistance against the Italians in south Somalia. She fled as many others. Barre Fiidow, one of the most known Somali poets from the now destroyed Somali National Theatre. His poem was much more interesting with regard to the link between the host and homeland.

currently a Canadian citizen, was also present[124]. Barre Fiidoow, a prominent Somali poet and playwright also participated.

With the announcement and the coordination of the cultural festival, Somalis brought significant people, institutions and events together, including Somali-Danish girl band, the Somali ambassador from Geneva as well as historical and cultural figures from Denmark, Canada and other European countries. The selection of a significant cultural institution such as the Music House was a milestone for the Diaspora image. The Music House is a major public institution (major cultural icon for the Danes and for Aarhus city in particular).

The invitation of the Somali ambassador was importantly symbolic. The ambassador is based in Geneva, working for a recognized but non-functioning government[125]. Bringing all these dimensions together, as table 9.3 shows, the Diaspora managed to distance itself from radicalization and succeeded to project its Diaspora transnational identity.

---

[124] The participation of the Somali cartoonist was important as the whole incident started with an attack of a Danish cartoonist. With his arrival the Danes become aware that the Somalis had also their own cartoonist that was also threatened by extremists (www.aminarts.com).

[125] The transitional Somali government controls few kilometers in the Capital Mogadishu. The rest of the country are either autonomous regions or are controlled by opposition armed groups

Table 9.3 Mobilization of the Somalis in Denmark

	Opportunity structures	Mobilizing structures	Framing structures
Local level	Mayor, Somali councillor, Somali Diaspora	City council, Music house, Somali associations and network	Attack on Danish cartoonist
National Level		Political parties, traditional qabiilah system Media commentator, expert	
Transnational level	The Somali Imam, Ayaan Hersi,	Kinship relations	Global war on terror, Islam Vs. the West

Informal Mobilization For Homeland Affairs

The Somali Diaspora associations held a two-day seminar at Kaløvig to evaluate and discuss their efforts. The seminar brought Somali activists and resource groups involved in community mobilization together[126]. In the discussions, Somali Diaspora members discussed their relationship with the homeland.

---

[126] In May 2010 thirteen Somali associations established Aarhus Somali to counter the municipality's political pressure. The associations considered the events successful as they managed mobilizing the community to held a parallel conference with cultural components that attracted significant media and public attention. To build on this gain, the association agreed to organize a weekend seminar for community activists. They selected Kaløvig centre, a seaside summer resort 30km outside Aarhus, as the seminar venue. This attractive green landscape contradicts the relatively poor residential areas most Somalis live. In this regard the Somalis try to move spaces beyond the familiar ethnic neighbourhoods.

Remittance constitutes the major link between Somali Diaspora in Denmark and the homeland. Somali associations in Denmark do not formally participate in the political activities in the homeland. This does not mean Somalis do not contribute. The same Diaspora formally involved in community organization and mobilization in the host country might informally contribute to Somali politics and development.

The humanitarian dimension is an exception. When droughts and other humanitarian challenges occur, the community collectively organizes and mobilizes. Another exception is when Somalia faces an external attack such as when the Ethiopian invasion occurred. The community then mobilized resources by arranging demonstrations and collecting funds for the homeland (Roble, Douglas F. Rutledge, 2008:149). Such informal humanitarian involvements often evolve to political involvement when Diaspora activists interact and study the homeland context properly (Sheffer, 2003: 207).

Community organization and mobilization in the UAE and Denmark: Similarities and differences

There are similarities and differences in the way in which Somali Diaspora mobilizes in Denmark and the UAE. Since the September 2001 attacks in the US Somalis, similar to other Muslim Diaspora, struggled to overcome suspicion and recurring accusations of extremism. In the UAE, the community was accused of financially sponsoring radicalization, warlordism and piracy in the homeland. In Denmark, the community, together with other Muslim Diasporas, was suspected of harbouring radical elements.

In addition, the two Diasporas, though in different ways, utilize cultural mobilizing structures such as traditional leaders and ethnic associations in order to negotiate and promote community interests. The two Diasporas also operate at trans-national level by interacting and linking to the homeland, host country and beyond.

The first difference between the two Diasporas relates to citizenship opportunity structures that each Diaspora accesses in the host country. The Somali Diaspora in the UAE has the advantage of residing in an Islam Arab country geographically and culturally close to Somalia and with a long historical relationship. Business opportunity structures provide higher competitiveness which in turn provides resources for a homeland-linked trade. An efficient utilization of homeland-oriented trade depends not only on the capability and the engagement of the business elite but also on the type of Diaspora, geographical and opportunity structures (Kitching, J., Smallbone, D., Athayde, R., 2009). The main challenge confronting the Diaspora in the UAE is the lack of citizenship rights. Because of this legal restriction, Somalis choose to operate informally in host country related mobilization activities, whereas they formally organize in their interaction with the homeland. Formality in this context means organizing and expressing community priorities and views openly in community assemblies and in the media.

The acquisition of citizenship is an important opportunity structure transforming Diaspora's socio-economic and legal conditions in relation to both host country and homeland. This is not the classical citizenship conceptualization assuming the naturalization process changing the individual's status and relationship in favour of the host country. In a post-modern context, acquiring citizenship has a trans-national consequence. For instance, the acquisition of Chinese Diaspora of American or Canadian citizenship facilitates a return to the homeland with an elevated status (Ong, 1999). In this regard, citizenship increases Diaspora's homeland involvement rather than the host country, which was also the original purpose of providing such citizenship.

Diaspora also responds positively to opportunity structures promoting better integration in the host country. In a situation with *"unwelcoming"* opportunity structures in which the host society for instance *"erects barriers of discrimination and exclusion"*, Diaspora might "isolate itself in becoming more insecure and informal" (Esman, 2009: 119). The utilization of existing political opportunities depends on the mobilization and the politicisation circumstances (Totoricagüena, 2004: 17). The opportunity structure also provides Diaspora with a chance to engage at trans-national level for involvement in homeland affairs from a distance (Karishnamurti, 2007: 57).

In the UAE, *qabiilah* relations, although modified, still prevail. Apart from the conflict mediation among the Somalis, the *qabiilah* network provides welfare, particularly for individuals who might suddenly lose their residence permit. Despite the absence of a welfare state, Somalis in the UAE exhibit self-confidence in managing their livelihoods and at the same time contributing to the development of the country (Wharfage, 2009).

In contrast, the Somali Diaspora in Denmark organizes and mobilizes formally in relation to the host country while pursuing informal activities in relation to the homeland. This is mainly to do with the existence of citizenship opportunities and interaction with the host institutions. Most Somalis in Denmark are either citizens or hold a permanent resident status with expanded social and political rights. Although they often become the subject of political rhetoric and exclusion, they have formal rights to organize and pursue civil liberties. Though authorities recently have introduced anti-immigrant restrictive legislations. However, the inclusion of the Somalis into the Danish welfare system affects the community positively. Most obvious is the fact that the state- sponsored social and institutional protection reduces dependency on the Somali *qabiilah* relation and thereby *qabiilah-ism*. If the *qabiilah* network originally provided belonging, security and welfare, the Danish state takes many of these prime functions. Similar to other citizens, Somalis refer to the authorities in times of social, health and employment challenges. *Qabiilah* relations might exist theoretically but in the Danish context, it loses its basic functions, except for limited informal applications for homeland politics among elder, usually unemployed, Somali men engaged in heated *"fadhi kudirir sessions"*. Though homeland relationship takes place informally, the digitalization and cyberspace provide opportunities for transnational activism in which cyber technologies expand Diaspora's engagement in the homeland and beyond (Totoricagüena & Reno, 2007: 18). As an institution, *qabiilah* relation among the Somalis in Scandinavia is, at least officially, replaced by a Pan-Somali framing and sometimes also by multi-ethnic framing.

The second difference is the character of mobilizing structures. Both Diasporas face an internal division influencing their relationship with the homeland. The Diaspora in the UAE is divided into *qabiilah* and regional lines. *Qabiilah* and the regional divisions although they exist in Denmark, are not formal and visible. In the UAE, this division is formal and visible.. The reason is probably the proximity to Somalia, where there are frequent visits and continuous interaction with homeland *Qabiilah* leaders. Often *qabiilah* and regional mobilizations take place in the UAE.

Finally the two cases differ on the framing opportunities. Somalis in Denmark frame ideas and values promoting Somali and Islamic identities occasionally combined with the adapted Danish identity. The basic ideas bringing the community together emanate from being Somalis and Muslims, while remaining legally integrated into the Danish society.

We should expect an opportunity structure providing citizenship and extended rights to transform Diaspora with regard to mobilizing and framing structures. But it seems the opposite happens, as the Somali Diaspora case in Denmark illustrates, Diaspora mobilization rests on religion and ethnic identity. The general anti-immigrant discourse in the society often emphasizing religion and ethnicity explains the diversion to identity politics.

The Somali Diaspora in the UAE do not formally frame socio-religious and cultural issues, as there are no significant religious and cultural differences. Instead, they organize cultural and national festivities linking to the homeland. The Somali Diaspora in the UAE qualifies a trade Diaspora [127].

Diaspora mobilization depends on the political opportunities (the institutional and legal conditions), the mobilizing opportunity (the associational, organizational and networking possibilities) and the framing opportunities (the opportunity to express ideas and values to mobilize) both in relation to the host environment and to the homeland. The two Somali Diaspora cases in Denmark and the UAE illustrate how differences in opportunity structures influence Diaspora mobilization. For instance, the Diaspora in Denmark pursues formal mobilization in relation to the host country. The conduct is in accordance with the associational tradition in Scandinavia, where citizens establish civil society groups to mobilize and participate in the society through specific networking and group formation activities.

In contrast, the Diaspora in the UAE refrains from organizing formally, at least officially, in relation to authorities in the UAE. Instead, the Diaspora's formal organization and mobilization targets the homeland. If Somalis in the UAE need to mobilize officially, they will have to do it within business framing arrangements. Such trade-oriented structural priority brings the business elite at the top of the community structure.

Similarly, framing religious and anti-ethnic discourse in the Danish society strengthens the traditionalizing tendencies of the Somali Diaspora in Denmark. As a consequence, it influences the way in which the community mobilizes. Although the community accesses democratic citizenship opportunities, it is the mosque centres, the elders and religious leaders that play prominent roles in community leadership and mobilization. Clearly, the differences of the mobilizing structures between Somali Diaspora in

---

[127] Cohen 2006 in his archetypal classification of Diasporas described The Chinese and the Lebanese as trade Diasporas, whereas, he argued, the Jewish, the Palestinian, the Armenians and probably the Africans are victim Diasporas.

Denmark and in the UAE are linked to the different opportunity structures in the two host environments. The Danish system provides a political structure allowing certain rights to Diaspora, whereas the structures in the UAE do not allocate people the rights to engage formally with governmental authorities.

There is strategic difference in the way in which the two Diaspora engage with their homeland. For the Diaspora in Denmark, the permanent legal and institutional status makes the community to be less preoccupied with homeland affairs formally. This is not the case for the UAE Diaspora. Due to their temporal legal status, they need to retain and consolidate their position in the homeland. These activities manifest in qabiilah and regional dynamics and relations.

In general the different aspects of Diaspora experience are interconnected, as figure 91. Shows, for instance migration not just leads to Social transformation but also influences on how Diaspora organize and mobilize. In return Diaspora organization and mobilization impacts the migration process as mobility is an integrated part of Diaspora experience and even survival. The opportunities for Diaspora to link and interact at transnational level, while pursuing hybrid form of social relations makes Diaspora activities and strategies to be fixed in particular host country and homeland context.

Figure 9.1   Diaspora formation

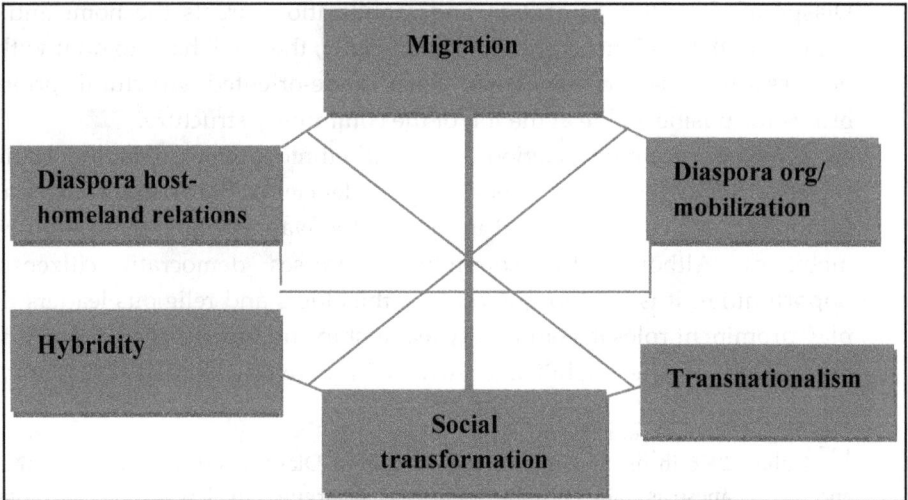

This raises the question of whether studying Diaspora mobilization should focus on the internal decisions and prioritizations within the Diaspora community or on the external host country and homeland opportunities motivating and influencing Diaspora's behaviour. The two Somali Diaspora cases of Denmark and the UAE suggest the need to combine the internal and external conditions and constellations eventually leading to Diaspora organization and mobilization.

CHAPTER 10

CONCLUSION

This research focused on Somali Diaspora social transformation, space formation and community organization and mobilization in Denmark and the UAE. The Somali community became an incipient Diaspora with an expanded global network in various parts of the world retaining and increasing homeland involvement. In many ways the migration has been an accumulative process spanning from the periods of colonial to post-colonial times. The fact that dictatorial regimes ruled meant they followed divide and rule strategies dispersing the Somalis across the world. What is remarkable is that in spite of the scattering Somalis remain connected to each other and to the homeland. It remains difficult for many Somalis to come to terms for the trauma from their involuntary migration and pursue normal life.

As an active member of this Diaspora, employed over a decade as a municipality official, specializing in ethnic integration issues in Aarhus, Denmark and researcher, the author of this study has over the years struggled to bridge the gap on how e.g. Somalis perceive themselves compared to how the host society generally judges them. One feels obliged to contribute with a nuanced explanation on the conflicting ideas and interpretations on the Somali Diaspora conduct. Insider researchers, with multiple, often contradicting, social imaginations and epistemological perspectives, have the privilege to access, observe and interpret how and why different world views and realities converge or diverge. The downside of this advantage is the need to disguise one's real identity by refraining from exposing one's academic background, leading to ethical dilemmas (*cf.* Chapter 4).

Thus, this research provide the processes and the dynamics of particular community scattered across the world to a settlement in two different contexts in examining internal social cohesion and realignment, Diaspora space formation and community organization and mobilization. In addition the research provides a complementary insight by critique how others construct Somali settlement in the two contexts. The specificity with the Danish context relates to the elitist managed public discourse that continuously portrays Somalis, and other ethnic communities, as threatening social entities with endless challenges to integrate into the Danish society (*cf.* Chapter 6).

This research employed the comparative case approach and closely observed by not relaying on secondary sources. The aim was to avoid what Ronald Barthes called the *"monitorial mode" i.e.* presenting data exclusively based on secondary sources and not necessarily from direct field work (Cannon, 2006: 53). By using primary data differences and similarities of two Somali Diaspora cases in Denmark and the UAE, the research introduces empirically grounded analysis to better understand varying Diaspora manifestations.

The research further utilized conceptual intellectual resources from thinkers with eastern and western background (*cf.* Chapter 5). Such an approach is essential not just to surmount the existence for socio-cultural, economic and political gaps between the host society and the Diaspora community, but also to depict potentially subjugated knowledge not often expressed and appreciated in the public discourse. In addition, methodologies such as active participation in *"fadhi ku durir"* sessions and focus groups, community social events and entering informal dialogue with community leaders have further enabled the access to valuable empirical sources not obtainable through formal data questionnaire methods.

Theoretical and conceptual ideas developed by eminent scholars both from the west and east can elucidate the Diaspora's experience in minimizing the analytical gap and in understanding the Diaspora's social dynamics. Bringing scholars from diverse civilizations into the discussion will help us to simultaneously achieve indigenization and universalization of knowledge production. The application of indigenous research methods combined with reference to non-western conceptualization qualifies this research as a modest contribution to not only research on Somali Diaspora in Denmark and the UAE but also to the emerging scholarly debate on incipient diasporas. Although representing differing intellectual worlds or civilizations, the scholars as shown (*cf.* Chapter 5) share certain epistemological and ontological commonalities.

This concluding chapter aims not to repeat the empirical findings analyzed and summarized in (*Cf.* Chapter 7, 8 and 9). Instead, under main headings, the chapter tries to connect central empirical findings to the conceptual dimensions in the research and its relevance for Diaspora scholarship. Finally, the chapter concludes with general remarks on Diaspora research and prospects for future research activities.

1) Development and social transformation: From structural Hegemony to Counter-Hegemonic Resistance

Migration transforms social relations, following a structural imposition in the host environment. Such social changes affect gender and intergenerational relations. Modernization theorists interpret the process as an indication of changing traditional family structures. Responding to host country socialization schemes, immigrant women and young generations have the opportunity to contest and renegotiate pre-constructed homeland-oriented social hierarchies. State institutions promote social integration, preventing the maintenance of traditional structures that cause exclusionary *assabiya* (anomie). Thus gender and intergenerational Diaspora transformations reflect a natural response to integration opportunities immigrants acquire in the host country providing them with institutional, formal platforms to distance themselves from their homeland traditions.

The question is: what transformation do the Somali Diaspora experience? Somalis both in Denmark and the UAE have largely maintained their tradition and culture. But following migration and adjustment to the host countries, such relationships gradually change. The research has found the Danish welfare system in a way transforming the Somalis by partially disrupting the traditional kinship relationship as a social, economic and security sustaining institution. In contrast, the absence of a welfare state consolidates the traditional social mechanism among the Somali Diaspora in the UAE, where Somali kinship relationship maintains its socio-economic significance *(cf.* Chapter 7). Despite the obvious community traditionalization, the UAE provides the Diaspora with modern infrastructure enabling the UAE Diaspora to be active in trade, business and communication as well as renewing itself and attracting trans-national Somali Diaspora.

Though kinship relationship among the Somalis in Denmark loses its traditional significance, in response to recent Danish traditionalization emphasizing national identity politics, Somali Diaspora reacted with increasing religious orthodoxy and national identity orientation. The religious discourse is almost absent among the Somali Diaspora in the UAE where cultural and religious affiliations are depoliticised and thus not contested.

Somali Diaspora in Denmark and the UAE also confront gender and intergenerational challenges. In Denmark, the relative economic opportunity for Somali women provided by the welfare state coupled with the economic marginalization of Somali men disrupted the traditional Somali family hierarchy. The gender challenge in the UAE is different, as Somali male-female disagreement appears to be an internal family dispute. The intergenerational conflict in Denmark emerges from the youngsters' lack of ability to relate to Somali culture while in the UAE, it is mainly due to the *"Arabization"* of the Somali children causing tension *(cf.* Chapter 7).

The Diaspora social transformation and development in relation to gender and intergenerational transformations appears more complex than the one provided by structuralist explanations. What emerged seems to be a hybrid combination from tradition of the homeland in its confrontation with the challenges in the host country environment. Therefore it is not a straight forward restructuring gender and intergenerational relations (Vertovec, 2009: 6-7). The depth of change is not measurable or reducible to behavioural characteristics manifested by Diaspora in the host country. What defines the major characteristics lies in the intersection between the host country and the homeland. That means if young Diaspora member returns to the traditional ancestry environment they will be able to bring that aspect of their invested tradition without any problem. They can also adapt to in the host country circumstances. What they have is a complex adaptable identity and single independent of circumstances. People relate to homeland and host country values if they find it suitable to improve the overall social condition and objectives. The essential is obtaining relative independence to select, combine and diversify. Gender and intergenerational transformations do not indicate a departure or disrespect from homeland structures and institutions. It is rather an attempt to achieve structural position and recognition with the intention to contribute to and modify societies.

In Foucaultian terms social transformation represents a response to existing discursive power relations. Gender and intergenerational challenges constitute social and organizational action to respond to existing asymmetric power relations, whether modern or traditional (Anthias, 1998). It is an attempt to inject one's own voice in a hierarchically- erected homeland and host societies. In this regard, women and young people in the Diaspora pursue dual resistance engagement aiming at both home and host society structures.

2) Diaspora Space: Does it reflect cultural persistence or economic Entrepreneurship?

In general, people adjust to spaces designated to them by society in accordance with the division of labour and the development parameters in the society. For instance, workers will be closer to industrial sites so that they are closer to production spaces *"resting on a social relation in which the principle of production manifests in the form of the people into class categories"* (Morrison, 2006: 60). People might relate to cultural and moral values, but the crucial point is the prioritization of the economic and developmental dimensions (Armstrong, 1976). Consequently, immigrants will occupy neighbourhoods they find relevant for their economic and cultural wellbeing.

Diaspora spaces might also emerge due to the creativity and engagement of individuals and groups wanting to improve their social, cultural and economic conditions. The spaces could be created from the interaction between *"the individual group's rhythmic and arrhythmic practices and the collective society"* (Cresswell and Merriman, 2011: 191). Such spaces link to multiple national and transnational spaces with continuing transferability and exchange of cultural, social and economic capitals. Sometimes people might decide to form socio-cultural spaces suitable for their wellbeing. On other occasions, they may find economic entrepreneurship appropriate for personal as well as community success (Smart and Hsu, 2004). Diaspora continuously creates, transfer and adjust resources through complex networks at the local, national and trans-national levels. In this regard the spaces represent

"movements of emancipation and identity. In struggles against existing nation-states, to embrace the very imaginary they seek to *escape"* (*Appadurai*, 1994: 418).

Finally, Diaspora spaces represent counter hegemonic resistance spaces reflecting experiences of asymmetric power relations. Through specific space formations Diaspora engage in a discursive counter hegemonic subjugated power through hybrid and transgression exercises to navigate constraints in the mainstream society (Werbner, 2001). If spaces happen to be cultural it is because people want to have their culture and need spaces where they can present and exercise their own culture. If it is an economic entrepreneurship space, it is because there exists an economic marginalization in the society and the only way to remedy is to establish trans-national ethnic businesses.

Diaspora's socio-cultural and economic spaces do not represent segregation or a decline but trans-national hybrid spaces not exclusively linked to the homeland nor to the host country (Faist, 2000).

We find that Diaspora's social and cultural relations with the homeland and the constraints and opportunities existing in the host country and how Diaspora utilizes such opportunities, determine Diaspora space formation and conduct. For instance in the UAE, fairly open business and trading conditions help Somalis create Diaspora spaces of the economic entrepreneurship type or category. Clearly Somalis created the Diaspora space because evidences show the existence of numerous Somali tycoons and leading Somali female entrepreneurs with global reach (*cf.* Chapter 8). In comparison when it comes to Diaspora space formation in Denmark, the evidence of socio-economic development hardly exist which shows the limits of independent Somali Diaspora pursuing entrepreneurship is limited.

Socio-cultural, economic transformation and opportunity structures influence the Somali Diaspora mobilization. In Denmark, Somalis organize and mobilize in response to host country challenges. Denmark is a country called *"an association country"* where people through organization access public support. Thus, the Somali Diaspora conduct reflects this structure, eventually producing a dominant group of educated and traditional cultural entrepreneurs. Such mobilization occurs within the traditional cultural frame. In contrast, the Diaspora in the UAE refrains from organizing formally, at least officially, in relation to the UAE authorities. Instead, their formal organization and mobilization target the homeland. If Somalis in the UAE need to mobilize officially, they will have to do it within business type organization and frameworks, *i.e.* trade-oriented structural priority inevitably bringing the business elite at the top of the community structure (*cf.* Chapter 9).

Similarly, framing religious and anti-ethnic discourse in the Danish society traditionalizes the Somali Diaspora in Denmark where the mosque centres, the elders and religious leaders play prominent roles in community leadership and mobilization. We find that for the Diaspora in Denmark, the permanent legal and institutional status make them less worried about residential matters which translate into less formal preoccupation with homeland affairs. This is not the case for the UAE Diaspora, who due to the temporal uncertain legal status constantly searches for ways to consolidate their position in the homeland. These activities manifest in kinship and regional orientation dynamics.

3) Community mobilization: From ideological focus to issue emphasis

Diaspora mobilization within the mainstream institutional frames indicate the capacity of the community for changing and adjusting to fit is in accordance with existing norms and values in society. Acts of informality, on the other hand, mean a decline (*anomie or assabiya*) representing re-traditonalization of the society. The professional community mobilization is in line with the dominant social values in the country. The ideological formal mobilization is always superior to the informal mobilization, which is specific and might lead to the fragmentation of the society. As Eisenstadt tells us, this include social mobilization through media, urbanization and economic change (Eisenstadt, 1966: 118).

Diaspora community mobilization takes place at multiple levels and with multiple purposes. The mobilization depends on the resources available to people and their capability to utilize and transform these opportunities. The more Diaspora link and access to particular resources, the more formalized and sophisticated they become. The key point then is the diversification, transferability and adaptability of Diaspora conduct (cf. Sokefeld, 2006).

Formalization and structuring of community mobilization fit the hegemonic order rather than Diaspora prioritization. It is through informal organization and mobilization that the Diaspora counterbalances the dominant structure. Though informal mobilization results from exiting exclusionary mechanism in the society, if properly managed, it could challenge the mainstream (Pollock, 2006: 189). The informal mobilization is different and necessary as it focuses on alternative competing dimensions. With the informal mobilization, the Diaspora obtains a critical voice.

An important question is whether the Diaspora mobilizes due to traditional values and beliefs linking the community to the homeland or whether the community organizes to overcome certain host country obstacles?. Certainly the Diaspora uses ideological frames for mobilization, but community mobilization appears to be largely issue driven. The Diaspora mobilizes around momentous challenges the community finds necessary at particular times. Thus Diaspora mobilization depends on several factors. First the identification of the issue or the problem. Secondly, the interpretation and reinterpretation of the issue internally within the community and externally by potential allies that will have to support such

Abdulkadir Osman Farah

mobilization efforts. Finally, the careful consideration of mobilizing and framing opportunities (*cf.* Chapter 9).

What is interesting is that, Somali Diaspora can mobilize around pressing issues in the host country, while remaining divided and probably more ideological in relation to homeland mobilization. At other times, Diaspora can conduct humanitarian mobilizations responding to the suffering and to the need for humanitarian support in the homeland.

Institutionalized culture plays a significant role in Diaspora mobilization. Members refer to commonalities defining them as a group and differentiating them from the surrounding environment. Similarly, religion has a significant intellectual power providing Diaspora with moral authority and legitimacy (Vertovec, 2000: 63).

The existence of cultural exclusion, in the form of not properly socializing and interacting with the Danes, coupled with systematic barriers in the employment market exclude the Somalis in Denmark[128]. Somalis respond with increased segregation in the form of inward oriented community organizations with emphasis on religiosity.

In contrast, the exclusion against the Somali Diaspora in the UAE emanates less from the cultural gap and more from the absence of legal citizenship rights. The UAE exclusion leads to expanded Somali creativity and entrepreneurship combined with intensive homeland investment and an eventual return. In addition with the increasing number of middle class Somalis with resources and western citizenship, the UAE gradually consolidates its position as a global Diaspora centre economically, socially and politically linking worldwide Diaspora with each other and with homeland (*cf.* Chapter 7, 8 and 9).

4) Citizenship and recognition: The dialectics of moderation and tradition

Access to citizenship rights represents a formal recognition of the individual as an equal partner in state and society affairs. The acquisition of citizenship is supposed to replace the informal interaction and relationship between people. Formal citizenship requires formalized and structured

---

[128] This trend changes when there is economic growth and Somalis and other ethnic group temporarily enter the job market, e.g. under the economic boom between 2000-2007, many Somali and other ethnic groups entered the employment market in Denmark (www.statbank.dk)

208

relational patterns where people relate to independent neutral institutions that mediate and support. The first represents moderation while the latter refers to informality and tradition.

There exist various citizenship forms the Diaspora exploits depending on the host state and society. Diaspora can acquire formal or informal citizenship. Another possibility is a flexible citizenship depending on the social, economic, cultural and political activities that people conduct (*cf.* Baubock &Faist 2010: 300-301).

Informal citizenship suits marginalized communities while formal citizenship brings communities into the mainstream. Exercising informal citizenship forms beyond state and society boundaries provides opportunities for Diaspora to challenge the status quo and problematize the assertive formal citizenship (Bauböck, 1994). Formal citizenship might promote social progress, but it is through informal citizenship Diaspora acquire empowered voices.

Diaspora has, due to their trans-national nature, complicated traditional citizenship arrangements. The research finds formal citizenship, combined with expanded social citizenship in liberal democratic countries can empower Diaspora communities. However, such citizenship might undermine the possibilities for informal citizenship (*cf.* Chapter 6).

In addition, the Diaspora phenomenon do not just relate to state and society formalizations but also to Welstein's world system distinction of periphery, semi-periphery and core (Wallerstein, 1991: 143). Obviously the core provides formal citizenship and the semi-core and periphery mainly offer informal citizenship. Diaspora communities want to combine both. They conduct secondary migration and trans-national mobility to access formal and informal resources on different locations. So far, in the current state centred international system, few countries and states are able to offer both formal and informal citizenships.

Diaspora communities develop and integrate in certain aspects while segregating in others. Normally, tradition comes under pressure as Diaspora adjust into host country circumstances. Moderation tendencies such as gender conflicts and intergenerational challenges emerge, but the goal is not to abandon traditions. Sometimes it is a struggle to re-contextualize tradition, i.e. instead of such traditional values linking to the homeland; women and youth in Diaspora insist the universality of such traditions.

Finally the study observes citizenship regimes and host society perceptions on the Somali Diaspora leading to different Diaspora space formations, organization and mobilization. Welfare and citizenship accessibility in Denmark give the Somali Diaspora an opportunity to organize formally, while maintaining an informal relationship with the homeland constituents. On the other hand, the lack of formal citizenship for most Somalis in the UAE makes Somalis clinging to informal citizenship through allies, networks and personality cultivation. At the same time, Somali Diaspora in the UAE formally engages in the homeland with investment and resettlement prospects.

In Denmark, the political rhetoric against immigrants is mainly negative. Both politicians and the media, particularly those from right wing constituents, profile immigrants as detrimental to Danish culture and political system. This perception has since 2001 gained significant ground. In contrast, the media and politicians in the UAE do not consider immigrants as a threat to the country's existence; on the contrary, they praise immigrants for keeping the country prospering. This study did not find any degrading statements in the reviewed media reports and political declarations (*cf.* Chapter 6). Nonetheless the UAE Diaspora suffers from other legal deficiencies.

The public role Diaspora performs depends on the host country's institutional and political structures. Diaspora can play a passive or an active role in both the homeland and host country economic and political affairs depending on the democratic and non-democratic institutional structures in the host country (Shain and Barth, 2003).

Obviously, democratic and non-democratic societies differ on how they deal with their Diasporas. Although in democratic societies, Diaspora openly becomes the subjects of negative media portrayal; liberal states have long abandoned to control, assimilate or exclude their Diasporas (cf. Cohen, 1996). In non-democratic countries, like the UAE, Diasporas do not confront constant public media and political scrutiny, but they enjoy few democratic and institutional rights.

TABLE 10.1   MAIN FINDINGS OF THE SOMALI DIASPORA IN DENMARK AND THE UAE

	Denmark	UAE
Diaspora social transformation	• Gender & intergenerational transformation conditioned by state intervention	• Gender & intergenerational transformation conditioned by legal and economic constraints
Diaspora space formation	• Socio-cultural spaces (mosques, community centres) and capital	• Socio-economic spaces & capital
Diaspora mobilization	• Formal host country mobilization based on Socio-cultural values and frames • Informal homeland mobilization (politics, humanitarian, remittance)	• Informal host country mobilization of Socio-economic and national values • Formal host country mobilization (Politics, regionalism, *qabiilism*, humanitarian, remittance)
Diaspora citizenship	• Community with formal citizenship & in search of informal citizenship	• Community with informal citizenship & in search of formal citizenship • Increasing number of global Somali Diaspora with flexible citizenships

5) Migration and Diaspora Formation

Migration is often conceptualized as a migration process from a homeland to host countries either voluntary or due to expulsions resulting from hostile political, social and economic conditions in the home country. The conventional understanding stipulates migration gradually leading to

Diaspora formation. The reality is much more complex as circuit and nomadic migrations not necessarily create Diaspora. In addition, certain diasporas became Diaspora without migration. These include many diasporas in the former Soviet Union and in the Somali context, Somalis both in Ethiopia an Kenya finding themselves classified as Diaspora while still in their homelands. Colonial powers did not just draw new boundaries in Africa, they also generated external and internal rural-urban migrations. Thus we need to re-evaluate the migration pattern to include return, circular, temporary, secondary, cyber and many other migration types.

This study shows the emergence of Diaspora communities and the diversity within Diaspora groups across gender, class and intergenerational aspects mainly resulting from host country socio-economic and political conditions. Thus migration leads to significant social transformations representing a mixture of continuity and discontinuity in relation to the homeland.

With regard to Diaspora formation another important aspect is the difference between Diaspora in the core, the periphery and the semi-periphery (*cf.* Patterson, 2001). These Diaspora formations experience different socio-economic and political conditions. Although Diaspora appear independent from fixed structural conditions, the host state and society character determines whether Diaspora succeeds or it becomes economicall, socially and politically excluded and marginalized. This confirms the transf ormative factors not just lying with the Diaspora but also with citizenship opportunities.

6) The Diasporization and de-diasporation of Diaspora

Scholars disagree on the definition of Diaspora mainly distinguishing the classical Diaspora, referring to the Jewish, and contemporary Diaspora, meaning all other modern and post-modern diasporas (Reis M., 2004). The processes of diasporization and de-diasporizations are nonetheless more complex (Cho, 2010: 134). There is a debate on *"Diaspora Diaspora"*, elucidating the existence of Diaspora within the Diaspora (Brubaker, 2005). This research considers Diaspora as an ongoing process in which Diaspora formations differ and depend on numerous issues, *e.g.* historical factors, homeland international status, geographical proximity to the homeland and citizenship opportunities in the host country, in the homeland and beyond.

In this regard, we differentiate an open Diaspora continuously renewing itself as the Somali Diaspora in the UAE and somewhat less open Diaspora as is the case in Denmark. The survival of Diaspora depends on whether the country is open and attracts additional migration. When Diaspora is open for inputs from additional migration, it transforms and renews itself. For instance, the UAE hosts more diversified Somali Diaspora including a recent Diaspora, conducting secondary migration from various countries, and attracted by the opportunities for informal citizenship and the possibility to combine business entrepreneurship with flexible citizenship.

In contrast, Denmark remains host for somewhat relatively *"stagnant Somali Diaspora"*. Diaspora has serious difficulties in renewing and attracting inputs from different sources following the tightened migration rules. Such Diaspora might disappear, assimilate or become marginal in the future. Nonetheless, virtual opportunities such as the internet support the Diaspora to survive. Consequently, the new generation can change the Diaspora, but they could be more assimilated and might sever homeland relations.

Final Remarks

In an increasingly complex world, it is difficult to maintain the idea of an agent-structure relationship. We can no longer discuss, as modernization social scientists did, a dominant structure social actors need to adjust. Instead, we can refer to multiple strategies and structures, *i.e.* more or less objective and subjective structures. A structural-oriented approach can explain some dimensions of social change rationality, but we obviously need to supplement with actor-oriented analysis.

Thus, the essentialist, evolutionary structural oriented approach proposes a linear progress from *hadara* to *badawa* as Ibn-khaldun informs us, or from a mechanical, social stage to organic structure as Durkheim recommends. The scholars have a point as people appreciate certain modernization tendencies. However, their conclusion on social structures conditioning progress rather than individual interpretation and internalization is somewhat exaggerated. People are far from mindless creatures subordinate to modern structures. Thus the ontological centrality on hegemonic state and society progression requires modification.

We also need to pay attention to the spiritual human capability to resist. Once Machiavelli, one of the founders of political science discipline, argued in his book *"the Prince"* that the end justifies the means (Michavelli [Goodwin] 2003: 13). By this he meant that we should march towards the end without speculating about how much exclusion and destruction the applied force results. This approach will not work in a world filled with not just one prince but with rival competing princes with multiple priorities. We therefore need to acknowledge multiple possibilities to reaching multiple ends.

Structural approaches might be suitable for analysing the processes of inclusion from state and society perspectives. But structural, institutional approaches will have difficulties in grasping non-institutional, national and international dimensions. A purely structural approach will for instance have difficulties in accounting for the Somali Diaspora member who works at a Danish post office in the day-time, but functions as vice-president of a political organization in Somalia through frequent communication and late-night skyping. This is not necessarily a distinction of the private and public spheres or the separation of the system world from the life world. This is a case where the individual Diaspora simultaneously and trans-nationally operates within two or more independent structures. Analysis focusing on structural exclusion might help us explain why individuals enter homeland politics rather than host country politics.

In this context, social critics such as Foucault and Mazrui caution us the fact human relationship is not just developmental and organizational but is also, to a certain extent, problematic through power exercise and exclusion. Often state and society power monopolization appears relatively observable, the challenge, however, lies with the exposition of resistance to monopolization and inequality. Analysing people's response to unequal power relationships contains valuable insights on not just how people adjust to power structures but also on subverting and eventually shifting to *wassatiyah* (middle position) to avoid marginalization (Al-Qaradawi, 2007). Ramadan (1998) also refers to the middle position with an attempt to conceptualize Euro-Islam that suits the Muslim Diaspora in Europe rather a religious condition reflecting the tradition in Muslim countries.

We should probably find some kind of intermediate position to understand both structure and the actor perspectives. This will require us to shift to the middle and not to take for granted any grand narratives. Somali Diaspora processes in Denmark and the UAE confirm that social constructivism so far provides the most suitable epistemological and ontological frame to observe and analyse Diaspora communities.

Bourdieu, Sen and others (*cf.* Chapter 5) propose the need to accept people's ability and judgement to pursue multiple strategies for socio-economic achievement. Eventually, society as a whole benefits from inputs from individuals and communities. Hence emphasis on social cohesion and

214

capacity building at micro and meso levels improves human capability as well as social quality.

Improving human dignity, values and quality of life remain central to social transformation processes. Humans are not just material beings. If that were the case, the Somali Diaspora in Denmark would not have expressed discontent. From a materialistic perspective, Somalis have a better life in Denmark compared to the one they would have sustained in an impoverished, civil war torn African country, or in a semi - or periphery host context. However, there is no evidence they now enjoy a proper quality of life. There is always something missing and humans are always preoccupied not on what they have on hand but on what they lack. We probably need to imagine whether humans are able to combining macro institutional frames with what Giri refers to as human passion (Giri, 2007).

This study compared/contrasted and analyzed Somali Diaspora in Denmark and the UAE. The theoretical construction of bringing various perspectives together with creative methodological approach enhances the level of the study. The strength of this study is bringing out from original data through interviews the Somali Diaspora side and perception of life in Denmark and the UAE. Key independent variables were taken and this were a) the nature of social Diaspora formations b) the formation of Diaspora spaces both in the UAE and Denmark c) Diaspora community organization and mobilization in the two contexts. Having taking these key independent variables this study has in different contexts managed to contribute to empirically grounded observations showing the dynamics of Somali Diaspora condition. What will be interesting is be to complement the study of the Somali Diaspora side in the UAE and Denmark with those engaged in way or another with the Somali Diaspora in the UAE and Denmark. This research used a primary data ion the Somali side and secondary data on the UAE and Denmark. The next challenge is to increase the primary data from the Diaspora side and include primary from both the UAE and Denmark in order to deepen our understanding and reflection on the Somali Diaspora phenomenon. There is also an important potential in pursuing further the western and non-western theorization of social transformation involving migration and Diaspora condition. There is a need to access classic and modern Arabic Islamic sources with social change, migration and community formation. Building on Ibn-khaldun's work we were partially able to do that in this study. The main contribution of this research is two levels. One is the conceptual contribution based on the comparison and the application of the work of classical theorists from the east and the west and this is original. The second is the original data collected from Denmark and the UAE that permitted us to observe empirical grounded appreciation on the social transformation, Diaspora space formation, and community organization and mobilizastion of the Somali Diaspora.

In conclusion, humans have a physical body they strongly guard to preserve, a heart to project sympathy or aversion, and most importantly a mind to think and measure. Thus, humans, including Diaspora, are in eternal search for a comprehensive well-being, i.e. an embedded ambition not confinable to institutional or structural frames. In the end human agency matters whether in the Diaspora or not.

216

Appendix A s- List of interviews

Respondents	Age	Gender	Marital status	Occupation	Commcontr.	Homeland (region)	Host country	Migration type	Period in Diaspora
Interview 1	39	Male	Mar-Ch	Imam-student	Active org.	SS	DK	Refugee	15 years
Interview 2	43	Male	Mar-Ch	Munic-employee	Active org.	SS	DK	Refugee	20 years
Interview 3	38	Female	Mar-Ch	-	Not active	-	DK	-	15 years
Interview 4	63	Male	Mar-Ch	Retired	Not active	SS	DK	Refugee	18 years
Interview 5	55	Male	Mar-Ch	Music teacher	Active org.	S	UAE	Migrant	23 years
Interview 6	26	Male	Mar-Ch	Business man	Active org	S	UAE	Refugee	1 0 years
Interview 7	69	Male	Single	Retired	Active org.	SS	UAE	Refugee	30 years
Interview 8	46	Male	Married	private company	Not active	S	UAE	Migrant	20 years
Interview 9	45	Male	Married	Munic-emp	Not active	SS	UAE	Refugee	14 years
Interview 10	60	Male	Mar-Ch	Bus driver	Active org.	SP	DK	Migrant	42 years
Interview 11	41	Male	Mar-Ch	Oil worker	Active org.	SPS	UAE	Migrant	10 years
Interview 12	30	Male	Mar-Ch	Business	Active org.	S	UAE	Refugee	10 years
Interview 13	55	Male	Married	Business	Active org.	SP	UAE	Migrant	11 years
Interview 14	54	Male	Mar-Ch	Engibusiness	Active org.	SS	UAE	Secmigrant	10 years
Interview 15	45	Male	Married	Broker	Not active	S	UAE	Migrant	10 years
Interview 16	47	Male	Married	Crane owner	Not active	S	UAE	Migrant	Noinform
Interview 17	49	Male	Married	Port worker	Not active	S	UAE	Refugee	Noinform
Interview 18	46	Male	Married	Port worker	Not active	S	UAE	Refugee	Noinform
Interview 19	23	Male	Single	Port worker		S	UAE	Refugee	10 years
Interview 20	75	Male	Married	Retired	Active	S	UAE/UK	Secmigrant	50 years
Interview 21	45	Female	Married	House wife	Not active	S	UAE	Refugee	11 years
Interview 22	46	Female	Mar-Ch	House wife	Active	SPS	UAE	Secmigrant	20 years
interview 23	35	Male	Mar-Ch	TV photgrPolice	Active	SY	UAE	Migrant	28 years
Interview 24	50	Male	Mar-Ch	Govemployee	Active	S	UAE	Migrant	30 years
Interview 25	40	Female	Mar-Ch	Employee	Active	S	UAE	Migrant	30 years
Interview 26	44	Male	Married	Broker	Active	SP	UAE	Refugee	10 years
Interview 28	52	Male	Mar-Ch	BrokBusines	Active	SP	UAE	Migrant	11 years
Interview 29	55	Female	Mar-Ch	police	Active	SS	UAE	Migrant	25 years
Interview 30	38	Male	Mar-Ch	Studentbusiness	Active	SS	UAE	Refugee	12 years
Interview 31	56	Male	Mar-Ch	Consultant	Active	S	UAE	Secmigrant	24 years
Interview 32	46	Male	Mar-Ch	BusinessPolitician	Active	SP	UAE	Migrant	30 years
Interview 33	25	Male	Married	Pol-busiss	Active	SS	UAE	Migrant	10 years
Interview 34	54	Male	Mar-Ch	Const- work	Active	SP	UAE	Migrant	28 years
Interview 35	62	Male	Mar-Ch	Different jobs	Not active	S	UAE	Migrant	42 years
Interview 36	36	Female	Single	Retired	Active	S	UAE	Migrant	8 years
Interview 37	48	Male	Mar-Ch	Hotel assistance	Active	SP	UAE/Canada	Refugee	10 years
Interview 38	34	Male	Married	Business IT	Active	SS	UAE	Secmigrant	7 years
Interview 39	57	Male	Mar-Ch	Oil worker	Not active	SP	UAE/Canada	Migrant	20 years
Interview 40	54	Male	Mar-Ch	Secschooltec	Active	SP	UAE	Migrant	25 years
Interview 41	35	Male	Mar-Ch	Business man	Active	SP	UAE	Migrant	14 years
Interview 42	45	Male	Mar-Ch	Business man	Not active	SPS	UAE/Canada	Secmigrant	10 years
Interview 43	63	Male	Mar-Ch	Retired	Not active	S	UAE	Migrant	37 years
Interview 44	38	Male	Single	Business man	Active	S	UAE	Refugee	10 years

Interview 45	47	Male	Married	Crane owner	Not active	S		UAE	Migrant	12 years

Appendix B - List of associations

Somali Diaspora organizations/associations in Denmark

Name	Role	Aim	Status	Contact
AarhuSomali	Community mobilization	Somali Integration in DK	Active	www.aarhusomali.dk
Somali Family association	Community empowerment	Somali integration in DK	Active	Aarhus, Denmark
Somali active women association	Women empowerment	Somali women & girls integration in DK	Active	Aarhus, Denmark
Somali-Danish Youth and sports organization	Youth sport and empowerment	Youth sport and integration in DK	Active	Aarhus, Denmark
Amal women association	Youth and women empowerment	Integration	Active	Esbjerg, Denmark
Danish Somali Association	Community empowerment	Integration & leisure time activities	Active	Aalborg, Denmark
Danish Somali Friendship Association	Community empowerment	Improve contacts between Danes and Somalis	Active	Aarhus
Danish Somali Friendship Association	Community organization	Danes Somali relationship	Active	Vejle

218

Danish Somali Friendship Association	Community Organization	Sport and leisure time activities	Active	Randers
Somali Cultural Association	Community organization and mobilization	Culture and art development and performance	Active	Kalunborg
The Somali Union	Community organization and mobilization	Quran and religious teaching & leisure time activities for youth and others	Active	Aarhus
Somali Youth Association	Community Organization and Mobilization	Sports and cultural activities for youth and educational activities	Active	Aarhus
Somali-Danish IFTIN Association	Community organization and empowerment	Academic and studying activities for young people and sports activities	Active	Aarhus
Somali Association for Help to parents	Community organization and empowerment	Support initiatives for parents with integration problems	Active	Aarhus
Somali Integration and Family Association	Community organization and empowerment	Promoting integration of families	Active	Copenhagen

Somali Cultural Association	Community organization and empowerment	Cultural activities festivals	Active	Fredericia
Somali Cultural Association	Community organization and empowerment	Somali-Danish cultural exchange	Active	Kolding
Somali Culture and Media Association	Community organization and empowerment	Media activities to promote integration	Active	Aarhus
Somali Family and Cultural Association	Community organization and empowerment	Promoting coexistence, tolerance and integration	Active	Silkeborg
Somali Women Association	Community organization and empowerment	Promoting integration and understanding between the Somalis and the Danes	Active	Vejle
Somali Women Association	Community organization and empowerment	Empowering women, families and children to better integrate in Denmark	Active	Aalborg
Somali Women Association	Community organization and empowerment	Building understanding between Somali families and other ethnic groups in Denmark	Active	Odense
Somali	Community	Promoting	Active	Copenhagen

Women Association	organization and empowerment	integration of the Somalis in Denmark		
Somali Relief Association	Community organization and empowerment	Contributing to the development in the homeland	Active	Copenhagen
Somali Youth Association	Community organization and empowerment	Supporting Somali youth and children to better integrate in Denmark	Active	Kolding
Somali Danish Friendship Association	Community organization and empowerment	Promoting better relationship between Somalis and Danes	Active	Holstebro
Somali Women Activities	Community organization and empowerment	Helping Somali women to contribute and progress	Active	Holstebro
Somali Media and Women support	Community organization and empowerment	Providing media and information for Somali women and their families	Active	Copenhagen

Somali Diaspora organizations/associations in the UAE

Name	Role	Aim	Status	Contact
Somali Chamber	Business Community	To promote Somali Business projects in	Active	Dubai

of Commerce	Organization and mobilization	the UAE		
Somali Business Association	Organization remittance associations	To promote better business engagement and remittance	Active	Dubai
Somali Women Association	Community organization and empowerment	Help vulnerable youth, women and families both in the homeland and host country	Active	Abu-Dhabi
Somali Youth Association	Community organization and empowerment	Arranging national and cultural festivities	Active	Sharjah
Somali Youth Association	Community organization and empowerment	Organizing cultural national holidays and supporting youth and children's homework	Active	Abu-Dhabi

Appendix C- Interview Guide

Questions	Analytical dimensions
1) How did you become and immigrant? 2) Were you politically active in Somalia? 3) How did you choose a country to immigrate?	Migration history/profile
4) What do think about the Somali Diaspora? 5) What is your relationship with them?	Inter-Diaspora relationship
6) Do you feel integrated in your host country?	Adjustment in the

	host country
7) What are the major challenges in the host country? 8) What does holding citizenship in the host country mean to you? 9) How do you feel about being in diaspora? 10) Do you play a specific role among the Diaspora? 11) Are you politically active in the host country?	
12) What kind of challenges do Somali Diaspora confront in the Host country? 13) Who is to be responsible? 14) How do host country institutions affect you?	Challenges in the host country
15) What kind of opportunities exist in the host country?	Opportunities
16) Are you involved in organizational activities?	Organizational and associational contribution
17) What does qabiil affiliation mean to you?	Identity
18) Do you have a relationship with your homeland? 19) How do you explain this relationship? 20) What role does religion play in your diasporic life?	Relationship and homeland engagement
21) Do you get support from formal Somali institutions	Interaction with

in the host country?	homeland and its institutions
22) What are the motivations for your involvement in the homeland?	
23) Are you politically active in the homeland?	
24) How do you think you can help Somalia?	
25) How frequently do you travel to your homeland?	

About the informant

Gender	
Age	
Current job	
Highest level of education	
Civil status	
Host country	
Homeland region	
Period in Diaspora	
Residence status- citizen or else	

References

Aalbers, M. B. (2002). "The neglected evidence of housing market discrimination in the Netherlands". *Radical Statistics Journal*, 79/80, pp. 161–169.

Abdi Ismail *Samatar* (1992). Destruction of State and Society in Somalia: *Beyond the Tribal Convention*. The Journal of Modern African Studies, 30, pp 625-641

Abdi, C.M. (2007). "The new age of security: Implications for refugees and internally displaced persons in the Horn of Africa" *Development* 50 (4), pp. 75-81.

Abdiwahid Osman Haji (2001). *Somalia: a chronology of historical documents 1827-2000*. Indiana University Press.

Abdullahi M. Abdurahman (2007). "Recovering the Somali state: The Islamic Factor" in Farah et el (eds.) *Diaspora and state reconstitution in the Horn of Africa* Adonis & Abbey, London.

Abu-Laban, Y. (2002). "Liberalism, multiculturalism and the problem of essentialism". *Citizenship Studies*, 6 (4), pp. 459-482.

Adamo, Silvia (2008). "Northern exposure: The new Danish model of citizenship test". *International Journal on Multicultural Societies*, vol. 10, no. 1, pp. 10-28.

Adams J. Michael & Carfagna Angelo (2006). *Coming of age in a globalized world: the next generation*. Kumarian Press.

Adams Richard H. (1991). The effects of international remittances on poverty, inequality, and development in Rural Egypt. International food policy Research.

Adejumobi, S. (2001). "Citizenship, rights, and the problem of conflicts and civil wars in Africa". *Human Rights Quarterly*, 23 (1), pp. 148-170.

Afrax, M.D. (2000), "Somali theatre", PhD research, School of Oriental and African Studies, University of London, London.

Ahmed, A. Jimale (1995). *The Invention of Somalia*. Red Sea Press, pp. 117- 134

Ahmed, I. (2000) "Remittances and their economic impact in post-war Somaliland". *Disasters*, 24(4): 380-389.

Al Abed Ibrahim & Hellyer Peter (2001). *United Arab Emirates: a new perspective*. Trident Press.

Al Rasheed Madawi (1997). *Politics in an Arabian oasis: the Rashidis of Saudi Arabia*. I. B. Tauris.

Al-Ali, J. (2008). "Emiratisation: Drawing UAE nationals into their surging economy". *The International Journal of Sociology and Social Policy, 28*(9/10), 365–379.

Al-Azmeh Aziz (2001). *Muslim kingship: power and the sacred in Muslim, Christian and pagan polities*. I. B. Tauris.

Al-danij, Mohamed bin-tawit (2003). *(Rehlatul Ibn-Khaldun (Ibn-Khaldun's journey)*. Darul suweydi lilnashri wa tawsi.

Alejandro Portes; Luis E. Guarnizo; Patricia Landolt (1999). "The study of transnationalism: pitfalls and promise of an emergent research field". *Ethnic and Racial Studies*, Volume 22, Issue 2, 217 - 237

Alpers, Edward A. (1986). "The Somali Community at Aden in the 19th Century" *North-East African Studies*, 8/2-3 (1986), pp. 143-168.

Alpers, Edward A. (1997). "The African Diaspora in the Northwestern Indian Ocean: reconsideration of an old problem, new directions for research" *Comparative Studies of South Asia, Africa and the Middle East*, 1997 17(2):62-81.

Al-Qaradawi, Yusuf (1984). *Alsahwa-Al-Islamiya-beynal-juhud watadaruf.* (Islamic Awakening between faithlessness and extremism), Maktabah Wahbah.

Al-Salih Muhammad Adib (2007). *Mowqic almar'a al-muslima baynal-Islaam-wadacaawi al-tajdiid*. Maktabah Ubaikan.

AlSayyad Nezar & Castells Manuel (2002). *Muslim Europe or Euro-Islam: politics, culture, and citizenship in the age*. Lexington Books

Al-sharmani Mulki (2007). "Diasporic Somalis in Cairo: The poetics and practices of Soomaalinimo" in Kusow Abdi M. and Stephanie R. Bjork (eds.) *From Mogadishu to Dixon, The Somali Diaspora in a global context*. The Red Sea Press

Al-Sharmani, M. (2010). "Transnational family networks in the Somali diaspora in Egypt: Women's roles and differentiated experiences" *Gender, Place and Culture*, 17 (4), pp. 499-518.

Al-useyma, Ibn Rajab (1983). *Kashful kurbah fi wasf hal ahlul qurbah*. Darul-dacwa

Andersen Peter B. (2006). *Religion, skole og kulturel integration i Danmark og Sverige*. Tusculanum Press.

Andersen, Goul Andersen (2002). "Danskernes holdninger til indvandrere: en oversigt". Volume 17 of *AMID working paper series*. AMID, Akademiet for Migrationsstudier i Danmark.

Andersen, Hans Skifter(2010). "Spatial Assimilation in Denmark? Why do Immigrants Move to and from Multi-ethnic Neighbourhoods?". *Housing Studies*, 25: 3, 281 — 300

Andersen, J., Larsen, J.E., Moller, I.H (2009). "The Exclusion and Marginalisation of Immigrants in the Danish Welfare Society: Dilemmas and Challenges". *International Journal of Sociology and Social Policy*, 29 (5-6), pp. 274-286

Andersen, J.G. (2002) "Danskernes holdninger til indvandrere. En oversight", AMID Working Paper Series No. 17/2002.

Andersen, John (2008). *Ressourcemobiliserende beskæftigelsespolitik strategier og erfaringer fra udsatte byområder* (eds.). Roskilde universitetsforlag.

Andersson, R. (1998). "Socio-spatial dynamics: ethnic divisions of mobility and housing in post-Palme Sweden" *Urban Studies,* 35(3), pp. 397–428.

AnnaLee Saxenian, 'Silicon Valley's New Immigrant High-Growth Entrepreneurs', Economic *Development Quarterly*, Vol. 16, No. 1 (2002), pp. 20–31.

Ansari, Humayun (2004). *The Infidel Within*. London, Hurst.

Anthias, Floya (1998). "Evaluating "Diaspora":Beyond Ethnicity". *Sociology,* 32(3), 557-80.

Appadurai, Arjun (*1990*). "Disjuncture and Difference in the Global Cultural Economy" in M. Featherstone (eds) *Global Culture*. London: Sage.

Arif Dirlik (2003). "Modernity in Question? Culture and Religion in an Age of Global Modernity". *Diaspora,* 12:2 2003.

Baali, Fuad (2005). *The science of human social organization: conflicting views on Ibn Khaldun's (1332-1406)* - Edwin Mellen Press.

Babu, B. Ramesh (1996). *Development strategies for Africa and Asia in the new global structure*. Academic books.

Ballard, Keith & Heshusius Lous (1996). *From positivism to interpretivism and beyond: tales of transformation in educational social research*. Teachers college press.

Ballard, R. (2001). "The impact of kinship on the economic dynamics of transnational networks: reflections on some South Asian developments". *Paper presented at workshop on Transnational Migration*. Princeton University, 29 June_/1 July 2001.

Barnes, Cedric (2006). *"U dhashay—Ku dhashay:* Genealogical and Territorial Discourse in Somali History Social Identities: Journal for the Study of Race". *Nation and Culture,* Volume 12, Issue 4, Pages 487 – 498.

Bartel, A. P. (1989) "Where do the U.S. immigrants live?". *Journal of Labour Economics,* 7(4), pp. 371–391.

Basch, L., Glick Schiller, N. and Szanton Blanc, C. (eds.) (1994). *Nations Unbound Transnational Projects, Postcolonial Predicaments and Deterritorialised Nation-States.* Langhorne: Gordon and Breach.

Bassel, L. (2007). "Refugee women and la république: Participation in the French public sphere". *Parliamentary Affairs,* 60 (3), pp. 467-481.

Bauböck, R. (2009). "The rights and duties of external citizenship". *Citizenship Studies* 13 (5), pp. 475-499.

Bauman Zygmunt (1997). *Postmodernity and its Discontents.* Cambridge: Polity Press.

Bauman, Robert (2007). *The Complete Guide to Offshore Residency, Dual Citizenship and Second Passports.* Sovereign society.

Bauman, Z. (1998). *Globalization: The Human Consequences.* New York: Columbia University Press.

Beardsworth, Alan and Teresa Keil (1992). "The Vegetarian Option: Varieties, Con-   versions, Motives and Careers ." *Sociological Review,* 40 :253-93.

Berger Maria, Galonska Christian, Koopmans Ruud (2004). "Political integration by a detour? ethnic communities and social capital of migrants in Berlin". *Journal of Ethnic and Migration Studies, Volume 30,* Issue 3, 2004, Pages 491 – 507.

Bernard, Helander (1991). "A Modern History of Somalia: Nation and State in the Horn of Africa". *Africa;* 1991, Vol. 61 Issue 3, p414-415.

Bertram, I.G. and Watters, R.F. (1985). "The MIRAB economy in South Pacific microstates". *Pacific Viewpoint,* 26(3): 497_/519.

Besteman Catherine (1998). "Primordialist Blinders: A Reply to I. M. Lewis" *Cultural Anthropology.* Vol. 13, no. 1 (1998), pp. 100-108.

Besteman, Catherine (1999). *Unravelling Somalia: Race, Violence, and the Legacy of Slavery.* Philadelphia, PA: University of Pennsylvania Press, pp. 284.

Bhabha, H. K. (1994), The Location of Culture. London: Routledge.

Bloch, A. (2000). "Refugee settlement in Britain: The impact of policy on participation". *Journal of Ethnic and Migration Studies,* 26 (1), pp. 75-88

228

Boahen A. Adu (1990). *Africa under colonial domination 1880-1935*. University of California Press.

Bogdan R. C. & Biklen S. K (1992). *Qualitative research for education: An introduction to theory and methods*. Boston: Allyn & Bacon-pp-166-172.

Bourdieu Pierre (2000). *Pascalian meditations*. Standford University Press. Verso.

Bourdieu Pierre and Wacquant Loic (1998). *The State Nobility: Elite Schools in the Field of Power*. Standford University Press.

Bourdieu, P. (1977). *Outline of a Theory of Practice*. Cambridge: Cambridge University Press.

Bourdieu, P. (1984) *Distinction: a social critique of the judgement of taste*, Cambridge, MA: Harvard University Press.

Bourdieu, P. (1986) 'The forms of capital', in J. G. Richardson (ed.) *Handbook of theory and research for the sociology of education*, New York: Greenwood Press, 241–58.

Bourdieu, P. (1990). *The Logic of Practice*. Cambridge: Polity Press.

Bourdieu, P. (1993). *The Field of Cultural Production: Essays on Art and Literature*. Cambridge: Polity.

Bourdieu, P. (1998) *Acts of Resistance*. Cambridge: Polity.

Bourdieu, P. (1998). *Practical Reason: On the Theory of Action*. Cambridge: Polity Press.

Bowen, J.R. (2004) "Beyond migration: Islam as a transnational public space" *Journal of Ethnic and Migration Studies*, 30 (5), pp. 879-894.

Bowen, J.R. (2004) "Beyond migration: Islam as a transnational public space". *Journal of Ethnic and Migration Studies*, 30 (5), pp. 879-894.

Bragdon Clifford R. (2008).*Transportation Security*. Butterworth Heinemann.

Brah, Avtar (1996). *Cartographies of Diaspora: Contesting Identities*, London, Rouledge

Brochmann, G., Seland, I. (2010). "Citizenship policies and ideas of nationhood in Scandinavia". *Citizenship Studies*, 14 (4), pp. 429-443.

Bryceson Deborah Fahy & Vuorela Ulla (2002). (eds.). *The transnational family: new European frontiers and global networks*. Berg Publishers. Pp.276.

Bryman, Alan. (2008) *Social Research Methods* 3rd. edition. Oxford University Press.

Buckley-zistel, S. (2006). "Dividing and uniting: The use of citizenship discourses in conflict and reconciliation in Rwanda". *Global Society*, 20 (1), pp. 101-113.

CAMP (2009). *Wharfage, project by for the 9th Sharjah Biennial.* Bombay India.

Campbell Elizabeth H. (2006). "Urban Refugees in Nairobi: Problems of Protection, Mechanisms of Survival, and Possibilities for Integration". *Journal of Refugee Studies*, 2006, Vol. 19, No. 3.

Cannon, JoAnn (2006). *The novel as investigation: Leonardo Sciascia, Dacia Maraini, and Antonio Tabucchi.* University of Toronto Press.

Castells, Manuel (2001). The Internet galaxy: *reflections on the Internet, business, and society.* Oxford University Press.

Catherin Besteman (1996). Violent Politics and the politics of violence; The dissolution of the Somali nation state. *American Ethnologist*, Vol. 23, No. 3, Aug., 1996.

Catherine Besteman (1996). "Violent politics and the politics of violence: the dissolution of the Somali nation-state". *American Ethnologist*, 23(3):579-596.

Catherine O. and William J. Wilson (1988). "Race and ethnicity" In Neil J. Smelsor (eds.), *Handbook of Sociology*. 223- 242. Newbury Park, CA: Sage.

Cecile Rousseau, Taher M. Said, Marie-Josee Gagne & Gilles Bibeau (1998). "Between Myth and Madness: The pre-migration dream of leaving among young Somali refugees". *Culture, Medicine and Psychiatry* 22: 385–411, 1998.

Ceuppens, B., Geschiere, P. (2005). "Autochthony: Local or global? New modes in the struggle over citizenship and belonging in Africa and Europe". *Annual Review of Anthropology*, 34, pp. 385-407.

Chafer Tony (2002). *The end of empire in French West Africa: France's successful decolonization.* Berg.

Chariandy, David (2006). "Post colonial Diasporas". Post colonial text, 2(1), http://postcolonial.org/index.php/pct/article/view/440/159.

Chau, Donovan C. (2010). "The fourth point: An examination of the influence of Kenyan Somalis in Somalia". *Journal of Contemporary African Studies*, 28: 3, 297 — 312.

Cheater, A.P., Gaidzanwa, R.B. (1996). "Citizenship in neo-patrilineal states: Gender and mobility in Southern Africa". *Journal of Southern African Studies*, 22 (2), pp. 189-200.

Cheddadi, A. (1994). "Ibn-Khaldun (A.D.1332-1406/A.H. 732-808". *Prospects*, 24(1/2), 7-19.

Chipkin, I. (2003). "Functional' and 'dysfunctional' communities: The making of national citizens". *Journal of Southern African Studies*, 29 (1), pp. 63-82.

Chivallon, C. (2004), *La diaspora noire des Amériques: Expériences et théories à partir de laCaraïbe. Paris*: CNRS-Éditions.

Clarke, J. (2005). "New Labour's citizens: Activated, empowered, responsibilized, abandoned?". *Critical Social Policy*, 25 (4), pp. 447-463.

Clausen Allan Friis & Poul Storgaard Mikkelsen (2005). *Det multikulturelle samfund - og det danske*. Systime.

Clifford Geertz (1973). *The Interpretation of Cultures*. New York: Basic Books.

Clifford, J (1994). "Diasporas". *Cultural Anthropology*, 9(3) 302-338.

Cohen Robin (2003). *Global Diaspora: An Introduction*. Seattle, University of Washington Press.

Cohen Robin (2008). *Global Diaspora: An Introduction*. 6th edition, Seattle, University of Washington Press.

Cohen, R. (1996). "Diasporas and the nation-state: From victims to challengers". *International Affairs*, 72 (3), pp. 507-520.

Colegrove, Kenneth Wallace (1921). *American citizens and their government*. The Abingdon Press.

Collet, Bruce A. (2007). "Islam, national identity and public secondary education: perspectives from the Somali Diaspora in Toronto, Canada". *Race Ethnicity and Education*, 10: 2, 131 – 153.

Collins, Greg (2009) "Connected: Exploring the Extraordinary Demand for Telecoms Services in Post-collapse Somalia" *Mobilities*, 4: 2, 203 – 223.

Contini Paolo (1969). *The Somali Republic: an experiment in legal integration*. Routledge Taylor.

Cook, J. (2010). "Exploring older women's citizenship: Understanding the impact of migration in later life" *Ageing and Society*, 30 (2), pp. 253-273.

Copestake, J. (2008). "Wellbeing in International Development: What's New?". *Journal of International Development*, Volume 20, Issue 5, pages 577–597.

Coser, Lewis and translation by W. D. Halls (1984). *"Emile Dukheim: The Division of Labour in Society"*. Macmillan Press.

Cox, R.H. (1998). "From safety net to trampoline: Labor market activation in the Netherlands and Denmark". *Governance*, 11 (4), pp. 397-414.

Creswell, J. and Miller, D. (2000). "Determining Validity in Qualitative Inquiry". *Theory Into Practice* 39(3): 124–30.

Damm, A. P. & Rosholm, M. (2005). "Employment Effects of Spatial Dispersal of Refugees". CAM WP 2005-3 (Copenhagen: University of Copenhagen, Institute of Economics).

Danièle Joly, Robin Cohen (1989). *Reluctant hosts: Europe and its refugees.* Avebury

DAVID J. GRIFFITHS (2000). "Fragmentation and Consolidation: the Contrasting Cases of Somali and Kurdish Refugees in London". *Journal of Refugee Studies, vol. 13, No. 3.*

Dhingra & Prashad, Karma (2006). "Seeking Recognition: Patriotism, Power and Politics in Sikh American Discourse in the Immediate Aftermath of 9/11". *Diaspora* 15:1.

Dresch, Paul & Wendy James (2000). Introduction: Fieldwork and the Passage of Time. In *Anthropologists in a wider world: Essays on Field Research.* (eds.). Paul Dresch, Wendy James & David Parkin. New York.

Drysdale, John. (2000). *Stoics Without Pillows.* London, HAAN Associates.

Durkheim Emile (1973). "The Dualism of Human Nature and Its Social Conditions", in *On Morality and Society: Selected writings.* (eds.)Robert N. Bellah. University of Chicago Press.

Durkheim, E. ([1893]1984).*The Division of Labour in Society.* New York: Free Press.

Durkheim, E. (1995 [1912]) *The Elementary Forms of Religious Life,* trans. K.E. Fields. New York: Free Press.

Durkheim, E. [1897] (1965). *Suicide: A Study in Sociology.* New York: The Free Press.

Dwyer Peter (2005). *Understanding Social Citizenship: Themes and Perspectives for Policy.* University of Bristol.

Eisenhart, M. (1998). "On the Subject of Interpretive Reviews". *Review of Educational Research,* 68(4): 391–400.

Emerson, P. and Frosh, S. (2004). *Critical Narrative Analysis in Psychology.* London.

Engebrigtsen I. A 'Kinship (2007). "Gender and Adaptation Processes in Exile: The Case of Tamil and Somali Families in Norway". *Journal of Ethnic and Migration Studies.* 1469-9451, volume 33, Issue 5, Pages 727 – 746.

European Commission (EC 2002). "European Commission Strategy for the Implementation of Special Aid to Somalia" 2002-2007. Brussels: EC.

Faist Thomas & Bauböck Rainer (2010).(eds.). *Diaspora and Transnationalism: Concepts, Theories and Methods,* Amestardam University Press.

Faist, T. (2000). "Transnationalization in international migration: Implications for the study of citizenship and culture". *Ethnic and Racial Studies.* pp. 189-222.

Faith Winchester (2000). *Muslim Holidays.* Capstone Press.

Fangen, K. (2007). "Citizenship among young adult Somalis in Norway". *Young.* pp. 413-434.

Fangen, Katrine (2007). "Breaking up the Different Constituting Parts of Ethnicity: The Case of Young Somalis in Norway". *Acta Sociologica,* December 2007, vol. 50(4): 401–414.

Farah Abdulkadir Osman and Ali Abdi Yusuf. *"Hadraawi's Peace Journey (Socdaalka nabadda)..* Reaches Aarhus, Denmark 30 March 2004. www.hiiraan.com.

Farah, Abdulkadir Osman, Mammo Muchie, Joakim Gundel (2007). (eds*)."Diaspora and state formation in the Horn of Africa'* Adonis Abbey, London.

Filomeno Aguilar, Labour Migration and Ties of Relatedness (2009).*"Diasporic Houses and Investments in Memory in a Rural Philippine Village"* Research Eleven, 98:88.

Finer Samuel Edward (1999). The *history of government from the earliest times: The intermediate ages.* Oxford University Press.

Fish Jonathan S. (2005). Defending the Durkheimian tradition: religion, emotion and morality. Ashgate publishing.

Forsyth, D. R. (2006). *"Group dynamics".* 4th ed. Belmont, CA: Thomson/Wadsworth.

Foucault M. (1986). *The Use of Pleasure.* New York: Pantheon Books.

Foucault, M. (1974). *The Archeology of Knowledge.* London: Tavistock.

Foucault, M. (1980). *Power/Knowledge: Selected Interviews and Other Writings 1972–1977,* London:Harvester.

Foucault, M. (1980a). Questions of Method. In J. D. Faubio (Ed.), *Michel Foucault: Power* (Vol. 3, pp. 223-238). New York: The New Press.

Foucault, M. (1982). Afterword: The Subject and Power. in H.L. Dreyfus and P. Rabinow (eds.). " *Michel Foucault: Beyond Structuralism and Hermeneutics*, pp. 208–26. Brighton: The Harvester Press.

Foucault, M. (1984) 'Polemics, politics and problematisations: an interview with Michel Foucault' in Rabinow, P. (eds.) *The Foucault Reader*. London: Penguin, 381_90.

Foucault, M. (1984). 'The Ethic of the Care for the Self as a Practice of Freedom', *Concordia*, Vol. 6,1984, p. 14.

Foucault, M. (1988). 'The Spirit of the World without Spirit', in his *Politics, Philosophy, Culture*, L. D. Kritzman, ed., London: Routledge, 1988, p. 218.

Foucault, M. (1990). *History of Sexuality, Volume III, Care of the Self* (R. Hurley, trans). New York: Pantheon Books.

Foucault, M. (1991). "Governmentality."; *The Foucault Effect: Studies in Governmentality.*; in (eds.) Graham Burchell, Colin Gordon, and Peter Miller; Hemel Hempstead; Harvester Wheatsheaf; 87-104

Foucault, M. (1994). *Power.* (Vol. 3). *New York: The New Press.*

Foucault, M. (1995). *Discipline and Punish: The Birth of the Prison.* New York: Vintage Books.

Fowler, A. (1993). "Non-governmental organizations as agents of democratization: an African perspective". *Journal of International Development* 5 (3). pp. 325-339.

Freek, S. (2004). *Voices from the shop floor: The impact of the multicultural work environment on UAE.* Dubai: TANMIA.

Fremeaux, Jacques (2006). "Les colonies dans la grande guerre: combats et épreuves des peuples d'outre-mer « *14-18 Éditions.*

Friedman (1994). *Jonathan, Cultural Identity and Global process. SAGE.*

G., & Sklar, S.M. (1997). "Culture, race, and the economic assimilation of immigrants". *Sociological Forum*, 12(2) 233-277 .

Gaasholt, Ø. and Togeby, L. (1995). *Syv sind. Danskernes holdninger til flygtninge og indvandrere.* Forlaget Politiken,Aarhus.

Gerson and R. Horowitz (2002). Observational and interviewing: Options and choices in qualitative research. *Southeast Asian J. Trop. Med. Publ. Health*, 23 (1992), pp. 207–211.

Ghannushi, Rashid (1993). *Xuququl muwadina: Xuquq geyrul muslimiin fi-mujtamac-alislami (Citizenship rights: the rights of non-Muslims in Muslim society.* International Institute for Islamic thinking, London.

Ghosh, F. (2005). *Reduced Economic Benefit to the Refugees: Missing Recognition.* Aalborg.

Giddens Anthony (1991). Modernity and self-identity: self and society in the late modern age. Standford University Press.

Giddens, A. (1991). *The Consequences of Modernity.* Stanford University Press.

Gilroy Paul (1993). *The black Atlantic: modernity and double consciousness.* Harvard University Press

Giri, Ananta Kumar (2006). "Creative Social Research: Rethinking Theories and Methods and the Calling of an Ontological Epistemology of Participation". *Dialectical Anthropology (2006) 30:227–271.*

Glaser, B., & Strauss, A. (1967). *The discovery of grounded theory: Strategies for qualitative.* Transaction Publishers.

Glick Schiller, N. 2005. "Transborder Citizenship: An Outcome of Legal Pluralism within Transnational Social Fields". *Theory and Research in Comparative Social Analysis". Paper 25.*

Goffman, Erving (1959). *The Presentation of Self in Everyday Life, Garden City.* New York: Doubleday Anchor Books.

Graham, J.W. (1991). "An essay on organizational citizenship behavior". *Employee Responsibilities and Rights".* Vol. 4, nr. 4, 249-270.

Gramsci A. [1932] 1971. "The intellectuals". *Selections from the Prison Notebooks of Antonio Gramsci.* Transl. Q Hoare, GN Smith. PP-5-23. New York: Int. Publ.

Granovetter, M. S. (1973), 'The strength of weak ties', *American Journal of Sociology,* 78 (6): 1360-1380.

Greaves Nigel M. (2010). *Gramsci's Marxism: Reclaiming A Philosophy of History and Politics.* Troubador.

Griffiths, David (1997). "Somali refugees in Tower Hamlets: Clanship and new identities". *"Journal of Ethnic and Migration Studies, 23: 1,* 5 — 24.

Guba, E. G. (1990). The alternative paradig dialog. In E.G.Guba (eds.) *The Paradigm dialog* (pp.17-30), Newbury Park. CA: SAGE.

Gundel, J. (2003). The Migration-Development Nexus: Somalia Case Study. In Van Hear, N. and Nyberg Sørensen, N. (eds.) *The Migration-Development Nexus.* Geneva: IOM.

Gundelach, P. and Torpe, L. (1999). Befolkningens fornemmelse for demokrati: foreninger, politisk engagement og demokratisk kultur', in Andersen, J.G., Christiansen, P.M. Jørgensen, T.B.,

Togeby, L. and Vallgaarda, S. (eds.) *Den Demokratiske Udfordring*. Copenhagen: Hans Reitzels Forlag 70–91.

Hamidullah Mohamed (1985). *Magnatul- alwataiq alsiyasiyah lil ahdnabahwih"* Beirut, Lebanon.

Hansen P. (2008). "Circumcising Migration: Gendering Return Migration among Somalilanders". *Journal of Ethnic and Migration Studies,* Volume 34, Issue 7, 2008, Pages 1109 - 1125

Hansen, P. (2004). "Migrant Remittances as a Development Tool: The Case of Somaliland. Migration Policy Research Working Paper Series No 3. Copenhagen" *University of Copenhagen, Department of Policy Research and Communications.*

Hansen, P. (2008). "Circumcising Migration: Gendering Return Migration among Somalilanders". *Journal of Ethnic and Migration Studies,* 34: 7, 1109 — 1125.

Hantrais, L. (1996). "Comparative Research Methods", *Social Research Update,* Issue *13,* Guildford: University of Surrey.

Helander Barnard (1996). The Hubeer in the Land of Plenty: Land, Labor, and Vulnerability among a Southern Somali Qabiilah. In (eds.) *The Struggle for Land in Southern Somalia: The War behind the War.* C. Besteman and Lee V. Cassanelli, eds. *Boulder, CO: Westview Press.*

Herbst, Jeffrey Ira (2000). *States and power in Africa: comparative lessons in authority and control.* Princeton University Press.

Herrera Lima, F. (2001). Transnational families: institutions of transnational social space. In (eds.) Pries, L. *New Transnational Social Spaces . London: Routledge 77_/93.*

Höhne, Markus V. (2006). Political identity, emerging state structures and conflict in northern Somalia. *The Journal of Modern African Studies,* 44:3:397-414. Cambridge University Press.

Holstein, J.A. and Gubrium, J.F. (1995). *The Active Interview.* London: SAGE.

Holsten J. (2009). "Dangerous Spaces of citizenship: Gang talk, rights talk and rule of law in Brazil". *Planning Theory,* 8 (1).pp. 12.31.

Hondagneu-Sotelo, P. (1994). *Gendered Transitions: Mexican Experiences of Migration.* University of California.

Hopkins, Gail(2010). "A changing sense of Somaliness: Somali women in London and Toronto", *Gender, Place & Culture 17: 4, 519 — 538.*

Horst, Cindy (2008). *Transnational nomads: how Somalis cope with refugee life in the Dadaab camps.* Berghahn Books.

Horst, Cindy(2008). "The transnational political engagements of refugees: Remittance sending practices amongst Somalis in Norway". *Conflict, Security & Development.* 8: 3, 317 — 339.

Houtsma M. Th (1993). *A. J Brill's First encyclopaedia of Islam.* 1913-1936. Brill.

http://wardheernews.com/Articles_09/August/Abow/14_Prof_Dalxa_Vs_Ambassad or_Ali_Amerika.html

http://www.statistikbanken.dk/statbank5a/default.asp?w=1280, august 2009

Human Rights Watch (2007). Th e *UAE's Draft Labor Law: Comments and Recommendations.*availableat

<hrw.org/backgrounder/mena/uae0307/.

HUMPHREY, JAMES HARRY (2007). *ISSUES IN CONTEMPORARY ATHLETICS.* NOVA PUBLISHERS

Hussain, M. (2007). *Muslims in the EU: Cities Report Denmark. Preliminary Research Report and Literature Survey, EUMAP Project.* – Open Society Institute, Budapest and New York, NY.

Hussain, Y., Bagguley, P. (2001). "Citizenship, ethnicity and identity: British Pakistanis after the 'riots". 2005 *Sociology* 39 (3), pp. 407-425.

Hyndman, Jennifer(2010) "Introduction: the feminist politics of refugee migration', *Gender, Place & Culture"* 17: 4, 453 — 459.

Ibn- khaldun (1958). *The Muqaddimali: An Introduction to History.* (INn. Three Volumes.) Translated by FRANRZO SENTHAL(B. ollingen Series XLIII.) New York: Pantheon Books, (Volume I, cxv, 481 pp).

Ibn Khaldun (1969). *The Muqaddimah: An Introduction to History.* trans. Franz Rosenthal" Bollingen Series XLIII, 3 vols. Princeton N.J 1958. Edited and abridged by N.J. Dawood 1969.

Ibn Khaldūn [1958]. *The Muqaddimah: an introduction to history, Volume 1, translation by Franz Rosenthal.* Princeton University Press.

Ibn Khaldun, A. (1415)[1995]. *Muqaddimat Ibn Khaldun* al-Juwaydi. (eds.). Beirut, Lebanon.

Isin Engin Fahri & Wood Patricia K. (1999). *Citizenship and identity.* Sage Publications ltd.

Issa-Salwe Abdisalam & Olden M. Anthony (2008). "Somali web sites, history and politics" *Aslib Proceedings,* vol. 60, issue 6, pp. 570-582.

Issa-Salwe Abdisalam M. and Anthony Olden (2008). "Somali web sites, history and politics". Centre for Information Management, Thames Valley University London UK.

Issa-Salwe, (2009). "Abdisalam M. The Internet and the Somali Diaspora: The Web as a New Means of Expression". *digitalcommons.macalester.edu.*

Itzigsohn, J. & S. G. Saucedo (2002), 'Immigrant incorporation and socio-cultural transnationalism', *International Migration Review*, 36 (3): 767-798.

Jaeger, D. A. (2000). Local labour markets, admission categories and immigrant location choice. Working paper, (Princeton, NJ: Hunter College, Princeton University).

Jagd, Christina (2007) *Medborger eller modborger? Dansksomalieres kamp for at opbygge en meningsfuld tilværelse i det danske samfund - gennem et arbejde*. PhD. Book, Copenhagen University.

Jain Ravindra K (1998). "Indian Diaspora, globalization and multiculturalism: A cultural analysis". *Contributions to Indian Sociology, November 1998 vol. 32 no. 2 337-360.*

Jenkins, Richard (2006). "Telling the frost from the tree, local images of national change in a Danish town". *Ethnos,* Vol., 71:3, Sept. 2006 (pp. 367-389).

John J. Patrick, Richard M. Pious, and Donald A. (2001). *The Oxford Guide to the United States Government.* Oxford University Press.

John Kitching, David Smallbone and Rosemary Athayde (2009). "Ethnic Diasporas and Business Competitiveness: Minority-Owned Enterprises in London". *Journal of Ethnic and Migration Studies,* Vol. 35, No. 4, April 2009, pp. 689_705.

Jones-Correa, M. (1988). *Between Two Nations: The Political Predicament of Latinos in New York City.* Cornell University Press.

Kahin Mohamed H. (1997). *Educating Somali children in Britain.* Trentham books.

Keane, D., McGeehan, N. (2008). "Enforcing Migrant Workers' Rights in the United Arab Emirates". *International Journal on Minority and Group Rights.* Volume, 15, Issue 1, 1 March 2008, Pages 81-115.

Khun Eng, Kuah-Pearce (2006). "Moralising Ancestors as Socio-moral Capital: A Study of a Transnational Chinese Lineage". *Asian Journal of Social Science,* Volume, 34, Number 2, 2006 , pp. 243-263(21).

Kinnvall, C., Nesbitt-Larking, P. (2010). "The political psychology of (de)securitization: Place-making strategies in Denmark, Sweden, and Canada". *Environment and Planning D: Society and Space,* 28 (6), pp. 1051-1070.

238

Kissau Kathrin and Hunger Uwe (2010). "The internet as a means of studying transnationalism and Diaspora". *Diaspora and Transnationalism Concepts, Theories and Methods*, in eds. Rainer baubock & thomas Faist. Amsterdam University Press.

Kleist N. (2010). "Negotiating Respectable Masculinity: Gender and Recognition in the Somali". Diaspora, *African Diaspora* 3, 185-206.

Kleist Nauja (2008). "Mobilizing "the Diaspora": Somali transnational Political Engagement". *Journal of Ethnic and Migration Studies*, Vol. 34, No. 2, pp. 307_323.

Kleist, Nauja & Hansen, Peter (2007): "Performing Diaspora – Studying the mobilization of a Somaliland transborder citizenry". in Farah, Osman, Muchie, M. & Gundel, J. (eds.): *Somalia: Diaspora and State Reconstitution in the Horn of Africa*. London: Adonis and AbbeyPublishers Ltd.

Knijn, T., Kremer, M. (1997). "Gender and the caring dimension of welfare states: Toward inclusive citizenship". *Social Politics* 4 (3), pp. X-361.

Kraxberger, B. (2005). "Strangers, indigenes and settlers: Contested geographies of citizenship in Nigeria". *Space and Polity* 9 (1), pp. 9-27.

Kremer, Monique (2007). *How welfare states care: culture, gender and parenting in Europe*, Amsterdam University.

Kristainsen & Ryen (2002). "Enacting their business environments: Asian entrepreneurs in East Africa". *African and Asian Studies*, 1 (3), pp. 165-186.

Kühle, Lene (2006). *Moskeer i Danmark: Islam og Muslimsk bedesteder*. Univers.

Kuhn, T. S. (1962). *The Structure of Scientific Revolutions*. Chicago University Press.

Kureer, Henrik & Lundgren, Svend Erik (2006). *International økonomi: B-niveau*. SYSTIME.

Kurthen Hermann (1999). "Welfare Policies and Immigrants' Citizenship" in eds. Kurthen *et al. Immigration, citizenship and the welfare state in Germany and the United states: immigrant incorporation*. Emeral Publishing.

Kusow Abdi M. (2004). "Contesting Stigma: On Goffman's Assumptions of Normative Order Spring". *Symbolic interaction*, Vol. 27, No. 2, pp.179–197.

Kusow, A. (1998). *Migration and identity processes among Somali immigrants in Canada.* Book, Wayne State University, Michigan (Ann Arbor, MI, UMI).

Kusow, Abdi M. (2004) (eds.). *Putting the Cart Before the Horse: Contested Nationalism and the Crisis of the Nation-State in Somalia,* Trenton, NJ: The Red Sea Press.

Kvale, S. (1995). "The Social Construction of Validity". *Qualitative Inquiry* 1(1): 19–40.

Kvale, S. (1997). *Interviews. An Introduction to Qualitative Research Interviewing.* London: SAGE.

Labov,W. (1972). "The Transformation of Experience in Narrative Syntax". In W. Labov (eds.) *Language in the Inner City: Studies in the Black English Vernacular.* Philadelphia, PA: University of Pennsylvania Press.

Lacoste, Yves (1984). *Ibn Khaldun: the birth of history and the past of the Third World*

Laitin David D. (2004). "The De-cosmopolitanization of the Russian Diaspora: A View from Brooklyn in the Tar Abroad". *Diaspora, 13:1.*

Laitin, David D (2004). "Creating transnational social spaces". *Diaspora* Vol. 13 Issue 1, pp.315-35.

Lal, Barbara. (1997). "Ethnic identity Entrepreneurs: Their Role in Transracial and Intercountry Adoptions". *Asian and Pacific Migration Journal,* 6: 385-413.

Larsen, J.E. (2005). *Fattigdom og social eksklusion i Danmark – Tendenser i Danmark over et kvart arhundrede.* Socialforskningsinstituttet, København.

Lee-Treweek Geraldine (2000). The Insight of Emotional Danger: Research Experiences in a Home For Older People', in G. Lee-Treweek and S. Linkogle (eds.) *Danger in the Field: Risk and Ethics in Social Research,* pp. 114–31. London: Routledge.

Levitt, Peggy, and Nina Glick-Schiller. 2004. "Conceptualizing Simultaneity: A Transnational Social Field Perspective on Society." *International Migration Review* 38: 1002-1039.

Lewis I. Lewis (1951). "Force and fission in Northern Somali Lineage structure". *American Anthropologist,* vol. 63 (1), pp. 94-112.

Lewis I. M. (2008). Understanding Somalia and Somaliland: culture, history, society. Columbia University Press.

Lewis, I. M. (1999). *A pastoral democracy.* London: Lit Verlag/James Currey.

Lewis, I. M (1994). *Blood and bone: the call of kinship in Somali society*. Red Sea Press.

Lewis, I. M. (1961). *A Pastoral Democracy: A Study of Pastoralism and Politics Among the Northern Somali of the Horn of Africa*, London: James Currey, 1961, Reprint 1999.

Lewis, I. W. (1962). "Historical Aspects of Genealogies in Northern Somali Social Structure". *The Journal of African History*, 3: 35-48

Li, P.S. (1977) "Occupational achievement and kinship assistance among Chinese immigrants in Chicago". *Sociological Quarterly, 18*, 478-489.

Lincoln, Y. S. & Guba, E. G. (2000). Paradigmatic controversies, contradictions and emerging confluences. In Y. S. Lincoln & G. uba (Eds.), *Handbook of Qualitative Research (pp. 163-188)*. Thousand Oaks, CA: SAGE.

Lincoln, Y.S. and Guba, E.G. (1985). *Naturalistic Inquiry*. Thousand Oaks, CA: Sage Publications.

Lindley, Anna (2009). "The Early-Morning Phone call: Remittances from a Refugee Diaspora Perspective". *Journal of Ethnic and Migration Studies*, 35: 8, 1315 — 1334.

Little, P. D. (2003). *Somalia: Economy Without State*. Oxford: James Currey.

Lofland J, Lofland LH. (1984). *Analyzing Social Settings: A Guide to Qualitative Observation and Analysis*, 2nd edn. Wadsworth: Belmont, CA.

Lofland John (1996). *"Social Movement Organizations: Guide to Research on Insurgent Realities"*. New York: Aldine De Gruyter.

Lofland John, Lofland, Lyn H. (1995). Analyzing social settings: a guide to qualitative observation and analysis. Wadsworth

Ludvigsen Lise (2007). Religion i det senmoderne samfund: mellem kritik og forsvar. Systime.

Luling Virginia (2006). "Genealogy as theory, genealogy as tool: aspects of Somali qabiilah". *Social identities, vol. 12, No. 4: pp. 471-485.*

Machiavelli Niccolò (2003).The Prince. Translated by Rufus Goodwin.

Malik, Kenan (2009). *From Fatwa to Jihad*. London: Atlantic Books.

Mamdani Mahmood (2002). *When victims become killers: colonialism, nativism, and the genocide in Rwanda*. Princeton University press.

Mandaville, Peter (2011). "Transnational Muslim solidarities and everyday life". *Nations and Nationalism*, Volume 17, Issue 1, pages 7–24.

Abdulkadir Osman Farah

Mansur, A. (1995). Contrary to a Nation: The Cancer of the Somali State. In Ahmed, A. (eds.)*The Invention of Somalia*. Lawrenceville, NJ: Red Sea Press.

Marchal, R. (1996). *Final Report on the Post Civil War Somali Business Class,* European Commission, Somalia Unit, Paris.

Marchal, Roland (2007). "Warlordism and terrorism: how to obscure an already confusing crises? The case of Somalia" *International Affairs,* Vol. 83, Issue 6, pp. 1091-1106, November.

Marcus, G.E. (1981). "Power on the extreme periphery: the perspective of Tongan elites in the modern world system". *Pacific Viewpoint, 22(1): 48_/64.*

Markakis, John (1986). "Radical military regimes in the Horn of Africa" in (eds.) *Military Marxist regimes in Africa.* John Markakis and Michael Waller, Rouledge.

Marpil, Jose (2009). "The Place of Sacrifice: qurbani and Transnational Circuits among Bangladeshis in Lisbon". *Analise Social, vol. 44, no. 190, pp. 71-103.*

Marx Karl (1933). *Wage-Labour and Capital*. International publishers.

Massey, D. S. (1985). "Ethnic residential segregation: a theoretical synresearch and empirical review". *Sociology and Social Research*, 69, pp. 315–350.

Mattausch, J. (1998). "From subjects to citizens: British 'East African Asians". *Journal of Ethnic and Migration Studies*, 24 (1), pp. 121-141.

May Roy & Charlton Roger (1989). "Warlordism and Militarism in Chad". *Review of African Political Economy, Volume 16, Issue 45, Pages 12 – 25*

Mazen, Hashem (2010) 'The Ummah in the Khutba: A Religious Sermon or a Civil Discourse?', *Journal of Muslim Minority Affairs*, 30: 1, 49 — 61.

Mazrui Ali A. (1963). "Edmund Burke and Reflections on the Revolution in the Congo". *Comparative Studies in Society and History*, Vol. 5, No. 2 (Jan., 1963), pp. 121-133

Mazrui Ali A. (1968). "From Social Darwinism to Current Theories of Modernization: A Tradition of Analysis". *World Politics*, Vol. 21, No. 1 (Oct., 1968), pp. 69-83.

Mazrui Ali A. (1977). "Boxer Muhammad Ali and Soldier Idi Amin as International Political Symbols: The Bioeconomics of Sport and War". *Comparative Studies in Society and History*, Vol. 19, No. 2 (Apr., 1977), pp. 189-215.

242

Mazrui Ali A. (1985). "Religion and Political Culture in Africa". *Journal of the American Academy of Religion*, Vol. 53, No. 4, 75th Anniversary Meeting of the American Academy of Religion (Dec., 1985), pp. 817-839.

Mazrui Ali A. (1994). "Islamic Doctrine and the Politics of Induced Fertility Change: An African Perspective". *Population and Development Review*, Vol. 20, Supplement: The New Politics of Population: Conflict and Consensus in Family Planning (1994), pp. 121-134.

Mazrui Ali A. (2001). "The digital revolution and the new reformation'. *Harvard International Review*, Vol. 23, No. 1, Spring 2001, available online at: ,http://hir.harvard.edu/articles/1001/.

Mazrui Ali A. (2004). Islam and the United States: streams of convergence, strands of divergence, *Third World Quarterly, Vol. 25, No. 5, pp 793–820.*

Mazrui Ali. A. (1993). The introduction, in Ali A. Mazrui (eds.) *General history of Africa: Africa since 1935, UNESCO, 1-23.*

Mazrui, Ali A. (2001) 'Pretender to Universalism: Western Culture in a Globalizing Age', *Journal of Muslim Minority Affairs*, 21: 1, 11 — 24.

McAdam, Doug, *John D. McCarthy, and Mayer N. Zald (1988).* Social Movements *in Neil J. Smelsor (eds.), Handbook of Sociology: 695-737.* Newbury Park, CA: Sage.

McAdam, Doug, Sidney Tarrow, and Charles Tilly (2001). *Dynamics of Contention.* Cambridge: Cambridge UP.

McCarthy, John, and Mayer Zald (1977). "Resource Mobilization and Social Movements: A Partial Theory." *The American Journal of Sociology* 82 (1977): 1212-41).

McGown Rima Berns (1999). *Muslims in the Diaspora: the Somali communities of London and Toronto.* University of Toronto Press.

McGown, Rima Berns (1999). *Muslims in the Diaspora: The Somali Communities of London and Toronto,* University of Toronto, Pp. 302.

McKay, J. (1982). "An exploratory synresearch of primordial and mobilizationist approaches to ethnic phenomenon". *Ethnic and Racial Studies,* 5 (4), 395-420.

Meadwell, H. "(1989). "Cultural and instrumental approaches to ethnic nationalism". *Ethnic and Racial Studies*, Volume 12, Issue 3, Pages 309 – 328.

Mehler Andreas Melber Henning Walraven Klaas Van (2008). Africa Yearbook 5: Politics, Economy and Society South of the Sahara. Brill.

Mercin, Galent (2010). *International Sociological Association*, Gothenburg, Sweden.

Merton, Robert (1972). "Insiders and Outsiders: A Chapter in the Sociology of Knowledge". *American Journal of Sociology*, 78 (July): 9–47.

Midtbøen, A.H. (2009). "Nationality reform and divergent conceptions of integration in the Scandinavian countries | [Statsborgerrettslig revisjon og integrasjonspolitisk variasjon i de Skandinaviske landene]" *Tidsskrift for Samfunnsforskning*, 50 (4), pp. 523-550.

Mishra Sudesh (2006). *Diaspora criticism*. Edinburgh University Press.

Mitchell, K. (1997), 'Different diasporas and the hype of hybridity', *Society and Space* 15 (3): 533-553.

Moallem Minoo (2000). "Foreignness" and Be/longing: Transnationalism and Immigrant Entrepreneurial Spaces". Comparative Studies of South Asia, Africa and the Middle East, Vol. XX Nos. 1&2. Pp-200-210.

Mohamed Mohamed-Abdi and Verity Johnson (2003). Mapping Somali civil society. NOVIB, SOMALIA.

Mohamoud Abdullah A. (2006). State collapse and post-conflict development in Africa: the case of Somalia (1960-2001). Purdue University.

Morison, Linda A. , Dirir, Ahmed , Elmi, Sada , Warsame, Jama and Dirir, Shamis (2004). "How experiences and attitudes relating to female circumcision vary according to age on arrival in Britain: a study among young Somalis in London". *Ethnicity & Health*, 9: 1, 75 — 100.

Muchie Mammo and Li Xing (2006) (eds.). *Globalization, inequality, and the commodification of life and well-being.* Adonis-Abbey Publishers, London.

Muhammad Umar Al-mishri (1998*). Bilad al-Qarn al-afriqi: Nusus Wawathaiq minal-masadir al-arabiya* (Horn of Africa Countries: Reports and Information from Arab sources).

Muhumed Mahamud Ugas (2008). Achieving Effective Results Through Strategic Plan: The Case of African rescue committee (PhD research). Author house.

Mukhtar, Haji Mohamed (1995). "Islam in Somali history: fact and fiction" in (eds.) *The invention of Somalia*. Ali Jimale Ahmed. Red Sea Press.

Murdie, R. A. (2002). "The housing careers of Polish and Somali newcomers in Toronto's rental market". *Housing Studies, 17(3), pp. 423–443.*

Musterd, S., Ostendorf, W. & Breebaart, M. (1998). *Multi-ethnic Metropolis: Patterns and Policies.* (Dordrecht: Kluwer Publications).

Nadje Al-Ali, Richard Black, Khalid Koser (2001). "Refugees and transnationalism: The experience of Bosnians and Eritreans in Europe". *Journal of Ethnic and Migration Studies*, Volume 27, Issue 4, 2001, Pages 615 – 634.

Nagel, C.R., Staeheli, L.A. (2004). "Citizenship, identity and transnational migration: Arab immigrants to the United States". *Space and Polity* 8 (1), pp. 3-23.

Najjar, Abd Allah (1973). *Al-Islam Fi Somal (Islam in Somalia).* Majlisul Ala lishuunil Islamiya.

Nasif, Majdi (1974). *Thowratul-Somal-Ardulbukhuur-Waluduur (Somali revolution: The Land of Incense and Perfume).* Maktabah Matbuli.

Nauja Kleist (2008) *Spaces of Recognition An analysis of Somali-Danish associational engagement and diasporic mobilization.* PhD book, Copenhagen University

Nazir Sameena & Tomppert Leigh (2005). *Women's rights in the Middle East and North Africa: citizenship and justice.* Rawman & Litllefield.

Neubauer John (1999). *Cultural history after Foucault.* Transaction books.

Neuman, W. L. (2000). *Social research methods: Qualitative and quantitative approaches.* Boston: Allyn & Bacon.

Noack Sascha (2007). *Doing Business in Dubai and the United Arab Emirates.* Grin.

Ø. Gaasholt *and* L. Togeby, *I Syv Sind.* Danskernes holdninger *til* flygtninge *og* indvandrere *(Aarhus: Forlaget Politica, 1995).*

Olwig, K.F. (2001). New York as a locality in a global family network. *in Foner, N. (eds.) Islands in the City: West Indian Migration to New*

York . *Berkeley, Los Angeles and London:* University of California Press, 142_/60.

Olwig, Karen Fog, Paerregaard Karsten (2007). *Integration: antropologiske perspektiver*. Museum Tasculanum Press.

Olzak, Sue (1992). *The Dynamics of Ethnic Competition and Conflict. Stanford, CA:* Stanford University Press.

Omer, A. (2002). *Supporting Systems and Procedures for the Effective Regulation and Monitoring of Somali Remittance Companies (Hawala).* Nairobi: UNDP Somalia.

Omer, A. (2004). *"QUESTS (Qualified Expatriate Somali Technical Support): Involving Diaspora Expertise in the Rebuilding of Somalia". Paper presented at the 9th Somali Studies International Conference, 3–5 September, University of Aalborg, Aalborg, Denmark.*

Omer, A. and El Koury, G. (2004). "Regulation and Supervision in a Vacuum: The Story of the Somali Remittance Sector". *Small Enterprise Development* 15(1): 44–52.

Ong, A. (1999). "Muslim feminism: Citizenship in the shelter of corporatist Islam". *Citizenship Studies* 3 (3), pp. 355-371.

Organization of the Petroleum Exporting Countries (OPEC) Monthly Oil Market Report (June 2007). available at www.opec.org/home/Monthly%20Oil%20Market%20Reports/ 2007/pdf/ MR062007.pdf>.

Ostergaard, K., Sinclair, K. (2007). "Danish Muslims, the Cartoon Controversy, and the Concept of Integration". *Global Dialogue,* 9 (3-4), pp. 65-74.

Paolini, A. J. (1999). *Navigating modernity: Postcolonialism, identity, and international relations Boulder:* Lynne Rienner.

Papastergiadis Nikos (2000). *The turbulence of migration: globalization, deterritorialization, and hybridity,* Blackwell.

Park, Robert E. (1967) The foreign language press and social progress. (1920*) In Ralph H. Turner (eds), Robert E. Park *on Social Control Control and Collective Behavior: 133-144. Chicago:* University of Chicago Press.

Parsons Stephen D. (2003). *Money, time, and rationality in Max Weber: Austrian connections.* Routledge

Patterson, Rubin (2006). "Transnationalism: Diaspora and Homeland Development". *Social forces,* vol. 84.

Pedersen, S. and Jensen, H.Z. (2002). *Befolkningens holdninger til at indføre begrænsninger i antallet af flygtninge i Danmark.* Nyt fra Rockwool Fondens Forskningsenhed, Juni 2002, pp. 12-14.

Peletz Michael G. (1995). "Kinship Studies in Late Twentieth-Century Anthropology". *Annual Review of Anthropology*, Vol. 24: pp. 343-372.

Pendakur, K., & Penda.kur, R. (2002). "Language as both human capital and ethnicity". *International Migration Review*, 36(1), 147-177.

Pérouse de Montclos, M.A. (1997). "Minorities and discrimination, exodus and reconstruction of identities: the case of Somali refugees in Mombasa", October, *ORSTOM*, France.

Perouse de Montclos, M-A. (2003). *A Refugee Diaspora - When the Somalis Go West.* In Koser, K. (eds.) *New African Diasporas.* London: Routledge.

Petterson, Rubin (2006). *"Transnationalism: Diaspora-Homeland Development"* Social forces vol. 84, 4.

Peutz, N. (2006). Embarking on an anthropology of removal, *Current Anthropology*, 47 (2), pp. 217-241.

Phuong Catherine (2004). *The international protection of internally displaced persons. Cambridge University Press.*

Pickering W. S. F. (1975). *Durkheim on religion: a selection of readings with bibliographies, Volume 1.* Routledge.

Popper, K. R. (1972). *Objective Knowledge.* London, *Oxford University Press.*

Popper, K.R. (2002). *The Logic of Scientific Discovery.* London: Routledge.

Portes , Alejandro (2010). "Migration and Social Change: Some Conceptual Reflections". *Journal of Ethnic and Migration Studies*, 1469-9451, Volume 36, Issue 10, First published 2010, Pages 1537 – 1563

Portes, A. & Bach, R. L. (1985). *Latin Journey: Cuban and Mexican Immigrants in the United States.* (Los Angeles, CA: University of California).

Portes, A. (1998). "Social capital: its origins and applications in modern sociology". *Annual Review of Sociology, 24, pp. 1–24.*

Quraishi, Muzammil (2005). *Muslims and crime: a comparative study.* Ashgate Publishing.

R. Cohen (1996). "Diaspora and the nation state: From victims to challengers" *International affairs*, 72, 1 (1996), 507- 520).

Ramadan, T. (1998). *To Be a European Muslim: A study of Islamic sources in the European context.* Leicester: The Islamic Foundation.

Rasmussen Tove & Bøggild Anders (2008). Social polarisering i Århus Kommune, Rapport 1:Social polarisering og fattigdom i

Århus Kommune 1996-2005, Socialrådgiveruddannelsen i Århus, VIA, University College.

Reinharz, Shulamit (1992). *Feminist Methods in Social Research*. Oxford: Oxford University Press.

Roald, Anne Sofie (2004). *New Muslims in the European context: the experience of Scandinavian converts*. Brill.

Roble Abdi and Rutledge Douglas F. (2008). *The Somali Diaspora: a journey away*. University of Minnesota Press

Roche, J. (1999). "Children: Rights, participation and citizenship". *Childhood* 6 (4), pp. 475-493.

Roger Charlton and Roy May, 'Warlords and militarism in Chad', *Review of African Political Economy* 16: 45/6, summer 1989.

Roitman, J. (2007). " The right to tax: Economic citizenship in the Chad Basin". *Citizenship Studies* 11 (2), pp. 187-209.

Romano Amy (2004). A Historical Atlas of the United Arab Emirates. Rosen publishing group.

Rose, N (2000). "Community, citizenship, and the third way". *American Behavioral Scientist* 43 (9), pp. 1395-1411.

Rose, N. (1996). "The death of the social? Re-figuring the territory of government". *Economy and Society* 25 (3), pp. 327-356.

Ryan G. W and Bernard H R (2003). "Techniques to Identify themes". *Field methods,* 15: 89-109.

S. Vertovec & R. Cohen (1999). *Migration, Diasporas and transnationalism.* Edward Elgar.

Sadouni, Samadia (2009) "God is not Unemployed': Journeys of Somali Refugees in Johannesburg". *African Studies, 68: 2, 235 – 249.*

Safran , W (1991). "Diasporas in Modern Societies: Myths of Homeland and Return". *Diaspora*, 1:83–99.

Safran, W. (1991*).*"Diasporas in modern societies: Myths of homeland and return*". Diaspora,* 1 (1991): 83-99.

Said, E. (1979). *Orientalism . New York: Vintage Books. Said, E. (1991). Cultural imperialism .* New York: Vintage Books.

Said, Edward W. (1993). *Culture and imperialism.* Vintage books.

Salama, S. (2006, June 25). *New Emiratisation drive. Gulf News. Retrieved January 13, 2009, from* http://archive.gulfnews.com/indepth/ *labour/Emiritisation/ 10049370.html.*

Samatar Abdi Ismail (1992). "Destruction of State and Society in Somalia: Beyond the Tribal Convention Author". *The Journal of Modern African Studies,* Vol. 30, No. 4: pp. 625-641.

Sand Shlomo & Lotan Yael (2010). *The Invention of the Jewish People.* Verso.

Sassen Saskia (2002). *Global networks, linked cities*. Routledge.

Sassen, S. (1995*)*. Immigration and local labour markets, in: A. Portes (eds.). *The Economic Sociology of Immigration, pp. 87–127*. (New York: Russell Sage).

Saye, Albert Berry (1979). *American constitutional law: cases and text*, West Pub. Co.

Schierup Carl-Ulrik, Peo Hansen Migration, Stephen Castles (2006). *citizenship, and the European welfare state: a European dilemma*. Oxford University Press.

Schierup, C.-U., (1994). "The right to be different: multiculturalism and the racialization of Scandinavian welfare politics; the case of Denmark". *Innovation, 7* (3), pp. 277-288.

Schiller et al. (2009). "Towards a comparative theory of locality in migration studies: migrant incorporation and city scale". *Journal of ethnic and migration studies* [1369-183X]., 2009 vol.:35 iss:2 s.:177.

Schmidt, Garbi (2011). "Law and Identity: Transnational Arranged Marriages and the Boundaries of Danishness" *Journal of Ethnic and Migration Studies, 37: 2, 257 – 275*.

Scott, John and Marshall, Gordon (2009). *A Dictionary of Sociology*. Oxford University Press.

Seale, C. (1999). *The Quality of Qualitative Research*. London: SAGE.

Seidman, G.W. (1999). Gendered citizenship: South Africa's democratic transition and the construction of a gendered state , *Gender and Society* 13 (3), pp. 287-307.

SF Alatas (1995). "The Sacralization of the Social Sciences". *De Sciences Sociales des Religions*, Year 1995 Volume 91 Issue 91 pp. 89-111.

Shain, Y (1999). *Marketing the American creed abroad: Diasporas in the US and their homelands*. Cambridge University Press.

Shain, Yossi (2007). *Kinship & diasporas in international affairs*, University of Michigan.

Sharam Alghasi, Thomas Hylland Eriksen, Halleh Ghorashi (2009). *Paradoxes of cultural recognition: perspectives from Northern Europe*. Ashgate.

Sheffer G. (1986). *Modern Diasporas in international relations*. 1986, Croom Helm.

Sherrell Kathy and Hyndman Jennifer (2006). "Global Minds, Local Bodies: Kosovar Transnational Connections Beyond British

Columbia". *Refuge: Canada's periodical on refugees*, Vol 23, No 1 (2006): Refugee Diasporas and Transnationalism.

Siim, B. (1998). "Vocabularies of citizenship and gender: Denmark". *Critical Social Policy*, 18 (3), pp. 375-396.

Simon Blackburn (2008). *The Oxford Dictionary of Philosophy*. Oxford University Press.

Simons, A. (1995). *Networks of Dissolution: Somalia Undone*. Oxford: Westview Press.

Singh Nagendra Kr (2002). *International encyclopaedia of Islamic dynasties*. Anmol publications.

Smith, G., (1999). "Transnational politics and the politics of the Russian diaspora". *Ethnic and Racial Studies* 22 (3), pp. 500-523.

Smith, G., Wales, C. (2000). "Citizens' juries and deliberative democracy". *Political Studies* 48 (1), pp. 51-65.

Snow, D., Morrill, C., & Anderson, L. (2003). "Elaborating analytic ethnography: Linking fieldwork and theory". *Ethnography, 4, 181-200.*

Sokefeld, Martin (2006). "Moblizing in transnational space: A social movement approach to the formation of Diaspora" *Global networks*, 6 (3), (July 2006), 265-84).

Soysal, Y.N. (2000). "Citizenship and identity: Living in diasporas in post-war Europe?". *Ethnic and Racial Studies 23 (1), pp. 1-15.*

Soysal,Y. N. (1994). *Limits of citizenship: Migrants and post-national membership in Europe*. University of Chicago Press.

Spickard Paul R. *(2005). Race and nation: ethnic systems in the modern world.* Routledge, Taylor & Francis group.

Staeheli, L.A., Thompson, A. (1997). "Citizenship, community, and struggles for public space". *Professional Geographer* 49 (1), pp. 28-38.

Stake, R. (2000). 'Case Studies', in N.K. Denzin and Y.S. Lincoln (eds.) *Handbook of Qualitative Research*, pp. 435–54. Thousand Oaks, CA: Sage Publications.

Stake, R. E. (1995). *The art of case study research*. Thousand Oaks, California: Sage.

Statham, Paul. (1999). "Political Mobilization by Minorities in Britain: Negative Feedback of 'Race Relations". *Journal of Ethnic and Migration Studies* 25, 597-626.

Stephen Sarah (2005). *Refugees and the Rich-World Fortress*. Resistance books.

Stone Gregory P. (1962). Appearance and the self', in Arnold Rose (eds.) *Human Behaviour and Social Processes*, Boston: Houghton-Mifflin, pp. 86_118.

Strauss Anselm L. and Corbin Juliet M (1998). Grounded theory in practice. Sage

Strenski Ivan (1997). *Durkheim and the Jews of France*. University of Chicago Press.

Subrahmanyam, Sanjay (1998). *The Career and Legend of Vasco da Gama*, Cambridge University Press.

Suryadinata Leo (2000). *Nationalism and globalization: east and west*. Institute of South East Asian studies.

Swyngedouw, E (2005). "Governance innovation and the citizen: The Janus face of governance-beyond-the-state" *Urban Studies*, 42 (11).

Tarrius, A. (2001), 'Au-delà des États-nations: des sociétés de migrants', *Revue européenne des migrations internationales* 17 (2): 37-61.

Terterov Marat (2006). Doing Business with the United Arab Emirates. GMB publishing.

The World Bank (2005). *Conflict in Somalia: Drivers and Dynamics*.

Thunø, M. (2003). "Channels of entry and preferred destinations: The circumvention of Denmark by Chinese immigrants". *International Migration*, 41 (3), pp. 99-134.

Tibi, Bassam (2007). "Migration Story: From Muslim Immigrants to European "Citizens of the Heart". A; Fletcher F. *World Affairs* , 147.

Togeby, L (1999). "Migrants at the polls: An analysis of immigrant and refugee participation in Danish local elections". *Journal of Ethnic and Migration Studies*, 25 (4), pp. 665-684.

Togeby, Lise (2004). "It depends... how organizational participation affects political participation and social trust among second-generation immigrants in Denmark", *Journal of Ethnic and Migration Studies*, Volume 30, Issue 3, Pages 509 – 528.

Tollolyan K (2007). *The nation and its others, Sociology of Diaspora*. Rawat Publications.

Tololyan, K. (1996). "Rethinking Diasporas: Stateless Power in the Transnational   Moment". *Diaspora, Vol. 5 No. 1, 3-34.*

Tololyan, Kachig (2002). "Redefining Diasporas: old approaches, new identities, the Armeinian diapsora in an international context". *Occasional paper*. London.

Tracey Reynolds (2007). "Caribbean families, social capital and young people's diasporic identities". *Cultural Dynamics*, 19: 193.

Tsakloglou, P. and Papadopoulos, F. (2002). "Aggregate level and determining factors of social exclusion in twelve European countries". *Journal of European Social Policy*, Vol. 12 No. 3, pp. 211-25.

Turner Stephen P. (1996). *Social theory and sociology: the classics and beyond.* Wiley Blackwell

Turner, B.S. (2001). "The erosion of citizenship". *British Journal of Sociology* 52 (2), pp. 189-209.

Turton E. R. (1974). "The Isaq Somali Diaspora and Poll-Tax Agitation in Kenya, 1936-41". *African Affairs*, Vol. 73, No. 292, July, pp. 325-346.

Umut, Erel (2010). "Migrating Cultural Capital: Bourdieu in Migration Studies". *Sociology*, vol. 44, no. 4, August, pp. 642-660.

UNDP Somalia (1998). *Human Development Report: Somalia 1998.* UNDP.

UNDP Somalia (2001). *Human Development Report: Somalia 2001,* UNDP Somalia.

UNHCR (2000). *The State of the World's Refugees,* Oxford University Press, Oxford.

Van Amersfoort, H. (2004). 'Gabriel Sheffer and the Diaspora Experience'. *Diaspora*, 13 (2-3), pp. 359-374.

Van Kempen, R. (2003). Segregation and Housing Conditions of Immigrants in Western European Cities, Eurex Lecture 7, 13 March. Available at http://www.shiva.uniurb.it/eurex/syllabus/lecture7/ Lecture7-VanKempen.pdf.

Van Oorschot, W., Abrahamson, P. (2003). "The Dutch and Danish miracles revisited: A critical discussion of activation policies in two small welfare states". *Social Policy and Administration,* 37 (3), pp. 288-304.

Van Valsen, Jaap (1967). The extended case method and Situational Analysis. In (eds.) A. L. Epstein,London: Tavistock. *the Craft of Social Anthropology.* London Tavistock Publications.

Vertovec Steven (2009). *Transnationalism.* Taylor and Francis.

Vertovec, Steven. (1999). "Conceiving and researching transnationalism". *Ethnic and Racial Studies* 22) no. 2: 1–13.

Vora, N. (2009). Book Abstracts International, A: *The Humanities and Social Sciences* 69 (7), pp. 2769.

Wagner, Peter *et al.* (1991). *Discourses on society: the shaping of the social science disciplines.* Springer.

Waldron, S., and N.A. Hasci (1995). *Somali Refugees in the Horn of Africa: State of the Art Literature Review*, Nordiske Afrikainstitutet.

Wallerstein M. Immanuel (1991).*The capitalist world-economy: essays.* Cambridge University Press.

Walters, Ronald W. (1993). *Pan-Africanism in the African Diaspora: An analysis of modern afro-centric political movements*. Detroit: Wayne State University Press.

Waters, J. (2003). "Flexible citizens? Transnationalism and citizenship amongst economic immigrants in Vancouver" *Canadian Geographer*, 47 (3), pp. 219-234.

Waters, Mary (1999). *Black Identities.* New York: Russell Sage.

Weber, M. (1922). The Theory of Social and Economic Organization. New York: Free Press.

Weber, M. (1930). *The Protestant Ethic and the Spirit of Capitalism.* London: George Allen and Unwin.

Weber, M. (1946). *From Max Weber: Essays in Sociology.* New York: Oxford University Press.

Weber, M. (1968). "Economy and Society" (eds.) Guenther Roth and Claus Wittich, New York: Bedminster Press.

Weber, M. (1981). *General Economic History.* New Brunswick, NJ: Transaction.

Weber, M. [1904] (1949). The Methodology of the Social Sciences. New York: The Free Press.

Werbner, P. (2000). "Divided loyalties, empowered citizenship? Muslims in Britain". *Citizenship Studies*, 4 (3), pp. 307-324.

Werbner, P. (2002). "The place which is diaspora: Citizenship, religion and gender in the making of chaordic transnationalism". *Journal of Ethnic and Migration Studies*, 28 (1), pp. 119-133.

Werbner, P. (2005). "The translocation of culture: 'Community cohesion' and the force of multiculturalism in history". *Sociological Review*, 53 (4), pp. 745-768.

Werbner, Pnina (1997). "Diasporic Political Imaginaries: A Sphere of Freedom or a Sphere of Illusions". *The Eastern Anthropologist*, vol. 50, no3-4, pp. 467-493.

Wiley, N. (1967). "The ethnic mobility trap and stratification theory" *Social Problems, 15*, 147-159.

Wilson, K.L., & Portes, A. (1980). "Immigrant enclaves: An analysis of the labour market experiences of Cubans in Miami". *American Journal of Sociology*, 86(2), 295-319.

Wolfson, N. (1997). Speech Events and Natural Speech', in N. Coupland and A. Jaworski in (eds.) *Sociolinguistics*, pp. 116–25. Basingstoke: MacMillan.

World Bank (1995). World Development Indicators CD-Rom, World Bank, Washington DC.

World Bank (2006). *Global Economic Prospects: Economic Memorandum*. World Bank Washington, DC.

World Bank (2006). *Somalia: From Resilience Towards Recovery and Development*, A Country Study.

World Bank (2007). Africa development indicators. World Bank.

ZAVODNEY, M. (1998). *WELFARE AND THE LOCATIONAL CHOICES OF NEW IMMIGRANTS*. FEDERAL RESERVE BANK.

INDEX

Sharjah, xii, 128, 145, 150, 151, 155, 156, 184, 226, 233
Sikh Diaspora, 63, 64, 79, 135
Somali National Movement, 16, 18, 184
Somali Patriotic Movement, 16, 18
Somali pirates, 185
Somaliland, xi, 15, 16, 28, 34, 90, 105, 139, 151, 156, 184, 229, 239, 242, 244
Sri Lankans, 100

T

Toronto, 31, 75, 234, 235, 240, 247, 248

Transitional Federal Government, 16
Trans-national hybrid spaces, 210
Turkey, 167
Tutsi, 89

Y

Yemen, 13, 15, 18, 19, 28, 123, 156

Z

Zimbabwean Diaspora, 133